# Emotions, Politics and W



A growing number of scholars have sought to re-centre emotions in the study of international politics, however an overarching book on how emotions matter to the study of politics and war is yet to be published. This volume is aimed at filling that gap, proceeding from the assumption that a nuanced understanding of emotions can only enhance our engagement with contemporary conflict and war.

Providing a range of perspectives from a diversity of methodological approaches on the conditions, maintenance and interpretation of emotions, the contributors interrogate the multiple ways in which emotions function and matter to the study of global politics. Accordingly, the innovative contribution of this volume is its specific engagement with the role of emotions and constitution of emotional subjects in a range of different contexts of politics and war, including the gendered nature of war and security; war traumas; post-conflict reconstruction; and counterinsurgency operations.

Looking at how we analyse emotions in war, why it matters, and what emotions do in global politics, this volume will be of interest to students and scholars of critical security studies and international relations alike.

**Linda Åhäll** is Lecturer in International Relations at Keele University, UK.

**Thomas Gregory** is Lecturer in Politics and International Relations at Auckland University, New Zealand.

## Interventions

Edited by: Jenny Edkins, Aberystwyth University and Nick Vaughan-Williams, University of Warwick

The Series provides a forum for innovative and interdisciplinary work that engages with alternative critical, post-structural, feminist, postcolonial, psychoanalytic and cultural approaches to international relations and global politics. In our first 5 years we have published 60 volumes.

We aim to advance understanding of the key areas in which scholars working within broad critical post-structural traditions have chosen to make their interventions, and to present innovative analyses of important topics. Titles in the series engage with critical thinkers in philosophy, sociology, politics and other disciplines and provide situated historical, empirical and textual studies in international politics.

We are very happy to discuss your ideas at any stage of the project: just contact us for advice or proposal guidelines. Proposals should be submitted directly to the Series Editors:

- Jenny Edkins (jennyedkins@hotmail.com) and
- Nick Vaughan-Williams (N.Vaughan-Williams@Warwick.ac.uk).

'As Michel Foucault has famously stated, "knowledge is not made for understanding; it is made for cutting" In this spirit The Edkins - Vaughan-Williams Interventions series solicits cutting edge, critical works that challenge mainstream understandings in international relations. It is the best place to contribute post disciplinary works that think rather than merely recognize and affirm the world recycled in IR's traditional geopolitical imaginary.'

Michael J. Shapiro, University of Hawai'i at Manoa, USA

**Critical Theorists and International Relations**
*Edited by Jenny Edkins and Nick Vaughan-Williams*

**Ethics as Foreign Policy**
Britain, the EU and the other
*Dan Bulley*

**Universality, Ethics and International Relations**
A grammatical reading
*Véronique Pin-Fat*

**The Time of the City**
Politics, philosophy, and genre
*Michael J. Shapiro*

**Governing Sustainable Development**
Partnership, protest and power at the world summit
*Carl Death*

**Insuring Security**
Biopolitics, security and risk
*Luis Lobo-Guerrero*

**Foucault and International Relations**
New critical engagements
*Edited by Nicholas J. Kiersey and Doug Stokes*

**International Relations and Non-Western Thought**
Imperialism, colonialism and investigations of global modernity
*Edited by Robbie Shilliam*

**Autobiographical International Relations**
I, IR
*Edited by Naeem Inayatullah*

**War and Rape**
Law, memory and justice
*Nicola Henry*

**Madness in International Relations**
Psychology, security and the global governance of mental health
*Alison Howell*

**Spatiality, Sovereignty and Carl Schmitt**
Geographies of the nomos
*Edited by Stephen Legg*

**Politics of Urbanism**
Seeing like a city
*Warren Magnusson*

**Beyond Biopolitics**
Theory, violence and horror in world politics
*François Debrix and Alexander D. Barder*

**The Politics of Speed**
Capitalism, the state and war in an accelerating world
*Simon Glezos*

**Politics and the Art of Commemoration**
Memorials to struggle in Latin America and Spain
*Katherine Hite*

**Indian Foreign Policy**
The politics of postcolonial identity
*Priya Chacko*

**Politics of the Event**
Time, movement, becoming
*Tom Lundborg*

**Theorising Post-Conflict Reconciliation**
Agonism, restitution and repair
*Edited by Alexander Keller Hirsch*

**Europe's Encounter with Islam**
The secular and the postsecular
*Luca Mavelli*

**Re-Thinking International Relations Theory via Deconstruction**
*Badredine Arfi*

**The New Violent Cartography**
Geo-analysis after the aesthetic turn
*Edited by Sam Okoth Opondo and Michael J. Shapiro*

**Insuring War**
Sovereignty, security and risk
*Luis Lobo-Guerrero*

**International Relations, Meaning and Mimesis**
*Necati Polat*

**The Postcolonial Subject**
Claiming politics/governing others in late modernity
*Vivienne Jabri*

**Foucault and the Politics of Hearing**
*Lauri Siisiäinen*

**Volunteer Tourism in the Global South**
Giving back in neoliberal times
*Wanda Vrasti*

**Cosmopolitan Government in Europe**
Citizens and entrepreneurs in postnational politics
*Owen Parker*

**Studies in the Trans-Disciplinary Method**
After the aesthetic turn
*Michael J. Shapiro*

**Alternative Accountabilities in Global Politics**
The scars of violence
*Brent J. Steele*

**Celebrity Humanitarianism**
The ideology of global charity
*Ilan Kapoor*

**Deconstructing International Politics**
*Michael Dillon*

**The Politics of Exile**
*Elizabeth Dauphinee*

**Democratic Futures**
Revisioning democracy promotion
*Milja Kurki*

**Postcolonial Theory**
A critical introduction
*Edited by Sanjay Seth*

**More than Just War**
Narratives of the just war and military life
*Charles A. Jones*

**Deleuze & Fascism**
Security: war: aesthetics
*Edited by Brad Evans & Julian Reid*

**Feminist International Relations**
'Exquisite Corpse'
*Marysia Zalewski*

**The Persistence of Nationalism**
From imagined communities to urban encounters
*Angharad Closs Stephens*

**Interpretive Approaches to Global Climate Governance**
Reconstructing the greenhouse
*Edited by Chris Methmann, Delf Rothe & Benjamin Stephan*

**Postcolonial Encounters in International Relations**
The Politics of Transgression in the Maghred
*Alina Sajed*

**Post-Tsunami Reconstruction in Indonesia**
Negotiating normativity through gender mainstreaming initiatives in Aceh
*Marjaana Jauhola*

**Leo Strauss and the Invasion of Iraq**
Encountering the Abyss
*Aggie Hirst*

**Production of Postcolonial India and Pakistan**
Meanings of partition
*Ted Svensson*

**War, Identity and the Liberal State**
Everyday experiences of the geopolitical in the armed forces
*Victoria M. Basham*

**Writing Global Trade Governance**
Discourse and the WTO
*Michael Strange*

**Politics of Violence**
Militancy, international politics, killing in the name
*Charlotte Heath-Kelly*

**Ontology and World Politics**
Void Universalism I
*Sergei Prozorov*

**Theory of the Political Subject**
Void Universalism II
*Sergei Prozorov*

**Visual Politics and North Korea**
Seeing is believing
*David Shim*

**Globalization, Difference and Human Security**
*Edited by Mustapha Kamal Pasha*

**Imagining World Politics**
Sihar & Shenya, a fable for our times
*L.H.M Ling*

**International Politics and Performance**
Critical aesthetics and creative practice
*Edited by Jenny Edkins and Adrian Kear*

**Memory and Trauma in International Relations**
Theories, cases, and debates
*Edited by Erica Resende and Dovile Budryte*

**Critical Environmental Politics**
*Edited by Carl Death*

**Democracy Promotion**
A critical introduction
*Jeff Bridoux and Milja Kurki*

**International Intervention in a Secular Age**
Re-enchanting humanity?
*Audra Mitchell*

**The Politics of Haunting and Memory in International Relations**
*Jessica Auchter*

**European-East Asian Borders in Translation**
*Edited by Joyce C.H. Liu and Nick Vaughan-Williams*

**Genre and the (Post)Communist Woman**
Analyzing transformations of the central and Eastern European female ideal
*Edited by Florentina C. Andreescu and Michael Shapiro*

**Studying the Agency of Being Governed**
*Edited by Stina Hansson, Sofie Hellberg Maria Stern*

**Politics of Emotion**
The song of Telangana
*Himadeep Muppidi*

**Ruling the Margins**
Colonial power and administrative rule in the past and present
*Prem Kumar Rajaram*

**Race and Racism in International Relations**
Confronting the Global Colour Line
*Alexander Anievas, Nivi Manchanda and Robbie Shilliam*

**The Grammar of Politics and Performance**
*Edited by Shirin M. Rai and Janelle Reinelt*

**War, Police and Assemblages of Intervention**
*Edited by Jan Bachman, Colleen Bell and Caroline Holmqvist*

**Re-Imagining North Korea in International Politics**
Problematizations and alternatives
*Shine Choi*

**On Schmitt and Space**
*Claudio Minca and Rory Rowan*

**Face Politics**
*Jenny Edkins*

**Empire Within**
International hierarchy and its imperial laboratories of governance
*Alexander D. Barder*

**Sexual Politics and International Relations**
How LGBTQ claims shape international relations
*Edited by Manuela Lavinas Picq and Markus Thiel*

**Emotions, Politics and War**
*Edited by Linda Åhäll and Thomas Gregory*

# Emotions, Politics and War

Edited by
Linda Åhäll and Thomas Gregory

Routledge
Taylor & Francis Group
LONDON AND NEW YORK

First published 2015
by Routledge

2 Park Square, Milton Park, Abingdon, Oxfordshire OX14 4RN
711 Third Avenue, New York, NY 10017

*Routledge is an imprint of the Taylor & Francis Group, an informa business*

First issued in paperback 2017



*British Library Cataloguing in Publication Data*
A catalogue record for this book is available from the British Library

*Library of Congress Cataloging in Publication Data*
Emotions, politics and war / edited by Linda Ahall and Thomas Gregory.
pages cm – (Interventions)
Includes bibliographical references and index.
1. International relations–Psychological aspects. 2. Emotions (Philosophy) 3. Emotions–Political aspects. 4. War–Psychological aspects. I. Ahall, Linda, 1979- II. Gregory, Thomas, 1985-
JZ1253.E66 2015
355.0201'9–dc23
2014048209

ISBN: 978-1-138-78905-0 (hbk)
ISBN: 978-0-8153-7713-9 (pbk)

Typeset in Times New Roman
by Taylor & Francis Books

# Contents

# Notes of contributors

**Linda Åhäll** is Lecturer in International Relations at Keele University, UK, but during 2014-2016 working on the Militarization 2.0-project at Malmö University, Sweden. Her publications include *Sexing War/Policing Gender* (2015), *Gender, Agency and Political Violence* (co-editor, 2012) and journal articles in *Security Dialogue, International Feminist journal of Politics* and *Critical Studies on Security.*

**Victoria M. Basham** is Senior Lecturer in Politics at the University of Exeter. She researches feminist approaches to militaries, militarism and militarization. She edits *Critical Military Studies* and is the author of *War, Identity and the Liberal State: Everyday Experiences of the Geopolitical in the Armed Forces* (Routledge, 2013).

**Roland Bleiker** is Professor of International Relations at the University of Queensland. His current research examines how images, and the emotions they engender, shape responses to humanitarian crises. Recent publications include *Aesthetics and World Politics* (Palgrave, 2009/2012) and, as co-editor with Emma Hutchison, a forum on "Emotions and World Politics" in *International Theory* (Vol 3/2014).

**Neta C. Crawford** is Professor of Political Science at Boston University. She is the author of *Accountability for Killing* (2013) and *Argument and Change in World Politics* (2002) and journal articles including in *International Theory, International Security, Ethics & International Affairs, Midwest Studies in Philosophy, Foreign Policy,* and *International Organization.* She is co-director of the Costs of War Project, based at Brown University.

**K. M. Fierke** is Professor of International Relations in the School of International Relations at the University of St. Andrews. She is author of five books as well as numerous articles relating to constructivism and security and emotion, trauma and memory as they relate to political violence.

**Thomas Gregory** is Lecturer in Politics and International Relations at the University of Auckland. His research interests included violence, targeted killings and the ethics of war. He is currently working on a book project that focuses on the conceptualisation of civilian casualties in US counterinsurgency doctrine.

**Emmanuel-Pierre Guittet** is Lecturer in Political Violence, Terrorism and Security Studies at the *University of Manchester.* He is associate researcher at the *Centre for Research on Conflicts, Liberty, and Security* (CCLS, Paris).

**Jack Holland** is Senior Lecturer in International Relations at the University of Surrey. He is author of *Selling the War on Terror* and *Security: A Critical Introduction*, as well as of articles in journals such as *European Journal of International Relations* and *International Political Sociology.*

**Alison Howell** is Assistant Professor of Political Science and an affiliate of Women's and Gender Studies at Rutgers University – Newark. She writes about critical military and war studies, the global politics of medicine and psychology, and global inequality and justice. She is the author of *Madness in International Relations* (Routledge, 2011).

**Emma Hutchison** is a Postdoctoral Fellow in the School of Political Science and International Studies at the University of Queensland. Her research examines emotion and trauma in world politics. She recently completed her first book, *Affective Communities in World Politics: Collective Emotions After Trauma*, which is under contract with Cambridge University Press.

**Marjaana Jauhola** (PhD in International Politics, Aberystwyth University 2010) writes on gendered politics and 'respectability' in post-disaster and conflict contexts. Her publications include *Post-Tsunami Reconstruction in Indonesia: Negotiating Normativity through Gender Mainstreaming Initiatives in Aceh* (Routledge 2013). Currently she works on ethnographic film *Scraps of Hope.*

**Brian Massumi** is Professor of Communication at the University of Montreal. His most recent books include *Politics of Affect*, *The Power at the End of the Economy*, and *What Animals Teach Us about Politics.* He is co-author with Erin Manning of *Thought in the Act: Passages in the Ecology of Experience.*

**Rose McDermott** is the David and Marianna Fisher University Professor of International Relations at Brown University. She is a member of the American Academy of Arts and Sciences.

**Helen Parr** is Senior Lecturer in International Relations at Keele University, UK. Her publications include *British Policy towards the EEC, 1964–7* (2006), *The Wilson Governments Reconsidered* (2006, co-edited) and articles on British and French nuclear weapons policies. She is currently writing on British memory and experiences of the Falklands War.

**Ty Solomon** is Lecturer in International Relations at the University of Glasgow. He is the author of *The Politics of Subjectivity in American Foreign Policy Discourses* (University of Michigan Press), in addition to articles in

*International Studies Quarterly*, *European Journal of International Relations*, and other journals.

**Swati Parashar** is Lecturer in Politics and International Relations at Monash University, Australia. She researches feminist IR, critical security studies, gender, war and political violence. She is the author of *Women and Militant Wars* (2014) and has also published in journals such as *Cambridge Review of International Affairs* (2009; 2013) and *Studies in Conflict & Terrorism* (2011).

**Julia Welland** completed her PhD on masculinities and counterinsurgency in 2013 at the University of Manchester. She is now based in the Politics and International Studies Department at the University of Warwick and continues to research on gender, violence and militarism.

**Marysia Zalewski** is Professor in the School of Social Science, University of Aberdeen. She has published widely in the fields of feminism, gender, masculinity and International Relations; her book *Feminist International Relations: Exquisite Corpse* was published by Routledge in 2013.

**Andreja Zevnik** is Lecturer in International Politics at the University of Manchester. She is convener of Critical Global Politics research cluster at the University of Manchester and of British International Studies Association working group in Contemporary International Political Theory (CRIPT).

# Acknowledgements

When we first embarked on this project we were both based in the UK, and still blissfully unaware of what a curious experience trying to co-edit a book whilst living on opposite sides of the world was going to be. Many of the big editorial decisions were made during snatched conversations over social media, usually as one of us was just waking up and the other about to drift off to sleep. The time difference did, however, mean that production never ceased, which in turn meant that our poor contributors were receiving emails at all hours of the day. This book would have been impossible without the wonderful work they have produced, their ability to meet our, at times, tight deadlines without any fuss and their general enthusiasm for the project.

As series-editors, Jenny Edkins and Nick Vaughan-Williams have been very supportive of this endeavour and were a great help when we approached them with our ideas. The editorial team at Routledge also deserve our thanks for the support given to us and for making this journey as smooth as it has been during the last couple of years. Brad Evans graciously allowed us to reprint Brian Massumi's essay "The Remains of the Day", which originally appeared as part of his *Histories of Violence*-project. We would also like to thank Laura Shepherd for inviting us to do an Intervention-piece on the theme of emotions, security, affect in *Critical Studies on Security* in the early stages of this project, and we would like to thank Katherine E. Brown, Elina Penttinen and Michael J. Shapiro who were part of that project but unable to contribute to the larger book project. We also would like to thank Marysia, Swati, Julia and Jack for presenting their chapters on our panel 'Mapping Emotions, Politics and War' at the International Studies Association (ISA) conference in New Orleans 2015, Victoria Basham for doing a brilliant job as discussant, and Susanna Hast for joining our panel with a fantastic vocal performance. The ISA Methods Café organised by the wonderful Cai Wilkinson was also an excellent forum for testing these ideas. Can E. Mutlu was a great interlocutor at this event, as were the participants who came to join us for the session.

Linda would also like to acknowledge the research support of the School of Politics, IR, Philosophy and Environment (SPIRE) at Keele University, UK; the Swedish Research Council (Vetenskapsrådet); Global Political Studies at

Malmö University, Sweden, particularly Susan Jackson and the other Militarization 2.0-project members. Above all though, I would like to thank our inspirational contributors who make this book what it is: amazingly thought-provoking, and, of course, Tom, for sharing this journey with me. I am incredibly proud of this book.

Tom would like to thank Julia Welland, Jamie Johnson, Anita Lacey, Andrew Slack, Megan Daigle and Andreja Zevnik for conversations along the way, as well as Mandy Roberts for all her love, patience and support over the years. Maria Tanyag and Ben Abraham were wonderful research assistants during the preliminary stages of this project, so I would like to thank them for their work and the University of Auckland for providing financial support to make this work possible. Linda was the perfect co-editor and a pleasure to work with.

*Linda Åhäll, Malmö.*
*Tom Gregory, Auckland.*
*February, 2015.*

# Preface

*Neta C. Crawford*

> If a theory is not an edifice of truth and not a reproduction of reality, then what is it? A theory is a picture, mentally formed, of a bounded realm or domain of activity… . Theory isolates one realm from all others in order to deal with it intellectually… . The question, as ever with theories, is not whether the isolation of a realm is realistic, but whether it is useful.
>
> Kenneth Waltz, *Theory of International Politics* (1979: 8)

Most theories of politics and military strategy assume that humans are rational utility maximisers. Or theorists at least take for granted that 'the assumption of rationality is a productive one' (Schelling 1960: 4). In emphasising rationality, the structural realist picture of world politics effectively excises emotions from explicit analysis. On this view, to the extent that they are mentioned, emotions are understood to be private reactions, perhaps deliberately manipulated by leaders, or an unconscious pernicious influence on decision-making, in whose absence, or through greater discipline, a rational/correct decision would have been reached.

The assumption of rationality, or at least dispassion, is constitutive of the definition of war that most scholars of world politics use. Specifically, contemporary scholars define wars by the phenomenon of force-on-force battle, and they qualify an event as a war based on the resultant battle deaths. For example, in the Correlates of War project, the threshold of a thousand combatant battle deaths qualifies an event as war. 'We must define war in terms of violence. Not only is war impossible without violence (except of course in the metaphorical sense), but we consider the taking of human life the primary and dominant characteristic of war' (Small and Singer 1982: 205–206). While the threshold for the Uppsala Conflict Database is lower, their definition of armed conflict is similarly free of emotional tone. 'An armed conflict is a contested incompatibility that concerns government and/or territory where the use of armed force between two parties, of which at least one is the government of a state, results in at least 25 battle-related deaths in one calendar year' (Uppsala University 2014).

Early and pioneering work in International Relations theory has challenged the assumption of rationality and explored cognitions and motivated biases. Robert Jervis, Richard Ned Lebow, Janice Stein and Deborah Welch Larson pioneered and extended the use of cognitive psychology for the study of deterrence, brinkmanship, and war. They and others showed, through comparative case studies and process-tracing, that humans were subject to cognitive biases and limitations. The assumption of rationality needed to be amended, but the cognitive turn minimised emotion.

Robert Jervis came to see the neglect of emotions as a mistake. Nearly thirty years after the publication of *Perception and Misperception in International Politics* (1976), Jervis acknowledged that the book missed the emotional dimension. '*Perception and Misperception* completely put aside emotion. ... This was a major blunder' (Balzacq and Jervis 2004: 564–565). Jervis says, 'I would very much like to produce a study that shows how emotions and cognitions interact in politics, but at this point the challenge is simply too great' (Balzacq and Jervis 2004: 565).

While analytic and quantitative definitions of war tend to omit emotions and to focus on action in the 'battlefield', emotions permeate classical political theory and security studies (see Crawford 2000 and 2009). Indeed, earlier observers and practitioners of war understood that emotions could not be easily disentangled from 'rationality', beliefs or the motives for action. Brian Massumi (Chapter 2 in this volume) recalls Carl von Clausewitz's observation in *On War* (1984) that war is the continuation of politics by other means. *On War* is a long book, and Clausewitz says a great deal about many aspects of war, including, as Åhäll and Gregory note, emotions. Clausewitz noted the tendency to dismiss emotions: 'Theorists are apt to look on fighting in the abstract as a trial of strength without emotion entering into it. This is one of a thousand errors which they quite consciously commit because they have no idea of the implications' (1984: 138).

In fact, emotions are central to Clausewitz's analysis of war, which he says is a 'paradoxical trinity – composed of primordial violence, hatred and enmity, which are to be regarded as a blind natural force; of the play of chance and probability within which the creative spirit is free to roam; and of its element of subordination, as an instrument of policy, which makes it subject to reason alone' (1984: 89). Clausewitz does not consider emotions apart from the other elements of war. In his discussion of military genius, he says, 'Of all the passions that inspire man in battle, none, we have to admit, is so powerful and so constant as the longing for honor and renown' (1984: 105). Further, Clausewitz characterises combat as 'essentially ... an expression of hostile feelings' (1984: 137). He argues that 'even when there is no national hatred and no animosity to start with, the fighting itself will stir up hostile feelings: violence committed on superior orders will stir up the desire for revenge and retaliation against the perpetrator rather than against the powers that ordered the action. That is only human (or animal if you like), but it is a fact' (1984: 138). In stressing the importance of character, and especially of courage, Clausewitz acknowledges the fact that soldiers are not so fearless and unemotionally ruthless as contemporary stereotypes have sometimes portrayed and as basic training has worked to instill.

In a masterful over 1,600-page volume, *A Study of War*, Quincy Wright first defines war as 'the legal condition which equally permits two or more hostile groups to carry on a conflict by armed force' (Wright 1965: 8). Wright then concentrates on the phenomena that characterise war: military activity, high psychological tension level, abnormal law and 'intensive political integration' within the belligerent community. For Wright, as for Clausewitz, the feeling of hostility is at the core of the phenomenon. 'The individual loves his own group and hates the enemy group' (1965: 699). The authors in this volume extend some of those themes. For example, as Basham suggests in Chapter 10, soldiers' beliefs about gender, and the emotions associated with those beliefs, are to be managed and harnessed. As Howell shows in Chapter 11, empathy and compassion are mobilised alongside hate.

Why do we need to include emotions, beyond the obvious statement that they are present in world politics and war? I think this and other recent work on emotions suggests that it is not just that emotions are missing from analysis, and we ought to add another variable to our list of factors that may affect outcomes. Rather, emotions are constitutive of war and politics. Recent research on decision-making shows that humans are both thinking and feeling, and emotions are an inextricable element of social life. Just as it is impossible to separate emotions from cognition in a healthy brain, there is no way to divide the passionate from the 'rational' in politics (Damasio 1994). Ruthless efforts to relegate emotions to the residual may lead to incomplete description, mistaken analysis or ineffective policy prescriptions. In sum, emotions are everywhere in world politics, and we ignore them at our peril. As Jervis argues, 'as we learn more about the role of emotions, it becomes clear that we cannot even imagine life, let alone sensible life, without their playing a large role' (Balzacq and Jervis 2004: 567).

Just what role do emotions play? First, policymakers and strategists often try to manipulate the emotions of their opponents, using what might be called naive or folk theories of how emotions work. In other words, warriors and strategists know that emotions are part of war, and in some ways constitutive of it; they make assumptions about the way emotions work, and military doctrines aim to manipulate emotions. For example, many strategists assume that it is possible to successfully manipulate fear in war. The working assumption of deterrence theory is that if a threat is communicated clearly, and if the threat is sufficiently, well, 'threatening', the object of the threat – if they are rational – should back down. In other words, the rational deterrence model assumes that the deliberate production of fear works to get an adversary's attention and induce their compliance with your demands. Indeed, this belief – that fear can be successfully manipulated in others – is at the core of many behaviours we study, including brinksmanship, arms racing and negotiation. But, as I suggest elsewhere, there is good reason to suspect that the deliberate production of fear reliably causes an opponent to yield (Crawford 2000, 2009, 2014).

Second, emotions are not just deployed, they are the frames through which actors understand their world. As George W. Bush said on 20 September

2001 to a Joint Session of the United States Congress: 'Great harm has been done to us. We have suffered great loss. And in our grief and anger we have found our mission and our moment. Freedom and fear are at war.' As Robert Jervis argues, 'In the event of a large-scale attack, emotions would surely weigh very heavily. This is not to say that an emotion-based response would be wrong or to hold up unemotional calculation as the model of rationality' (Balzacq and Jervis 2004: 567).

Why, if emotions are everywhere in world politics, and deeply embedded in the assumptions of our theories, hasn't theorising about emotions become more central to the field? There are legitimate reasons, at the level of epistemology and ontology, for caution about the study of emotions in politics, although those concerns also point to fruitful avenues of research.

One reason for caution among social scientists is that much of the literature on emotions and politics, especially that which draws on neuroscience, is concerned with the micro, at the level of chemical signals and brain structures, sometimes reporting the results of functional magnetic resonance imaging (fMRI) and so on. The literature is focused on decision-making, and often describes processes that occur in fractions of a second, which ostensibly disappear. Further, much of the research emotion in politics concerns voting and political campaigns – areas that are of little interest to scholars of war and peace. In addition, with important exceptions, this literature has not gone far enough – to illuminate connections and causes from the micro to the political – to interest most theorists of international security. It appears to be stuck in the brain, an ostensibly private realm (for examples and exceptions, see Neuman *et al.* 2007).

Another concern is that emotions seem somehow very different from rational cognition, or at least the assumption of rationality. Emotions are ostensibly fleeting, impulsive and private. They appear to be here and then gone, a feature of agents and agency, rather than of process and structure. It is unclear how to measure emotions, gauge their intensity, or even distinguish genuine emotions from a manipulative display of feelings, and whether and when that distinction matters. The challenge is explaining how something so ostensibly ephemeral and mercurial as emotions may have enduring, structural effects.

But it is precisely these concerns that point to avenues for further research and theorising. Recognising that emotions are an inextricable element of human reasoning, there is a great deal we can learn from continued attention to the neuroscience of emotions if we take care to relate it to the evidence of foreign policy decision-making. In short, humans simply do not think the way we thought they did. Attending to the ways in which affect and cognition work together might sharpen our analysis and produce policy prescriptions that are useful in decision-making, diplomacy and negotiation. It would pay to revisit the assumptions and beliefs about emotion that are embedded in theories of world politics. Doing so would help us uncover the ways that unselfconscious (and perhaps untested) beliefs about emotions animate our paradigms.

For example, there is good reason to believe that the outcomes of the practice of deterrence so often do not match the predictions of deterrence theory because our theories and policies are mistaken about how leaders and states react to threats.

Emotions are not so mercurial as we often suppose. Rather, emotions are often institutionalised, incorporated and, eventually, deeply embedded in the processes and structures of world politics. The institutionalisation of emotions is perhaps the key thread that ties the agential aspects of emotions to the structures and processes of world politics. It is perhaps easiest to see the institutionalisation of emotion when new emotions have been dramatically evoked and policies pivot in response. When emotions such as fear and anger animate the policy process, become institutionalised in threat assessment and budgets, and prompt reactions by other states and organisations, the emotions have become institutionalised with long-term effects that can produce yet more emotions. Emotions are then part of a recursive process, constituting action and reaction dynamics, shaping perceptions and justifying policies. Security dilemmas and escalatory spirals are only one manifestation of the institutionalisation of emotions (Crawford 2014).

Scholars of world politics who make pictures of the world and the practices of war, as if from space, see great masses, dynamics and flows; others begin with beliefs and reasons, with agents who make the structures. Some scholars' pictures attend to the brain's anatomy; using fMRI they trace electrical impulses and blood flow in the brain. Others focus on the cellular level, as if from an electron microscope, with stains highlighting ever-smaller structures and activities, our gaze fixed on neurons and neurochemistry.

Work that explores the role of emotions in war, as the authors in this volume do, can offer pictures of world politics from every one of these views. Adding emotions is like adding colour to a black-and-white image. Work that reads world politics and war with emotions in the foreground, rather than as an element to be dismissed, or a distortion, offers a new set of lenses – actually, several new pairs. Not just lenses without scratches, but lenses with a different prescription, that help us know what was already there, perhaps unseen, indeed often erased, distorted or re-constructed. The challenge is to highlight how emotions work, while at the same time acknowledging that emotions are elements of the features of structure, agency and processes of world politics.

The scholars in this volume take the study of war to new and different landscapes, and provide fresh insights on familiar territory.

## Bibliography

Balzacq, T. and Jervis, R. (2004) 'Logics of mind and international system: A journey with Robert Jervis', *Review of International Studies*, 30(4): 559–582.

Clausewitz, C. (1984) *On War*, Howard and Paret (eds and transl.). Princeton, NJ: Princeton University Press.

Crawford, N. C. (2000) 'The passion of world politics: Propositions on emotion and emotional relationships', *International Security*, 24(4): 116–156.

Crawford, N. C. (2009) 'Human nature and world politics: Rethinking "Man"', *International Relations*, 23(2): 271–288.

Crawford, N. C. (2014) 'Institutionalizing passion in world politics: Fear and empathy', *International Theory*, 6(3): 535–557.

Damasio, A. R. (1994) *Descartes' Error: Emotion, Reason and the Human Brain*. New York: Quill.

Jervis, R. (1976) *Perception and Misperception in International Politics*. Princeton, NJ: Princeton University Press.

Neuman, R. W., Marcus, G. E., Crigler, A. N. and MacKuen, M. (2007) *The Affect Effect: Dynamics of Emotion in Political Thinking and Behavior*. Chicago, IL: University of Chicago Press.

Schelling, T. C. (1960) *The Strategy of Conflict*. Cambridge, MA: Harvard University Press.

Small, M. and Singer, J. D. (1982) *Resort to Arms: International and Civil War, 1816–1980*. Beverly Hills, CA: Sage.

Uppsala University (2014) Department of Peace and Conflict Research, Conflict Database. Available online at: www.pcr.uu.se/research/ucdp/definitions (accessed September 2014).

Waltz, K. N. (1979) *Theory of International Politics*. New York: Random House.

Wright, Q. (1965) *A Study of War*, Second Edition *with a Commentary on War Since 1942*. Chicago, IL: University of Chicago Press.

# 1 Introduction

## Mapping emotions, politics and war

*Thomas Gregory and Linda Åhäll*

The commemorations marking the centenary of the First World War have brought the lived experiences of those most affected by war back into view. In contrast to previous years, there has been a much greater emphasis on lived experiences of those touched by war. To mark the anniversary, *The Guardian* has opened up its website to readers, encouraging them to submit mementos of the war. Since its initial launch, there has been a steady stream of faded photographs, tattered postcards and old letters submitted to the site – memorabilia that provide a very different perspective from how stories of war are usually told. One entry, for example, describes in quite disconcerting detail the mood in the trenches following the execution of a soldier for desertion. The details, recorded in the diary of an army chaplain, recount the moment that the soldier – 'only a boy' – was led out to be shot. In a last-gasp effort to escape, the chaplain describes how he 'ran wildly across the broken ground, stumbling, panting, straining' before being caught and lined up against a sandbag, 'a pathetic figure of exhaustion and helpless appeal' (*The Guardian* 2014). A few hours later, clearly still uncertain about the rights and wrongs of the execution, the chaplain recorded his feelings again, 'the strain of this morning's tragedy has been rather much' (*The Guardian* 2014).

Along with the letters describing the misery of life in the trenches, the pain of being far from home, and the horrors of the conflict, there are numerous items that hint at the more enjoyable aspects of people's wartime experiences. Although these may represent nothing more than a brief respite in an otherwise terrifying experience, they point to experiences of war that are often overlooked.[1] One photograph shows three men sitting in a dugout in Egypt, grinning toward the camera from underneath their pith helmets as they drink tea from a cup and saucer. Other photographs show groups of soldiers standing around watching unsanctioned boxing matches, cheering on one side or the other as they try to find ways to pass the time. Still others tell of the boredom and monotony of trench life; variations of the phrase 'nothing exciting to report' are common. Of course, these items were not necessarily meant to be seen by anyone other than the intended recipient. They are not the memoirs of a great military leader or an important political figure, but the intimate reflections, thoughts and memories of ordinary people, perhaps hidden away at the back of an old drawer or left to collect dust in a loft. Still, these historical artefacts reveal aspects of their authors' experiences that are often forgotten, overlooked or simply pushed to the margins of political and academic debates on war.

In her influential essay 'The passion of world politics', Neta C. Crawford (2000) argues that emotions have been neglected in the study of global politics, despite that they actively shape the world around us. Her intervention was particularly thought-provoking as emotions, in the realm and study of 'high politics', security and war, tend to be seen as contrary to reason and rationality, and to be relegated to the private, feminine sphere, or seen as some kind of bodily aberration that needs to be subdued or overcome. Yet key ideas in the study of war, such as deterrence, cooperation and security, Crawford argues, simply do not make sense unless we take emotions into consideration. The security dilemma, for example, cannot be understood without some awareness of the fear, anxiety or apprehension that underpins the calculations of state leaders as they look at what their rivals are doing. The problem with the academic discipline of International Relations (IR), Crawford notes, is not that the emotions are absent, but that they are treated as undisputable and entirely unproblematic (2000: 118–121). In other words, it is because rationalist prejudices have traditionally dominated the discipline of IR that the role of emotions in global politics has been downplayed, ignored or denigrated, despite that emotions are essential to the way in which conflicts are both thought and fought.[2]

Although some contributions to IR acknowledged that psychological issues are important to perception and therefore, for example, key to understanding why state leaders go to war (see Jervis 1976), it is only more recently that a growing number of scholars have sought to re-centre emotions in our study of international politics.

Contemporary commemoration of war shows us what war meant and means to us. Such meanings are emotional, but such emotional meanings are also political. With this book we would like to make the simple point that we cannot make sense of war if we are unable or unwilling to pay attention to the sensual experiences of those affected. The contributors to this volume, therefore, proceed from the assumption that a nuanced understanding of emotions, affect and the somatic experience of the human body can only enhance our engagement with contemporary conflict and war (Sylvester 2011; McSorley 2012; Holmqvist 2013). Our overall aim is to provide a range of perspectives on the conditions, maintenance and interpretation of emotions that will both enhance scholarly understandings of war and interrogate the multiple ways in which emotions function and matter to the study of global politics. In this way, we hope to turn conventional approaches to conflict, IR and security on their head, not only by thinking about the embodied experiences of those affected by war and other forms of violence, but also by exploring the ways in which emotions function to re-inscribe the boundaries between the human and the non-human and differentiate between those who can be loved and those who cannot, those who should be feared and those who should not, those whose deaths can be grieved and those whose deaths cannot. In multiple ways, we hope this book will contribute to conversations about the practice, study and experiences of war that are frequently marginalised, silenced, forgotten or ignored despite their obvious importance.

Our final aim is to facilitate some conversations about how to study a topic that, at first glance, might appear rather difficult to grasp. The methods used and perspectives taken by the contributors to this book are by no means the only ways to engage with the topic methodologically; nevertheless, we hope these interventions can start a wider conversation on how to think seriously about the [political] role of emotions, feelings and affects in contemporary practices, experiences and representations of war. This is because, as Jon Elster argues, if we do not account for emotions, the things that happen in the world – from the mundane decisions we make in our everyday lives to acts of genocide on a much larger scale – would simply be unintelligible (Elster 1999: 403–4). This book is about, on multiple levels, making the politics of war intelligible.

## What are emotions?

It may seem like a relatively straightforward task to explain what counts as an emotion. After all, we are all familiar with the spectrum of emotional states, from the more negative feelings associated with anger, sadness and fear to the more positive experiences of joy, optimism, hope. However, our familiarity with these emotions can be quite deceiving; there is simply no agreed definition of what counts as an emotion. With this book, we do not attempt to offer a fixed definition of emotions. Instead, we echo Roland Bleiker and Emma Hutchison's call for 'a type of scholarly and political sensibility that could conceptualise the influence of emotions even where and when it is not immediately apparent' (2008: 128). With this caveat in mind, we now discuss the most important ways in which emotions have been theorised.

The *Oxford English Dictionary* describes an emotion as an 'agitation of the mind' or an 'excited mental state' that is commonly used to signify feelings such as 'pleasure, grief, hope, fear, etc.', derived from our relationships with others. According to so-called basic emotions research, there are six (or maybe five or seven) universal primary human emotions and a more tenuous set of secondary emotions (Wetherell 2012: 18). However, within this range, affective reactions do not seem to fit. To make matters worse, it is not always possible to distinguish between an emotion and a mood, or an emotion and a physical condition or bodily state. Going by the dictionary definition, one would be hard pressed to differentiate between an emotional state and a mood or temperament, which makes classifying states such as boredom, optimism, excitement or apathy incredibly difficult. Likewise, there appears to be a great deal of overlap between our emotional state and our physical condition. Let's think about how one can be a 'happy person' without being happy in that particular moment, or angry about structures of poverty without necessarily experiencing the physical conditions that we would normally associate with anger. Rather than being an emotional experience as such, these examples seem to be more of a value judgement about what is right and what is just – how emotions experienced are closely related to our normative beliefs as individuals. The idea that emotions simply signify feelings, in other words, seems insufficient.

Scholars arguing that emotions should be viewed as a cultural construct, which we follow here, take issue with approaches that focus on the cognitive dimension of our emotional experiences, and with studies on emotions that place more emphasis on physiological, neurological and biological dimensions of emotional experience.[3] Catherine A. Lutz, for example, argues that we need to 'deconstruct an overly naturalised and rigidly bounded concept of emotion, to treat emotion as an ideological practice rather than as a thing to be discovered or an essence to be distilled' (1988: 4). Such a focus, which has been used to great effect by postcolonial, feminist and queer theorists, means a focus on not just what emotions *are*, but also what they *do*. For example, Lauren Berlant has focused her attention on the *effects* of compassion in producing and maintaining exclusionary practices. The emphasis of compassion, she argues, is not on the experiences of those who are suffering, but on the experiences of those watching from afar (2004: 1–2; see also Spelman 1997; Sedgwick 2003; Welland, Chapter 9 in this volume).

Some of the most exciting work being done on such performative power of emotions is by Sara Ahmed. In *The Cultural Politics of Emotion*, Ahmed uses 'emotions' rather broadly, as the idea of 'impression', precisely to avoid making analytical distinctions between bodily sensation, emotion and thought, as if, she says, they could be 'experienced' as distinct realms of human 'experience' (Ahmed 2004: 6). Ahmed argues that emotions are not simply feelings that an individual undergoes, but are cultural constructs that help to 'shape the "surfaces" of individuals and collective bodies' (2004: 1). When we are scared, for example, we are responding not simply to some existential danger that this person or object poses, but to the cultural memories and shared social norms that have marked them as dangerous in our minds. Likewise, the hate we might feel towards certain groups of people cannot be understood as the manifestation of some innate dislike for them that is buried deep within us. Rather, it is the product of past encounters that have resulted in these groups being demarcated as a threat to our way of life (2004: 42). Moreover, this experience of hatred or fear is not a passive occurrence, but works to reaffirm the boundaries between us and them and to strengthen the notion that they are a group that should be approached with caution (2004: 63). As Ahmed explains, 'emotions work to differentiate between others precisely by identifying those that *can be* loved those that *can be* grieved, that is, by constituting some other as legitimate objects of emotion [whilst denying others the same privilege]' (2004: 191, emphasis in original).

Affect, by contrast, has traditionally been used as a noun to signify an inner disposition or feeling, or a mental state, mood or emotion. Affect can also be used as a transitive verb to indicate the ways in which something or someone may cause a particular *effect*, material or otherwise. In this sense, affect can be used to explain effects on the mind or feelings of a person, the ways in which someone can be impressed upon, moved and touched. It also signifies the material effects that can be made, the physical imprints that might be left after a particular encounter between two objects or the physiological impressions left upon the body.

Within the academic literature, affect has been used in a variety of different ways. Although there is no agreed definition of what affect is, studies of affect generally tend to move beyond a focus on single emotions to explore our ability to affect and be affected in more depth. To some, it is important to separate affect from emotion in the sense that, where emotions might be used to denote a more amplified, developed and coherent form of experience, affect is seen as something that is *before* emotion:

> Affect gives you away: the tell-tale heart; my clammy hands; the note of anger in your voice; the sparkle of glee in their eyes… Affect is the cuckoo in the nest; the fifth columnist out to undermine you; your personal polygraph machine.
>
> (Highmore 2010: 118)

Although there is disagreement to what extent affect is mainly biological and instinctive or social, an interest in affect necessarily involves a focus on bodies (human and non-human), and affect theorists thus often focus on embodiment – on the very fabric of the body and those forms of embodied experience that often remain unseen, unnoticed and unrecognised. In contrast to personal, and conscious, emotional experiences identified as 'feelings', affect resembles a flow of resonances, a form of emotional communication between body and mind that influences us, and is therefore often described as non-conscious, non-subjective or pre-personal. In other words, whereas emotion might capture the conscious thoughts, subjective experiences and normative judgements belonging to the individual, affect refers to a completely different order of activity where, as Nigel Thrift suggests, affect can be understood as a 'set of embodied practices' or as a form of 'indirect and non-reflective' thinking that never quite rises to the level of an emotion (2008: 175).

Others are careful not to overstate a distinction between emotion and affect. Margaret Wetherell uses affect as '*embodied meaning-making* that is mostly understood as *human emotion*' (Wetherell 2012: 4, emphasis in original); and while Brian Massumi would agree with Thrift that affect has another 'logic' than emotion, he argues that these two registers can be situated on the same continuum, viewing the former as a more qualified and coherent expression of the latter. Emotion, Massumi argues, can be viewed as a 'qualified intensity' or 'sociolinguistic fixing' of affect that has been imbrued with subjective content; emotion is 'intensity owned and recognised' (Massumi 2002: 28). Affect, to Massumi, is *that* feeling of dread that seems to creep up on you when walking home late at night: the goose-bumps that cover the skin, the tension in the shoulders, the hairs that stand up on the back of your neck that seem to appear when you catch a glimpse of a strange shadow or hear an unexpected sound (2002: 25). Similarly, William Connolly speaks of the 'thought-imbrued energies' that find expression in the 'timbre of our voices, the calmness or intensity of our gestures, our facial expression, the flush of our faces, the rate of our heartbeats, the receptivity, tightness, or sweatiness of our skin, and the relaxation or turmoil in our guts' (2002: 74).

The suggestion that affects can be understood as pre-personal and non-subjective does not mean that they are asocial, or that they can be located and contained within a single body (Massumi 2002: 35). In a recent textbook on affect theory, Gregory J. Seigworth and Melissa Gregg argue that there can be no pure state of affect because it 'arises in the midst of *in-between-ness*: in the capacities to act and be acted upon' (2010: 1). This 'in-between-ness', moreover, commonly described as 'stickyness', 'movement', or 'forces of encounter', means that affect is located in those intensities that pass body to body (human, nonhuman, part-body, and otherwise). This means that even our most intimate feelings do not really belong to us, but are an effect of the body's encounters with others. As Kathleen Stewart explains, affect can be seen as 'a connection of some kind that has an impact. It's transpersonal or pre-personal – it is not about one person's feelings becoming another's but about bodies literally affecting one another' (2007: 128). Perhaps the clearest example of what we mean here is Teresa Brennan's notion of an 'affective atmosphere', which she uses to refer to that feeling you get when you walk into a room and sense a particular mood in the air (Brennan 2004: 2). In this sense, affects are transmitted between bodies to the extent that the moods of others can have a physical and psychological impact on others without their consent. Sara Ahmed, however, points out how the affective atmosphere is also dependent on the baggage that we bring with us: 'What we will receive as an impression will depend on our affective situation' (Ahmed 2010: 36). In other words, even when we feel we have the same feeling, we do not necessarily have the same relationship to that feeling (Ahmed 2004: 10).

## Research on emotions, politics and war

Although the emotional and affective dimension of war has largely been ignored within the discipline of IR, there have been some important interventions. Perhaps most prominently, Jonathan Mercer has built on developments in psychology and neuroscience to argue that even the most hard-headed of rational-choice scenarios do not work unless you take into account the feelings of those expected to make a [rational] decision within these systemic constraints; Mercer shows how emotions are rational (Mercer 2005). Andrew Ross (2006) has highlighted the role of emotions in sustaining identities and norms in the international arena, for example, in order to understand why states choose to conform to certain international norms but violate others. Likewise, Ned Lebow argues that most actors (including states) frame their identities and interests in collective terms and therefore, he suggests, feelings of empathy might encourage states to cooperate rather than pursue purely self-interested initiatives (2005: 304). Similarly, building on social psychology research, Brent Sasley argues that states can and should be theorised as groups that have emotional reactions (2011).

These contributions, although adding to how emotions matter in IR, remain focused on how emotions matter to states, or to how statesmen and women are making decisions in the name of the state. As such, they do not explore emotions through the everyday experiences of those actually, personally, affected by war.

When it comes to research on emotions and war, much work has approached 'emotions' through 'feelings', predominantly negative. A lot of this work also centres around the terror attacks in the United States on 11 September 2001 and/or the ensuing 'war on terror'. Alex Danchev (2006), for example, reflects on emotions as military strategy, and argues that humiliation and shame were an essential part of the interrogation techniques used at Abu Ghraib, Guantanamo Bay and beyond. Similarly, Paul Saurette (2006) claims that American counter-terrorism initiatives cannot be understood without paying attention to the humiliation that Americans experienced when attacked and their desire to humiliate others in response; points that are echoed by Khaled Fattah and Karin M. Fierke (2009; see also Fierke 2014).

Furthermore, discussing emotion as affect, some scholars in and beyond IR have focused their attention on the manipulation, indeed the politics, of fear after the terror attacks in the USA in 2001, as a way of justifying security measures against unrealised future threats, both domestically and in the form of military interventions in Afghanistan and Iraq. Brian Massumi, for example, discusses affect in relation to the *pre-emptive* security measures taken in response to *potential* threats post-9/11: 'A threat that does not materialize is not false. It has all the affective reality of the past, truly felt' (Massumi 2010: 54). Ben Anderson explores the role of affect as morale of 'total wars'. Anderson argues, for example, that there is an affective dimension to aerial bombing campaigns such as the 'shock and awe' campaign in Iraq: it was not only designed to cause damage to the enemy, but was also a performative demonstration of America's military power and Iraq's violability and impotence (2010a: 181–182). In addition, the military strategy of counterinsurgency has meant 'population-centric operations', aimed at winning the hearts and minds of the local population in an attempt at preventing them from supporting the insurgency or resistance (see Chapter 9). The affective dimension to this policy, Anderson argues, is that by rebuilding local amenities, providing health-care and reopening schools, counterinsurgents are trying to create atmospheres of hope, respect and trust within the local population (2010b: 214).[4] Whether such a strategy of affect actually works is, of course, another matter.

Others have focused on emotions as individual and shared social experiences. Jenny Edkins, for example, has focused on our experiences of trauma, defined as an 'exposure to an event so shocking that our everyday expectations of how the world works are severely disrupted' (2002: 245). The events of 11 September can be considered traumatic, she argues, because they were 'outside the frameworks of normal social reality and thus outside the linguistic and other symbolic tools we have at our disposal for making sense of the world' (2002: 246, see also Edkins 2003). Trauma is also a theme that is addressed by Emma Hutchison (2010) in her work on the constitution of identity, security and community in the aftermath of the Bali bombing in 2002. Although trauma is often viewed as experience that isolates individuals and undermines any sense of community, Hutchison argues that the narratives used to make sense of a traumatic event can help to produce a sense of community and togetherness (2010: 66).

Moreover, acknowledging the role of emotions in war also means recognising how emotions form and impact upon us as researchers of war. In a forum edited by Christine Sylvester in *International Studies Review* (2011), emotional challenges in relation to being researchers of war were addressed. The point was made that not only do we need to remain open to the emotional experiences of those we are studying, but we also need to address our own emotional experiences as researchers. In the forum, both Megan MacKenzie and Swati Parashar reflect upon how, after having done fieldwork, they felt compelled to write emotions out of their research in order to be taken seriously by the discipline, effectively censoring their own emotions.

Within this literature, the terms emotion and affect are sometimes used interchangeably, whereas to some authors it is the distinction between emotion and affect that matters most. Others distinguish between macro and micro approaches to the study of emotions. And, within the micro perspective, some draw on developments within neuroscience and brain psychology and others on feminist engagements with bodies and embodiment. With this, by default limited and partial, discussion of a complex and at times contradictory area of research, we do not wish to offer one single definition of either of these ways to analyse the emotional. Rather, we encourage creativity as a method.

## Outline of this book

We have divided the book into two themed sections. The first looks at the different ways in which scholars have theorised the relationship between emotions, affect and war, focusing specific attention on competing methodological claims. The second, by contrast, focuses on the different ways in which emotional experiences of war can help us better understand contemporary practices of violence. Several chapters touch on both of these aspects. Thus the outline provided here is only one of many ways in which the chapters speak to each other. We hope our readers will find their own ways to connect and explore the methodological, empirical and analytical links between the thought-provoking chapters in this volume.

The first contribution (Chapter 2) is a reprint of Brian Massumi's essay 'The remains of the day', which was originally published online in 2013 as part of Brad Evans' multimedia project 'Histories of Violence'.[5] Massumi reflects upon the policy doctrine of 'preemption' as the remains of the 9/11 terror attacks. He argues that it is a logic that operates in the realm of affect; it is about 'gut-feeling' and it is about 'feeling the threat into reality', but it is also a self-operating logic that 'spreads its tentacles'. He concludes by offering a glimmer of hope: 'generosity' as a collectively practised political procedure to act as a counter-affective posture to pre-emption.

In Chapter 3, Marysia Zalewski offers a rather different reflection on the political power of emotions. By thinking about two Carries – the lead protagonist in the US drama *Homeland* and the main character in Stephen King's book *Carrie* – Zalewski reflects on some of the boundaries to which a focus on the role of emotions invites us. She notes how gender 'keeps appearing and re-appearing like an amorphous border guard'. Starting with a feeling, a personal encounter, an uncomfortable moment, Zalewski also illustrates the difficulty in theorising emotions academically. But, of course, if we are to break with our tendency in IR as 'uncurious methodological amateurs in regard to meaning making', Zalewski argues, it is important to explore the in-betweenness, the uncomfortable and the everyday as a way to disrupt the shortcomings of hegemonic approaches which simply re-articulate specific configurations of power relations.

In Chapter 4, Karin Fierke takes a more overarching approach as she explores collective, social and cultural aspects of human dignity and its negative counterpart, humiliation. In a similar way to state sovereignty, Fierke argues, human dignity is about existential value; however, it is about more than survival – it is about the importance of autonomy to the dignity of human life. She argues that, as a result of the fact that human dignity is seen as an existential value in international law, today there is a global emotionology; the norms that shape appropriate expression of emotion are global, which means that both awareness and expression of basal emotions such as human dignity and humiliation are facilitated.

Chapters 5 and 6 offer methodological discussions on emotions, politics and war. First, Ty Solomon calls on studies of war to focus on emotions through the role of the body. He argues that much work in IR and security studies still remains too disembodied. Solomon turns to recent literature on 'new materialism' in order to get at the corporeal and embodied aspects of identity/difference dynamics in the intersections of emotions, discourse and the body. He argues that a focus on bodies through materialism offers consideration to the role of the lived experience and materialisations of meaning that constitute the felt effects of emotions and discourses of (in)security. Then, in a chapter that focuses on anger, Swati Parashar also discusses emotions through the body. Parashar makes the point that feminists, convinced that 'the personal is political', have long theorised bodies as [gendered] sites of discursive practices, and a 'move' to also study emotions is not actually that great a step, or perhaps not even 'new' at all. Methodologically, Parashar focuses on feminist storytelling. By drawing on interviews with women in support of wars and armed conflict in Kashmir, India and Sri Lanka, she explores the relationship between anger and women's collective political action. She shows how anger is important to focus on in order to understand the reasons why women support violence, explanations that tend to be omitted in the narration of violent women's politics; but she also reflects on emotional encounters of the research process, how anger might play a role between the researcher and the researched. Parashar argues that if anger forms part of the researcher's self-reflection, it is possible to engage with it through mutual respect, compassion and empathy.

Chapters 7 and 8 offer two, albeit very different, approaches on method, for how to actually study emotions, politics and war. In Chapter 7, Marjaana Jauhola explains how she draws on ethnography and 'mindful research' as a method to study embodied, emotional experiences, in her case of boredom. Jauhola's chapter illustrates the emotional processes of a particular methodological approach to fieldwork. The aim of her chapter is to demonstrate how it is impossible to separate out emotions from being a researcher. Based on her street ethnographic study of punks in post-conflict/tsunami Banda Aceh, Jauhola argues that boredom can construct alternative ways to occupy the city and thereby functions to contest and rupture the political present. Jauhola also suggests that ethnographic and embodied encounters, as part of mindful research, offers affective and gendered maps of a city and thereby provides alternative ways of seeing the practice of politics.

In the final chapter of the first section, Chapter 8, Rose McDermott offers an epistemological alternative to Jauhola's embodied and sensory research design to study emotions, politics and war. Informed by research in psychology, McDermott argues that experimental methods, aimed at exposing and demonstrating causal, generalisable, universal aspects of human behaviour, can also be applied to studies of conflict, combat and trauma. For example, McDermott suggests, experiments are useful when it comes to establishing broader patterns, such as risk perception of threats. Her chapter thus offers both a defence of a positivist epistemological perspective, and a suggestion as to how experiments can complement other, more in-depth and subjective analyses of emotions and emotionality, politics and war.

The chapters in the second half of the book explore the theme 'Emotionality in war'. The first three chapters in this part do so by focusing on soldiers, soldiering experiences and contexts. First, in Chapter 9, Julia Welland reflects on the role of compassion in practices of contemporary war-making and, more specifically, the idea of the soldier as a compassionate actor. She exposes two different processes of compassion, based in two different meanings of compassion: as an emotion felt 'on behalf of another who suffers', but also as 'suffering together with another'. She shows not only how contemporary wars and counter-insurgency policy are justified through ideas about compassion, but also how compassion can work to conceal the ongoing violence and obscenity of war. Welland argues that in the two processes of compassion identified, compassion functions as a comforting device – not in the form of a care of others, but instead as comfort for those who express to experience it on behalf of those others' suffering.

In Chapter 10, Victoria Basham focuses on how the appropriate control and expression of emotion is integral to soldiering, and also how such regulation of emotion is profoundly gendered. More specifically, Basham focuses on expressions of boredom and joy. She argues that men's desire in warfare is prioritised while women's is marginalised. This means that, while expressions of combat as pleasurable for men are normalised and gender-conforming, similar expressions by women are not. Crucially, however, Basham points out that this is not based on the necessity for the military to function, but instead is a result of how the emotional spaces and temporalities to do with soldiering have long been gendered.

In Chapter 11, Alison Howell focuses on some of the emotional implications of soldiering by analysing Anglo-American armed forces' management of their soldiers' mental health. She notes that there has been a shift from stoicism to emotional self-governance. However, this also means that the responsibility for preventing mental ill-health among soldiers is placed not only on soldiers themselves, but on their families. Specific policies focusing on 'family fitness' as a way to achieve resilience, Howell argues, function to instrumentalise intimate relationships as the family (most often wives) become enlisted in the maintenance of soldiers' fitness for re-deployment in an affective economy of militarism. The family, Howell argues, is treated as a military instrument.

Several chapters in the second section of the book explore the politics of grief and trauma. In Chapter 12, Helen Parr reflects on the role of grief in relation to conservative nationalism and militarisation in Britain during the 1982 armed conflict with Argentina over the Falkland Islands. Parr explores the contrasting expressions of grief between the public display as formal commemoration and the emotions expressed through lived experiences, by soldiers as well as civilians. Parr argues that the display of grief was inherently gendered and that this forms part of the politics of how certain narratives and stories of war are more likely to be told, and thereby remembered, than others. In Chapter 13, Jack Holland turns his attention to the articulation of affect during and after the terror attacks in the United States on 11 September, 2001. By comparing ordinary citizens' experiences of the events on that particular day with how the US government framed the events of '9/11', Holland shows how the Bush administration tapped into, articulated and incorporated the affective responses of the general public. As a result, Holland argues that while the emotional experiences of citizens matter, during moments of perceived national crisis the state has the potential to control such affective narratives along particular political and policy agendas.

By reflecting on the work and life of British war photographer Don McCullin, in Chapter 14 Tom Gregory explores the relationship between photographs of human suffering and the emotional responses they may or may not engender. Building on Judith Butler's work on the politics of grief, Gregory suggests that war photographs provide us with an opportunity to think about the normative regimes that regulate our affective disposition and govern our emotional responses to scenes of death and destruction. Some of these themes are explored in greater depth by Emmanuel-Pierre Guittet and Andreja Zevnik in Chapter 15. Focusing on a broader range of photographs, they explore how representation of war works in a contemporary world saturated with images of violence. From the idea that every photo is always already simultaneously authentic and a copy, something between documentary and art, Guittet and Zevnik argue that war photographs should be engaged with as 'quilting-points of common societal narratives of heroism, cruelty or suffering... as indexes of something taking place'.

In the final contribution, Chapter 16, Emma Hutchison and Roland Bleiker explore the role of emotions in rebuilding war-affected communities. They show why it is important to pay closer attention to emotions linked to notions of identity, belonging and community in general, and for communities to actively embrace, acknowledge and express acceptance of the impact of violence and suffering involved in the trauma of war. To this end, Hutchison and Bleiker suggest that grief and trauma could be seen as two sides of the same coin, and that a politics of grief can function as an alternative way for communities to work through emotional trauma post-conflict, as a way to transform post-war emotions such as fear and anger to empathy.

The book ends with a concluding reflection around what is perhaps the most challenging part of emotions research: methods and methodology. We discuss different knowledge claims in emotions research, and pick up on two themes that we believe the content of the chapters of this book draw us towards, precisely because both have expanded the horizons for what can be considered 'politics' – aesthetics and feminism. For future research on emotions, politics and war, we encourage epistemological clarity, methodological diversity and, above all, creativity.

## Notes

1 On how the everyday of soldiering impacts the geopolitical see Basham 2013; on joy and IR see Penttinen 2013.
2 The reluctance to talk about the emotional dimension of conflict in IR, a discipline initially established to avoid another 'Great War', is somewhat ironic considering how important 'emotion' in its broadest sense is in the writings of some of the earliest and most influential theorists of war, such as Clausewitz.
3 See Clough and Halley (2007); Gregg and Seigworth (2010); Wetherell (2012) for more detailed overviews of various strands of 'researching emotions'.
4 See also Khalili (2011) for an analysis of the gendered character of these counter-insurgency campaigns.
5 For more information see http://historiesofviolence.com.

## Bibliography

Ahmed, S. (2004) *The Cultural Politics of Emotion*. Edinburgh: Edinburgh University Press.

Ahmed, S. (2010) 'Happy objects', in *The Affect Theory Reader*, Gregg and Seigworth (eds). Durham, NC: Duke University Press.

Anderson, B. (2010a) 'Modulating the excess of affect: Morale in a state of "Total War"', in *The Affect Theory Reader*, Gregg and Seigworth (eds). Durham, NC: Duke University Press.

Anderson, B. (2010b) 'Security and the future: Anticipating the event of terror', *Geoforum*, 41: 227–235.

Basham, V. (2013) *War, Identity and the Liberal State*. Abingdon: Routledge.

Berlant, L. (ed.) (2004) *Compassion: The Culture and Politics of an Emotion*. London: Routledge.

Bleiker, R. and Hutchinson, E. (2008) 'Fear no more: Emotions and world politics', *Review of International Studies*, 34: 115–135.

Brennan, T. (2004) *The Transmission of Affect*. Ithaca, NY: Cornell University.

Clough, P. with Halley, J. (eds) (2007) *The Affective Turn: Theorizing the Social*. Durham, NC: Duke University Press.

Connolly, W. (2002) *Neuropolitics: Thinking, Culture, Speed*. Minneapolis, MN: University of Minnesota Press.

Crawford, N. C. (2000) 'The passion of world politics: Propositions on emotion and emotional relationships', *International Security*, 24(4): 116–156.

Danchev, A. (2006) '"Like a Dog!": Humiliation and shame in the war on terror', *Alternatives*, 31: 259–283.

Edkins, J. (2002) 'Forget trauma? Responses to September 11', *International Relations*, 16(2): 243–256.

Edkins, J. (2003) *Trauma and the Memory of Politics*. Cambridge: Cambridge University Press.

Elster, J. (1999) *Alchemies of the Mind: Rationality and the Emotions*. Cambridge: Cambridge University Press.

Fattah, K. and Fierke, K. M. (2009) 'A clash of emotions: The politics of humiliation and political violence in the Middle East', *European Journal of International Relations*, 15(1): 67–93.

Fierke, K. M. (2014) *Political Self-sacrifice: Agency, Body and Emotion in International Relations*. Cambridge: Cambridge University Press.

Gregg, M. and Seigworth, G. J. (eds) (2010) *The Affect Theory Reader*. Durham, NC: Duke University Press.

*The Guardian* (2014) 'Guardian Witness: First World War'. Available online at: https://witness.theguardian.com/assignment/52751e38e4b01fc33230d4aa (accessed 18 May 2014).

Highmore, B. (2010) 'Bitter after taste: Affect, food and social aesthetics', in *The Affect Theory Reader*, Gregg and Seigworth (eds). Durham, NC: Duke University Press, 118–137.

Holmqvist, C. (2013) 'War, "strategic communication" and the violence of non-recognition', *Cambridge Review of International Affairs*, 26(4): 631–650.

Hutchison, E. (2010) 'Trauma and the politics of emotions: Constituting identity, security and community after the Bali bombing', *International Relations*, 24(1): 65–86.

Jervis, R. (1976) *Perception and Misperception in International Politics*. Princeton, NJ: Princeton University Press.

Khalili, L. (2011) 'Gendered practices of counterinsurgency', *Review of International Studies*, 37(4): 1471–1491.

Lebow, N. (2005) 'Reason, emotion and cooperation', *International Politics*, 42(3): 283–313.

Lutz, C. (1988) *Unnatural Emotions: Everyday Sentiments on a Micronesian Atoll and Their Challenge to Western Theory*. Chicago, IL: University of Chicago Press.

Massumi, B. (2002) *Parables for the Virtual: Movement, Affect, Sensation*. Durham, NC: Duke University Press.

Massumi, B. (2010) 'The future birth of the affective fact: The political ontology of threat', in *The Affect Theory Reader*, Gregg and Seigworth (eds). London: Duke University Press, 52–71.

McSorley, K. (ed.) (2012) *War and the Body: Militarisaiton, Practice and Experience*. Abingdon: Routledge.

Mercer, J. (2005) 'Rationality and psychology in international politics', *International Organization*, 59: 77–106.

Penttinen, E. (2013) *Joy and International Relations: A New Methodology*. Abingdon: Routledge.

Ross, A. G. (2006) 'Coming in from the cold: Constructivism and emotions.' *European Journal of International Relations*, 12(2): 197–222.

Sasley, B. (2011) 'Theorizing states' emotions', *International Studies Review*, 13: 452–476.

Saurette, P. (2006) 'You dissin me? Humiliation and post 9/11 global politics', *Review of International Studies*, 32: 495–522.

Sedgwick, E. (2003) *Touching Feeling: Affect, Performativity, Pedagogy*. Durham, NC: Duke University Press.

Spelman, E. V. (1997) *Fruits of Sorrow: Framing Our Attention to Suffering*. Boston, MA: Beacon Press.

Stewart, K. (2007) *Ordinary Affects*. Durham, NC: Duke University Press.

Sylvester, C. *et al.* (2011) 'The Forum: Emotion and the feminist IR researcher', *International Studies Review*, 13: 687–708.

Thrift, N. (2008) *Non-Representational Theory: Space, Politics, Affect*. London: Routledge.

Wetherell, M. (2012) *Affect and Emotion: A New Social Science Understanding*. London: Sage.

# Part I

# Researching Emotions

# 2 The remains of the day[1]

*Brian Massumi*

September 11, 2001: 'The day the world changed.' That was the refrain, in any case. It was a refrain that radiated in shockwaves from the impact at 'Ground Zero', as it came to be known. There was a gash in the way the world was, and people were agape at it. Everything, it was felt, had changed. Had it? Or: what precisely had changed?

Today, more than ten years later, the shockwaves have subsided, becoming a background ripple. Presidents have gone, and come. The rallying cry of the 'war on terror' that had been the US banner for eight years was itself banned from the lexicon of the current administration. The color was drained out of it, literally. The infamous color-coded terror alert system of the Bush years was replaced in late April of 2011 by a pared-down verbal alert system with just two words, 'imminent' and 'elevated'. Within days of this official black-and-whiting of terror, the personification of terror, Osama bin Laden, was dead. This was right around the time that the final details were being ironed out for withdrawal of US troops from Iraq. A month after that, Obama marks the beginning of the US troop withdrawal from Afghanistan as well. The withdrawals are not exactly a 'mission accomplished' moment. 'Mission fatigue' is more like it. 'Terror' and the 'war' declared against it had lost their luster, fading into the grey ambience of 'business as usual'. Now what is front-stage and center is the gridlock that seems to have become business as usual, at least in Washington. The more it changes, the weary grumble, the more it stays the same.

More than ten years later, what remains of the 'everything changed'? What remains of that day?

This is not just a question about one particular event, and about the cast of political and institutional characters it launched into an ill-defined 'war'. It is also a broader question of how we think about history: how we assess the impact of historical events that seem to mark thresholds or sudden breaks; how we can think about the forces that regather on the far side of the threshold to make it so that things continue, even so. What regathering historical forces connect the 'everything changed' to the 'more it changes, the more it stays the same'? How can we talk about change when the harder things fall, the more they stumble on?

As a way of beginning to address these questions, I'd like to talk about something that came into prominence in the aftermath of 9/11. I'd like to talk about preemption. First, a couple of preliminary comments:

To help answer our questions, preemption can't be thought of as simply a doctrine. Doctrines change as political actors and institutions turn over. Preemption was a doctrine – in the aftermath of 9/11, it became the stated war doctrine of the George W. Bush administration. But as a formative historical force with a power to regather itself and follow its own momentum, it overflowed the Bush administration and flowed into the Obama administration, and will likely flow beyond it. In addition, it can be argued that it overflowed the borders of the United States, going global.

Preemption in this sense is a tendency that cannot be reduced to a time- and place-specific doctrine. Tendencies are self-propagating. They have a power to repeat their operations in different times and places. Doctrines must be applied. Tendencies are self-applying. They are self-driving. This makes them a force to be contended within their own right. The question, then, is how preemption constitutes a self-driving tendency that has to be construed as a force of history passing through shifts in doctrine and changes in casts of characters.

We'll start from the way preemption was formulated as a doctrine by George W. Bush in response to the 9/11 attacks – and then consider how what was encapsulated in that doctrine took on a momentum of its own.

This is the doctrine, Bush's own words:

> If we wait for threats to fully materialize, we will have waited too long. We must take the battle to the enemy, disrupt his plans and confront the worst threats before they emerge. In the world we have entered, the only path to safety is the path to action.

Now some might actually see this as an example of 'the more things change, the more they stay the same', because the right to preemptive attack has been a part of the practice of war for as long as there have been wars, and is a part of classical war theory and the law of war. However, in the past, preemptive attack was considered justified in response to 'a clear and present danger': the Bush doctrine changed danger to threat.

The first thing this does is shift the emphasis to the affective register. A clear and present danger is observable and, in principle, objectively verifiable, whereas a threat only has to be felt to be. It has a visceral reality that is self-confirming. If you feel threatened, you are – end of story. On 9/11 we felt it.

Although formalized as a State doctrine, preemption establishes a direct relation to life at its most visceral level. In other words, to affect – to what hits us in the gut so immediately that all we can do is reel, not yet reflect, not yet knowing how to act in response. Affect at this level of the visceral hit that suspends considered reflection and momentarily paralyzes action isn't what we normally think about as emotion. Through a triggering event like 9/11, it hits collectively, directly riveting a whole population to a situation it is not yet capable of categorizing. It braces us together in uncertainty, in the terror of not yet being able to answer the question, 'what just happened?'. Unlike an emotion, affect at this level it is less something we each have personally, than it is something that has us collectively. We are taken up together in the terror. We are vaulted into it together. We are agape, in suspense together. We are all in it together, in the disorientation of terror. We are swept up by it. We are moved by it.

Preemption establishes a direct link between the institutional level of policy – the formal level of collective organization – and the informal affective level of sweeping collective disorientation and agitated paralysis. With preemption, this political link to the level of affective immediacy becomes a motor of what happens. It goes off and running. It sets in motion an historical tendency that is difficult to put the brakes on once it starts. That tendency has a certain logic of its own.

I'm not saying that the connection of politics to a visceral level where reflection is momentarily suspended makes politics simply irrational. I'm saying that it gives preemption a logic of its own, and that to understand what changed on 9/11, and how it stays the same the more it changes, we have to understand that logic, and what's different about it.

There is something else that happens with preemption. There is another significant shift, this one concerning time. Classically, a preemptive attack is justified when there is 'a clear and present danger'. But threat inhabits the future. Threats don't clearly present themselves. They vaguely loom, and their looming casts a shadow on the present. A threat is how an uncertain future makes itself felt in the present. This has immediate consequences on the plane of action. Even in paralysis, it can change how we will be disposed to act. This viscerally felt, affective presence of an uncertain future has consequences for the future. In a weird way, threat is a way in which the future affects itself.

What I've just described is like a time-loop. The future comes back to the present to trigger a reaction that jolts the present back to the future, along a different path of action than would have eventuated otherwise. Threat is a strange animal: a future cause. It comes from the future, to act on the futurity from which it came. In a sense, threat makes future self-causing. There is a kind of short-circuit in time. A future cause (the looming of the threat) loops through affect in a way that effectively changes what goes down. Threat loops through affect to effect, never surrendering the future tense.

By contrast, the classical doctrine of preemption as it was understood pre-9/11 specifically referred to danger, not threat, as already mentioned. Danger involves the linear relationship between cause and effect that we are used to dealing with in our common-sense everyday lives. A situation clearly presents itself; its objective characteristics are analyzed; the analysis suggests reasonable paths of action; a direction is chosen, and the present marches the straight and narrow path to the future, as dictated by the decision. The effects of the decision flow logically, step-by-step, from it. Of course, all kinds of accidents can happen. The path can be miscalculated. The deliberations can be flawed, the implementation flubbed. But the point remains that there is an assumption that decisions affecting the future can be based on objectively verifiable, empirically present conditions, and that political response begins with deliberation and is guided by it. Here, the causes of things precede them in time. Their effects feed forward from the empirical past, through the observable present, and if all goes well, into a better future. It's all nicely ordered, comfortably linear.

All of this gets seriously twisted by threat. Because, once again, it's enough for a threat to be felt to make it real. It needs no objective validation to have an effect as a future cause. It doesn't operate in the realm of the objective. The future is precisely what is not yet objectively present. It's not empirically observable. Preemption operates in the realm of affect. Its concern is threat. If it is enough for threat to be felt for it to be real and effective, then it's logical that the actions that effectively flow from the feeling of threat are going to be justified affectively as well. With preemption, the justification for actions, the legitimation of political decision, tends to become fundamentally affective. It is reasonable to say that a shift of this magnitude marks a threshold where 'everything changes'. It's the death knell of centuries of politics that were supposed to be guided by the 'reason of State'.

To get a sense of how this works, consider Bush's well known rationales for invading Iraq: 1) Saddam Hussein had weapons of mass destruction; 2) Iraq was a haven for Al-Qaeda and would be used as a launching pad for further attacks.

The first rationale was vigorously discounted at the time by people objectively in a position to know, such as UN weapons inspector Hans Blix. It was subsequently found to be entirely lacking any factual foundation. What was Bush's response when he had to face up to the fact that he had embarked on a costly war on objectively false premises? Did he apologize for the thousands of allied lives lost? For the hundreds of thousands of Iraqi lives lost? Did he admit having made a mistake? No, he reaffirmed that his decision to invade had been right in spite of having no factual basis. Because, he said, we can be certain that if Hussein had had weapons of mass destruction, he would have used them. In a word, if he could have, he would have. Maybe it's true he couldn't have then. But had the US not invaded, he might have could-have later on.

What threat does is shift the mode of political decision from the objective to the conditional – the 'could have/would have' – and treat the conditional as a certainty. And it is a certainty – affectively speaking. Bush certainly felt that Hussein would have if he could have. This certainty is not an informed judgment about a set of objective conditions. It's a gut feeling that there is a potential for something to happen. The thing is, it is impossible to disprove a potential. Even if nothing has happened years later, nothing is disproven, because it might still happen years after that. There's nothing to say that it couldn't. No-one can know. The only certainty is that you have to act now to do everything possible to preempt the potential. In the vocabulary of Bush's Secretary of Defense Donald Rumsfeld, the only thing certain is that you have to 'go kinetic', even though you don't really know and can't know and know you don't know. There are known knowns, Rumsfeld famously said and there are known unknowns. But in the post 9/11 era of threat and terror, what we're dealing with and have to act on are the 'unknown-unknowns'. As Bush put it in the quote cited earlier, 'the only path to safety is the path to action' – against threats that have not yet emerged. What has not yet emerged can be nothing other than an unknown-unknown.

The best way to act when faced with the unknown-unknown of a felt threat vaguely looming is … quickly. Otherwise you may have acted too late. 'We will have waited too long', Bush warned. The only way to act quickly on an unknown-unknown is to act intuitively, using the same 'gut feeling' you used to feel the threat-into-reality. Bush, it is well known, prided himself on deciding with his guts. He once actually said he used his advisors primarily as 'mood rings'.

So not only does preemption locate our actions in a realm of affect; not only does it politically legitimate actions affectively; it makes affect what makes them. All of this short-circuits objective assessment or evidence-based reasoning. Hair-trigger action replaces deliberation. Rapid-response tactical capabilities replace considered strategy. Remember the outrage when members of Bush's inner circle were quoted by investigative journalist Ron Suskind, ridiculing what they called the 'reality-based' community. While you're off deliberating all nice and civil about what's really real, they said, we're busy making reality, in our gutsy, preemptive way. The phrase 'reality-based' was sarcastic. It's the height of illusion, they were saying, to treat a looming threat as if it were a clear and present danger that can be responded to in the old-fashioned way, as if the world were still orderly and linear. No, what's realistic is go kinetic with utmost urgency. And when you do that, you're not sitting back reflecting on the reality, you're making it, you're producing it. How can an approach to decision-making based on vaguely looming futurities that have not yet emerged, that are still in potential, that as-yet exist only in the conditional, as would-haves and could-haves, in a way that short-circuits the present of considered reflection into a future time-loop – how can that actually produce the real? How can action legitimately bootstrap itself into reality, from a grounding in affect and potential?

The answer is obvious if you think about the second rationale Bush gave for going into Iraq. Iraq, he said, was a staging ground for Al-Qaeda. Yes, the cynic might say. Iraq was a staging ground for Al-Qaeda and Al-Qaeda-like terrorist groupings – but only after the invasion, and as a direct result of that preemptive action. It was the US invasion that created the conditions for Al-Qaeda to move in and capitalize on the chaos and resentment the invasion unleashed. The retort to that, following the logic of preemption, is simple. It happened. That's the reality. Iraq did become a staging ground for terrorism – which only goes to show that the potential was there after all.

This isn't just stupidity or faulty reasoning. There is a perverse logic to it. Because if you accept that it's paramount to respond to threat, and that you have to act in response to it even if it has not yet fully emerged, or even if it hasn't really even begun to emerge, then you're facing a real conundrum. If you wait for the emergence, you'll have waited too long – too late. A terrorist threat can strike like lightning. Like lightning, it can strike anywhere and any time. But worse than lightning, it can strike anywhere at any time in any guise. This time it might be planes crashing into buildings. Next time it might be an improvised explosive device. Or a bomb in a subway. Or anthrax in the mail. No-one knows. This only makes the urgency of action all the more acute.

Faced with urgent need to act in the face of the unknown-unknown of a threat that has not yet emerged, there is only one reasonable thing to do: flush it out. Poke the soft tissue. Prod the terrain. Stir things up and see what starts to emerge. Create the conditions for the emergence of threat. Start the threat on the way to becoming a clear and present danger, and then nip it in the bud with your superior rapid-response capabilities. Make it real so you can really eliminate it.

I'm not saying that the Bush administration consciously decided to make Iraq a staging ground for terrorism. I'm only saying that the fact that their preemptive actions did in fact do that fits perfectly into the logic of preemption, and says something fundamental about what that logic implies. It is fundamental to the logic of preemption to produce what it is designed to avoid. That is the only way to give its urgent need to 'go kinetic' in response to threat something positive to attack.

This is what distinguishes preemption from the logic presiding over the previous age of conflict, the Cold War. The logic of the Cold War was deterrence: making something not happen. The goal, faced with the clear and present danger of nuclear Armageddon, was to hold it in potential, to make sure the threat was never realized, precisely by refraining from preemptive attack. What was fundamental to the logic of deterrence was the impossibility of a first strike – exactly what preemption requires. Deterrence exercises a negative power. In a way, its logic is the inverse of the logic of preemption. Its aim is to prevent the unthinkable from happening by transforming a clear and present danger into a threat, then to hold the threat in abeyance, so that it continues to loom over the present indefinitely, so that it doesn't follow any action path back to the future. The aim of deterrence was to suspend threat.

Preemption, by contrast, suspends the present. It puts us and our actions in that conditional time-loop of the would have/could have. It hangs us on a thread of futurity. It does this in order to make the would-have-been/could-have-been a 'will-have-been-in-any-case'. The job of preemption is to translate the unknown-unknown into a foregone conclusion. Preemption always will have been right, because it exercises a positive power, a reality-producing power to make things emerge.

There is a word for a reasoning that is always right regardless of the objective situation, and that always leads a foregone conclusion in any case. The word is tautological. The logic of preemption is a tautological logic. But that's just the half of it. The logic of preemption is a tautological logic that has the power to produce the reality to which it responds. In spite of being tautological, or because of the particular way it is tautological, preemption works. It operates. It operationalizes the future of threat in a way that really, positively produces a future. It is an operative logic.

I call an operative logic that is positively productive of what will really come to be, an ontopower – '*onto-*' meaning being. An ontopower is a power that makes things come to be: that moves a futurity, felt in the present, into a presence in the future. When threat becomes effectively tautological, and power becomes ontopower, everything has changed. We've entered a brave new world, a new regime of power, and a new political era. And yes, the more things change, the more they stay the same.

In a recent book, Andrew Bacevich, a life-long military careerist turned military critic, laments that:

> Since taking office, President Obama has acted on many fronts to adjust the way the United States exercized that leadership. Yet these adjustments have seldom risen above the cosmetic. … The global war on terror [begun by Bush has not only] continued [under Obama] … it has metastasized.

It has turned cancerous. It has turned into a self-driving tendency that has swept Obama up in it. The operative logic of preemption is not a logic he has – it has him. It has proven itself a self-propagating historical force, an operative historical logic whose 'rightness' is still, as always, a foregone conclusion. It has proven its ability to continue, as a tendency, across the break between administrations and the changes on the level of explicitly stated doctrine.

I will briefly go into how Bush's 9/11-fueled 'everything-changed' is now Obama's 'more of the same', despite the differences in doctrine, the change in the cast of characters, and the obvious differences in personal quality and leadership style. But before I do that, I want to draw out a bit more some of the implications of the recentering of war and politics on threat. On the way, I want to respond to an objection I've left my account open to.

The example of Al-Qaeda in Iraq, that was central to my argument that preemptive power is a productive power, is just one example. In many eyes it might seem a weak one, since it could be laid to unforeseen collateral effects, and dismissed as a mere anomaly or accident, or simply a product of a miscalculation. The point I want to make is that in the operative logic of preemption, more-or-less unforeseen effects are precisely what is and must be produced. If the situation is really one full of unknown-unknowns, in a perpetually crisis-ridden, ungraspably complex, increasingly chaotic world, then unforeseen effects will always accompany any action carried out according to any logic. That's a corollary of the foregone conclusion.

What's particular about preemption is that it makes a virtue of this. It turns this problem into something positive as well. It turns it into a mechanism that fosters its own continuation and proliferation. It can't make the unknown-unknown known. It can't pre-form or fore-see the exact nature of the reality it will produce. But if it is ready with fast-adapting rapid response capabilities, it can field the effects it brings into being, by immediately going kinetic in a follow-up action. When it flushes out threat, it can contrive to keep the emergence within parameters it can handle, more-or-less. There will be threat again. But if all goes well, it will be in more controllable parameters. Preemption can then re-legitimate itself affectively, and redeploy. In this way, to use the military theory jargon, the operative logic of preemption 'leverages' uncertainty. What preemptive power must do is remain poised to go kinetic again and again, in serial response to the exercise of its own ontopower. Every time it acts, it must already be poising itself to act again, with equal urgency. In that way, each of its actions will contain within it the seeds of the next action, and that action, the action after, so that the deployment of preemption cascades, bringing its affective legitimation by threat with it, step by step. Preemptive action has become self-driving.

It only stands to reason that, if terrorist threat is ever-present and proliferates in unforeseen ways, then the power mobilized against it must be similarly ever-present and proliferating. How could anyone argue that we shouldn't be capable of fielding uncertainty? We must always be poised for threat. We must assume the posture – even if the stated doctrine has changed. If we sit on our hands, all it will take to de-legitimate a government would be another terror attack that happened on its watch. No government can afford not to be in a posture of preemption. We must assume the posture at every moment – we must be poised to go kinetic at a moment's notice, whenever and wherever in the world that threat is felt to loom. Whenever and wherever. The realignment on time I mentioned earlier ends up driving a tendency for the logic set in motion to turn space-filling. The operative logic of preemptive is not only self-driving; it is self-expanding.

We watched this happen. Iraq was in fact used as a terror training ground. Terrorist techniques such as the improvised explosive device and suicide bombings were perfected there, then carried to the other front, Afghanistan, where they fueled a resurgent insurgency. The preemptive follow-up response on the part of the US was to expand the use of counter-terrorist tactics that matched the IED attack in terms of their ability to strike by surprise with lightning speed, and to morph themselves to the shape any kind of circumstance, taking any number of guises. The use of these techniques by the US military exploded. Chief among them were targeted assassinations using rapidly deployed special operations forces, and unmanned drone attacks. This escalation began under Bush, but was taken to new levels by Obama, who had criticized the war in Iraq and called for its winding down only in order to shift attention to Afghanistan, which he defined as the 'good war' and the right war. The right war overflowed to the wrong side of the border, into Pakistan.

The blowback from US cross-border drone attacks, and special operations in Pakistan, have energized activity elsewhere in the world: in Somalia, in

Yemen. Yet another proliferation. US drone attacks and special ops have followed. Preemptive US military intervention has expanded to yet another continent.

The invasions of Iraq and Afghanistan may be winding down. But the preemptive military posture of the US has only spread. And nowhere has terrorist threat stopped looming. Last month (July 2011) was the bloodiest for months for US military personnel in Iraq, and terrorist attacks in Afghanistan picked up spectacularly with the assassinations of the governor of Kandahar province and the mayor of Kandahar city. Even after the 'withdrawal' of US troops from Iraq, there will be a continuing US presence indefinitely into the future, as Obama's Secretary of Defense Robert Gates put it, in order to 'fill the gap in Iraqi Security Force operations'. This continuing presence will be in the form of five high-tech compounds outfitted for drone operations and housing aircraft and armored vehicles for rapid-response forays. The withdrawal from Afghanistan will similarly leave a permanent preemption-ready presence. That presence has unprecedented reach. According to best estimates, the US preemptive presence stretches across more than 750 bases around the world. The less focused it becomes on outright invasion, the more spread-out and tentacular it becomes. US special operations forces are now active in no fewer than 75 countries around the world and carry out an average of 70 missions a day. The number of countries 'serviced' is slated to rise to 120. A key advisor to General Petraeus, the commander of US troops in Iraq, then Afghanistan, and now incoming CIA director, was recently quoted marvelling at the reach of this 'almost industrial scale killing machine'.

Preemption doesn't go away. It spreads its tentacles. Things change. Boots on the ground may recede as drones advance, following the rhythms of public opinion and the electoral cycle of politicians' engrossment in domestic affairs. Nation-building might get backgrounded in favor of targeted assassination campaigns. But the operative logic of preemption only becomes more widespread and insidious. The more it changes, the more it stays the same, ever-expanding. To the point that it can be said to become the dominant operative logic of our times. Preemption octopuses on. Ontopower rules.

Significantly, one of the places it expands to is the 'domestic front'. Here's an example.

It's June 2010. G20 leaders will be meeting in Toronto, and protestors will be gathering in the streets. The threat of violence is vaguely, but insistently, felt. Preemptive policing becomes the order of the day. In anticipation of the demonstrations, a three-meter fence is constructed to create a security zone around the meeting locations. A major section of downtown Toronto becomes a no-go security zone. Based on publicly available legal information, protest organizers advise prospective protestors that they can approach the fence and that, if they're stopped by police, they have the right, under the Canadian Charter of Rights and Freedoms, not to identify themselves. Meanwhile, in closed session, the province of Ontario issues a special regulation. It will be in force for exactly one week, the week of the G20 meetings. What the law says is that if anyone comes within five meters of the perimeter fence, the police not only have the right to ask them for identification, but if the person refuses, the police can arrest them on the spot.

The regulation is not debated in the legislature. It is made in closed committee in direct response to a request by the Toronto chief of police. It is passed in secret – and no-one is told about it. Imagine the surprise of peaceful demonstrators, armed only with their legal rights pamphlet, when they find themselves in a mass detention center. How can this be interpreted as anything other than a device to positively produce illegality, in order to empower the police to make on-the-fly decisions leading to arbitrary imprisonment based on nothing more than a particular officer's gut feelings of which individuals constitute a threat (or, I should say, would if they could).

This wasn't the only productive preemptive policing method put to use. The classic device of seeding the crowds with police provocateurs to initiate violence was also used. A couple of police cars are set on fire at a location swarming with police, but thin in protestors. The police stand by and watch. The spectacular images of the burning splashes across the media. Other footage also surfaces, of what are ostensibly protestors in stereotypical anarchist outfits nonchalantly walking behind police lines, casually taking off their black block gear and joining the security line of the men and women in blue. This use of provocateurs is clearly meant to do two things. The first is to flush out the threats, to make them appear, so their emergence can be met by rapid police response, ready in waiting. It is not a minor point that this productive-preemptive operation requires the actions of the security forces to mimic the threat they are preemptively responding to – to the point of being indistinguishable from it. The forces for security must effectively become what they fight. They must, for a moment at least, become their own enemy, in order to meet the enemy on the same terrain of threat. They must cause exactly the kind of damage they are meant to prevent. Once again, produce to preempt: ontopower.

The other aim is to make threat felt through the circulation of fear-producing images. Affect, again. Once threat is felt and fear has taken us, the operative logic of preemption kicks in to make it a foregone conclusion that any action taken following that logic will have been right in any case. Whatever actions the police take will come across as justified, based solely on what was felt – the feeling of threat. Police actions are affectively pre-legitimated. 'Reality-based' decision making – political decision that is deliberative in nature and purports to respond in a linear and measured fashion to objectively verifiable conditions, in other words, public decision-making that follows the procedures we have been taught to associate with democratic governance – is short-circuited by the logic of preemption. This affective pre-legitimation of preemptive policing is meant to allow measures like the province of Ontario's secret perimeter law to pass, in the sense of slipping by, slipping through the gaps. If the threat was felt immediately and intensely enough, the fact that the measure contravenes the Canadian Charter of Rights might be overlooked.

The fact that its own illegality was designed to produce still more illegality, in order to give police response more favorable parameters, might well be forgiven. After all, it was just one week. Perhaps it will also slip by that hundreds of peaceful protesters were preemptively rounded up, even away from the perimeter fence, without even being asked to identify themselves, and kept without charge in a purpose-built detention center without access to legal counsel – another clear violation of civil rights. Whether or not this pre-legitimation of the exceptional police measures will work in the long run is up in the air.

Blowback is always a possibility (a commission has been appointed). My point is that what will determine whether it slips by or not is the affective force associated with the event. If the affective effect is strong enough, the foregone conclusion will continue to be that the actions were right.

Another important point is the expansion this Canadian example illustrates. The preemptive logic in play is operatively identical to the logic of preemption of the United States in the theater of war. But it's not in the United States, and it's not in the theater of war. There's no direct link between the Canadian response to the G20 protests and US military practice, and yet they end up being isomorphic, which is to say, operatively identical. This Canadian policing experience is not unique. Similar tactics were used in Denmark at the 2009 UN Climate Summit, and have been repeatedly put into practice in England, where preemptive detention of protestors has become routine enough to be given a brand name: 'kettling'. Preemption is well on its space-filling way.

The Toronto G20 example also shows that the operative logic of preemption has the power to migrate from the military sphere to the civil sphere, from warring to policing, without any direct line of causal connection from one to the other. Without missing a beat. The operative logic of preemption has the power to pilot itself along a migratory route of expansion that does not observe either the boundaries between nation-states or the divisions that have traditionally structured politics and society within the State. To use Bacevich's word: it has metastasized.

Perhaps the most significant implication of all of this is that the self-piloting of preemption places warring and policing in continuity with one another. The civil sphere and the sphere of war are now on the same operative continuum. This is a direct consequence of the protean nature of threat in an uncertain, complexly chaotic, perpetually crisis-ridden world. In the military think-tank jargon, we don't live in a 'world' any more: we live in a global 'threat environment', bubbling with threat. A new one can pop up in any form, when and where you least expect it. It can infiltrate from outside, or rise up from within. Threat potential is ever-present. Where will come from next? is the perpetual question. It is worth noting that neither terror-alert system had a category for 'safe'.

Norway. Massacre. For 24 hours the media are full of speculation on Al-Qaeda. The fact that the attacker turns out to be a white Norwegian born and bred almost makes the event more frightening. You just never know. But shouldn't we have known? Wasn't the archetype for 9/11 itself the bombing of the Oklahoma Federal building in 1995, perpetrated by another right-wing Christian fundamentalist?

We will always be in the position of should-have-known, because threat potential is the unknown-unknown. Every time, it will hit us with the same affective force of shock and surprise and agitated paralysis. We can only hope that next time it will have been preempted. Whenever we hear the siren, whenever we see the smoking rubble on TV, or the police cars burning. We are primed to reenter the continuum of preemption. Preemptive measures are automatically pre-legitimated. Preemptive action has self-authorized. The road is cleared for its tendency's self-driving to speed ahead. We are affectively disposed to let it pass. We have assumed the posture. Exceptional measures that short-circuit deliberative democracy can slip through the gaps again. Time and time again we will be hung out to dry on the circular thread of preemption's self-expanding.

Given the indeterminacy of threat and its propensity to surprise, preemptive mechanisms positively cannot limit themselves to the sphere of war. Or rather, the sphere of war must bleed across the line that has traditionally divided it from the civil sphere, and contaminate that sphere with its operative logic, from one end of it to another. The operative logic of preemption, as a self-driving tendency, constituting a historical force, is what military theorists call a 'full spectrum force'. By nature and by necessity, it covers the full spectrum of life. That is part of the very definition of the 'war on terror'.

When the civilian sphere gets annexed by the operative logic of preemption, it is no longer civilian. It's saturated by a war-derived logic. It is now paramilitary. Another way of saying this is that policing in the civil sphere becomes a degree of war. This is not the Cold War. It's the 'Long War', to use what has become the stock phrase. It's the war that never ends. War becomes as permanent as the looming of threat, and the forms it takes become just as tentacular and ever-changing.

Given this condition of all-encompassing permanent war stretching from one end of the spectrum to the other, changes in doctrine and the casts of institutional and individual characters do little more than toggle the war setting from one degree of war to another. With each felt threat, the setting moves to a new position on the continuum between policing and military intervention, or between paramilitary and military expressions of the operative logic of preemption. In the process, new combinations of policing and military intervention are invented and tried out: improvised preemptive device. The much-touted change of course in Iraq that started under Bush in 2006 with the announcement of his troop 'surge' is a case in point. It was presented as a major shift in doctrine from the Counterterrorism approach that had been synonymous up until that point with the 'war on terror'. Counterterrorism explicitly privileged preemptive military intervention. The new doctrine would be Counterinsurgency. The idea of Counterinsurgency was to toggle toward the formerly civil sphere. The emphasis would be on nation-building.

The Counterinsurgency motto is 'clear, hold, build'. But: in order to clear, you have to strike first. And in order to hold and build, you have to be ready to strike first again – to keep preempting. You have to assume the posture, and hold it.

Counterinsurgency was never the opposite of Counterterrorism. It never fundamentally called into question the logic of preemption and the infamous 'Revolution in Military Affairs' that preemption implied. It just repositioned the use of preemptive violence on the full spectrum. It toggled the setting away from preemptive invasion toward the kind of more punctual intervention we now see in Afghanistan, where going kinetic takes the preferential form of rapid-deployment special ops and drone warfare.

The policy shift to Counterinsurgency was in fact made to make more room on the spectrum for more preemptive policing. The role of the US would shift toward police/military training. Not to mention setting in place for the Iraqi government the kind of Orwellian high-tech surveillance systems that full-spectrum preemptive war requires in order to get enough information to even begin to flush out threats. Counterterrorism is widely recognized since 2006 to have failed in Iraq. What this means is that the emphasis on going kinetic attracted blowback. In response, Counterinsurgency toggled preemption more to the 'soft power' side of the spectrum, while keeping the means to go kinetic at a moment's notice in ready reserve: while holding the posture.

Counterinsurgency is now widely recognized to have failed in Afghanistan. A 'new' doctrine has just been announced this summer (2011). The new name for this doctrine is an old one: 'Irregular Warfare'. The more it changes … by now we know the drill.

Irregular Warfare is defined as a 'hybrid' combination of counterinsurgency and counterterrorism. In other words, it is an official recognition of what has been the de facto situation since 9/11: that the 'war on terror' (by whatever name) has always necessarily been a full-spectrum affair, with a built-in preemptive tendency to expand and proliferate.

Back to 9/11. The attacks of that day struck with an affective force of maximum magnitude. 'Everything changed' was on everybody's lips. The orderly unfolding of the world along known lines seemed to have been interrupted. The present was in suspense. Into the suspense moved the operative logic of preemption. Over the years, it has taken permanent hold, not in small part due to the endless creativity of this crisis-ridden world when it comes to suggesting threats. The tendency that came of this (the operative logic of preemption I've been talking about) has toggled along the full spectrum, and morphed into different hybrid combinations. When the toggle is set at the softest of soft power settings in what used to be the civil sphere – i.e., tentacular surveillance – you can be sure that an emergency toggle back to the hardest-of-hard preemptive power is ready and waiting. Ready and waiting for an affective legitimation event to kick in. It is now the permanence of war that looms over us as a foregone conclusion, in just as many morphings as its uncertain enemy, threat. In fact: in the image of the enemy. Threat/counter-threat, in mimetic embrace. You become what you fight. If that sounds exaggerated, ask a Pakistani villager in the drone zone, where civilian casualties have soared, what name they might apply to the United States.

The Toronto G20 example showed how mechanisms can be easily improvised for letting the logic of preemption slip through the gaps of the traditionally structured political landscape: escape-hatches from the traditional checks-and-balances. More worryingly, these are not just being improvised. They are being institutionalized. Exceptions to the rule are becoming integrated into the rules. Legal outs into extra-legal actions are being written into the law. Holes for arbitrarily decided preemptive action are being sewn into the fabric of our institutions. The exception to the rule is becoming the rule.

This is where Obama comes back in. It has been under Obama that the exception to the rule has become the rule, to an unprecedented extent. What perhaps characterizes Obama's administration more than anything else is the extent to which he has gone about systematically institutionalizing arbitrary decision in keeping with the exceptional logic of preemption. This began under Bush, with the Patriot Act. But it has not only been continued by the Obama administration, it has been consolidated by it. In his first interview after Obama was elected, Bush-era vice-president Dick Cheney snidely remarked that he was confident that as commander-in-chief Obama would come to appreciate the Bush administration's expansion of the executive power of arbitrary decision that Obama had criticized as a candidate. Right again.

In the Toronto G20 example, we saw the role that secrecy played. Secrecy also plays a key role in Obama's preemptive posturing. While ostensibly returning to the rule of law on the domestic front and reaffiriming respect for international law on the foreign policy front, Obama has actually been extraordinarily busy sinking holes in the fabric of the law designed to enable a return of just the sort of exceptional and extralegal measures that Bush was criticized for. The cover for these escape-hatches from the law in the law is the 'national security secret'. 'National security secret' is the name of the permanent opening for arbitrary preemptive decision. It is a nickname for the permanence of preemptive war. A few examples:

1 Obama officially renounces torture. At the same time, he appeals to the principle of the state secret to block any judicial oversight of 'enhanced interrogation techniques', opening the way for their exceptional use without fear of legal consequences for the perpetrators.
2 Obama reasserts the principle of habeas corpus, the principle that protects against unlimited arbitrary detention without appeal. At the same time, he asserts an exception for suspects considered terrorist threats. Given what we've seen about the malleability and indeterminacy of threat, and its way of short-circuiting objective evaluation and affectively legitimating foregone conclusions, this is a hole that that can easily rip into a full-spectrum gash.
3 Obama announces a desire to return to accepted norms of judicial procedure. At the same time, he institutionalizes trial by military commission

for individuals deemed 'unlawful combatants'. The concept of the military commissions is to lower the bar of what constitutes admissible evidence and to restrict a suspect's rights to legal defense – in short, to stack the decks. Obama is different from Bush on this. His idea has been to close Guantanamo and institute the military commissions on domestic soil: basically, to repatriate this form of exception.

4 Obama reaffirms US adherence to the Geneva Convention and the international laws of war. At the same time, he expands the Bush-era system of secret 'black sites' into which unlawful combatants disappear without a trace. In tandem with this, he unleashes the CIA, extending its mandate beyond information-gathering to military special-operation interventions, so that the CIA becomes a full-spectrum paramilitary force unto itself, carrying out its shadowy preemptive war games under the cover of secrecy provided by its black sites. In an inverse action, he issues secret Executive Orders giving the Pentagon's US Special Operations Command CIA-like surveillance capabilities, buckling the full-spectrum loop of exceptional force. This preemptive organ reports directly to the president personally without any form of judicial oversight or Congressional oversight, keeping it perpetually poised for instant delivery of extralegal action on demand.

5 Obama talks the talk of human rights, to relieved UN and European Union ears. At the same time, he walks the walk of targeted assassination. The practice of targeted assassination has expanded significantly under Obama. It is contrary to the laws of war and international norms concerning the right to a fair trial. But exception is regularly made. The fact that the US is still not a member of the International Criminal Court helps. Obama has even extended targeted assassination to US citizens.

6 Obama has waxed long on his respect for civil rights on the home front. At the same time, he used the national security rationale to institute exceptions to constitutional protections against unreasonable search and seizure. And he has expanded the high-tech surveillance system to unprecedented levels. Legal limits are placed on surveillance of private individuals' communications, but state secrets can be invoked to prevent judicial oversight, making the government's surveillance powers effectively unlimited. In parallel, Obama has declared war on whistle-blowers. Bradley Manning, the army private who spilled the Wikileaks beans, is just the best known and most spectacular case. Under Obama, individuals who leak government and military information are prosecuted with draconian zeal. It's to the point that Daniel Ellsberg, the man who helped end the Vietnam war by leaking the Pentagon papers, was recently moved to say that if Richard Nixon were alive today, 'he would feel vindicated that all the crimes he committed against me – which forced his resignation facing impeachment – are now legal'. Note the wording: 'legal crimes'.

7 Obama has assured the world that the United States will no longer embark on foreign war adventures at the drop of a hat. At the same time, he has removed the conduct of war from democratic oversight, a function

> invested in Congress by the War Powers Act. In this case he has done this not by changing the law, but simply by ignoring it. He is not the first to do this. But in the past, presidents have initiated war action, citing the role of the president as Commander-in-Chief, then gone back to Congress within the required 90 days for rubber-stamp approval for their fait accompli. This was Bush's approach. Earlier this year, Obama deployed the military in Libya without consulting Congress – and never went back to Congress for its rubber stamp. He said he didn't want to, and if he doesn't want to he doesn't have to, because he's the Chief. This can only be interpreted as a radicalization of the principle of the 'unitary executive' that Bush used to justify his arbitrary gut decisions and to shift the balance of power toward arbitrary executive decision exempt from the usual checks and balances.

The situation now is that extralegal powers, escape-hatches for the exercise of exceptional powers, holes of arbitrary decision, now perforate the fabric of government. Permanent sluices have been built in for the logic of preemption. Through these gaps preemption will continue to pass. It will continue to move through as an historical tendency that has become a force in itself, sweeping everyone up in its momentum, explicit doctrine aside.

It is important to emphasize this: the tendency I am diagnosing is self-operating. It operates independently of the personal qualities of those in power. As a person, I find Obama honorable and reasonable to a fault. No-one is more sincerely deliberative. No president in recent memory has shown such infinite patience for working out differences and reaching compromise. Rarely has the United States seen such dedication in a president to the civil sphere as the seat of deliberative representative democracy, to the point that he has even tried to play down that old standard, the politics of fear. And yet … he has been swept up. His return to the deliberative reason of traditional liberal democratic process has been a tragi-comic failure. Rarely has a president proven so painfully ineffectual. Rarely has the power of reason of State seemed so faint. But the way in which Obama has at the same time made the exception to the rules the rule, in the name of national security – that definitely works. It's likely to prove indefinitely effective. It is likely to be Obama's most lasting 'contribution'. It is what makes the 'everything has changed' of 9/11 just 'more of the same'. For the unforeseeable future. Because the unforeseeable future is threat, and that puts us right back in the loop.

Please don't misunderstand this as appeal to a more effective return to the liberal-deliberative model. This path has been effectively short-circuited. The circuits are burned. They won't be rewired anytime soon, if ever. The circularity of the future cause at the heart of preemption as a positive and productive power, as a force of history in its own right, has seen to that.

All signs indicate that political legitimation has moved onto an affective footing, as permanently and unrefusably as the spectrum of politics has moved onto a war footing. A logic of war has become the logic of politics. In the nineteenth century, Clausewitz said that war is the continuation of politics by other means. Now politics is the continuation of war by the same means. There is likely no going back. If resistance is possible, it must engage in that full-spectrum battlespace that has become the space of life. This means engaging the operative logic of preemption on its own terrains. This in turn means, in the most literal sense, a struggle for the future (perhaps through practices of slowness, against the preemptive addiction to rapid response?). It also means engaging it on the level of affect: reclaiming legitimation in a different affective key.

Not the key of hope. Hope is more of a deferral of the present to the future than it is a way of bringing the future into the present according to a different operative logic. To hope is to look dreamy-eyed toward the future – cringing with the half-acknowledged certainty that when the future comes, in this broken world, it will be enough to make you cry. The only way to keep up the spirit is to defer to the future again, eyes wet with hope all over again. Hopefully, there's a limit to our capacity for deferral.

Maybe there's an affective posture that has the same reality-producing power that preemption has, but to different effect. Perhaps there's a counter-affective posture to preemption that we can find right here in the present.

I can't say that I know what that might be. It's not for me to decide in any case. It's for all of us to collectively invent. But my hunch would be that it might involve a little thing called generosity. Not inculcated as a personal quality, but practiced as a political procedure.

## Note

1 This chapter is a reprint of Brian Massumi's essay 'The remains of the day', originally published online in 2013 as part of Brad Evans' multimedia project 'Histories of Violence' (http://historiesofviolence.com).

# 3 Stories of pain and longing

## Reflecting on emotion, boundaries and feminism through Carrie Mathison and Carrie White

*Marysia Zalewski*

> … the most useful work … is likeliest to occur near the boundary of what a writer can't figure out how to say readily, never mind prescribe to others.
>
> (Sedgwick 2004: 2)

There is some apprehension about theorising emotion, certainly amongst IR scholars. One concern is that emotion may simply become another thing to commodify within the discipline, assisting a methodological desire to be pluralistic. Analytic, ethical and creative purchase is easily eluded in this way. Though perhaps there is deeper trepidation as emotions are so much part of 'us' as people; they mark and make us in many ways, even if they are a counter-intuitively elusive part of what we are. We *know* emotions matter to us as people, but we are very unclear *how* they matter, or indeed, how *much* they matter in the context of war, politics and security, issues of consistent concern within IR presumably given the violence they are enmeshed in. At the same time, we also know that something more or other is necessary to make better sense of the ongoing challenges apparent on the contemporary international landscape. We are surely missing something in the quest to resolve what Stephen Chan refers to as the 'world's blood drenched conflicts' (2010: 370)? Certainly this is one reason Patricia Ticineto Clough offers for the turn to affect:

> … the increasing significance of affect as a focus of analysis across a number of disciplinary and interdisciplinary discourses is occurring at a time when critical theory is facing the analytic challenges of ongoing war, trauma, torture, massacre, and counter/terrorism.
>
> (Clough 2007: 1)

As part of the generic field of affect in the context of the 'aesthetic turn' in IR (Bleiker 2009), the analyses of emotion(s) offer the potential for more understanding, more possibility of effective action in the face of unacceptable violence, or as Roland Bleiker puts it, 'hope for a better world will, indeed, remain slim if we put all our efforts into one set of knowledge practices alone, no matter how compelling they may seem' (2009: 1). This all seems logical and reasonable enough. But we remain, rightly so, apprehensive and unsure. The terrain of emotion is chaotic, iridescent, quivering with uncontrollability, or certainly the fear, threat or hope of it. And we place a great deal of value in and on emotion, even when we don't like it, or even give it that name. Do we run the risk of evaporating the value of emotion if we too successfully analytically capture it? Or is it that our struggles around emotion expose more clearly some of the impossibilities of methodology and the ongoing challenges of formulating bits of knowing, feeling and sensing into useful and usable knowledge in a chaotic world? It turns out it's not so easy to write about emotion for an academic text.

I am suggesting, however, that we might turn, if obliquely and cautiously, to affect and aesthetics to help us think about 'how to' study emotion; 'how to' being a crucial question for methodology. Yet the 'how to' question is not comfortably answered using affective methods, for a number of reasons. One is that affectively following emotions does not easily lend itself to replication or, as the opening quote from Kosofsky Sedgwick suggests, it doesn't make it easy to know what to say readily, or indeed prescribe to others. How, for example, might one methodologically track a sense of discomfort, or something that doesn't feel quite right? Or, more disciplinarily pertinent, advise others how to track such things? How, unless writing a poem or a novel, can one represent a sense of emotional and affective intensity? I'm not sure, but I want to push at some of the boundaries that I think opening up questions about emotion draws us towards. These are theoretical, conceptual and methodological boundaries (where do we start? how can we look?) which I explore briefly in this chapter. But writing and thinking boundaries are also invoked in our dabbling analytically with emotion – the tidiness of the word on the page, the purity of the correct grammatical style, the neat encapsulation and articulation of a concept, or an idea, or the disciplinary framing of what counts; these are all at odds with the unfathomable character of emotion, and begin to indicate some of the boundaries that opening up questions about emotion provokes.

But I will start with a feeling, and embark on a brief affective journey from a feeling that something wasn't quite right. I do this as I understand theories of affect in the frame of aesthetics to facilitate working with what might be called anecdotes, such as a snippet of conversation. I also take working with affect and aesthetics to permit the development of alternate registers of sense-making, partly by tracking elusive connections (Zalewski 2013). Further, I think this kind of approach may help to open ways to think better, or rather alternately, about how emotion(s) labour to configure boundaries, not least in regard to gendered subjectivities and identities. Gregg and Seigworth offer evocative terms for this kind of work as they write about 'intensities' and 'resonances that circulate about, between and sometimes stick to bodies and worlds' (2010: 1). Sara Ahmed similarly writes about how emotions both shape the surface of bodies, and work to make things and bodies move (or become immobile) (2004). These emotionally laced intensities and resonances are oftentimes simultaneously hidden and visible. Teresa Brennan's opening line in her book evinces this doubled (edged) transmission of affect, 'is there anyone who has not, at least once, walked into a room and "felt" the atmosphere' (2004: 1)? The answer surely has to be no. However, conventional methodologies tend to disallow working on this register; as such, we regularly remain uncurious methodological amateurs in regard to emotions and meaning-making.

So I start with a feeling which leads me to think about the character Carrie Mathison from the US television series *Homeland*. I was first drawn to this character given her position in the world of high politics, even if through the medium of a television show – the epistemological and ontological power of popular culture is convincingly theorised. It seemed to me there must be a gendered story to tell here. But it was a fleeting conversation – an affective moment – which moved me to think about Carrie more deeply. And the more I followed Carrie around in thought, the more I was drawn to think about pain, longing, security and the steely evanescence of boundaries and how, so often, it is through the bodies of women that this paradoxical transience becomes apparent, even if 'only' felt.

As a character, Carrie is eminently interesting for many reasons: she is positioned as 'other' (of a sort) in the midst of the high politics of the US government/CIA/terrorism scenario she is engaged in, which is where the important security action is generally understood to be in contemporary international politics/relations. Her presence at the centre of this world is intriguing, given that she presents as an over-emotional, excessive woman; this writes the boundaries of sense (and methodology) differently for us, or it feels that way. One thing this may alert us to, is that if we want to think more deeply about the work of emotions, we may also have to write and think the boundaries of our work and writing differently too. This idea and my pursuit of Carrie Mathison led me to another Carrie, this time from Stephen King's book of the same name (1999). The two Carries seemed connected, if seemingly very different and separated by 40 years – a period echoing with the episodically vibrant politics and practices of feminism which, we might think, would have made the boundaries containing and constraining women crystal clear. Yet, when I thought more deeply, and affectively and affectionately, about the two Carries, their presence as women in their stories helped to augment my thinking about the elusive and illusive character of boundaries. Why might any of this matter? I think it might help with our thinking about our puzzles about violence, posed here as questions: how does violence come so easily? Because it does. How do some violences so readily appear as *other* than violence, depending on the body/bodies wielding them? It also might help with our puzzles around gendered violence, so heavily monitored and analysed, yet so little dented.

In the remainder of this chapter I will introduce Carrie from the television series *Homeland*, and then move to write about Carrie White from Stephen King's novel. In the subsequent discussion, I will return to reflect on the questions and ideas I introduce here.

## Carrie Mathison

I start with a fragment of an everyday conversation between colleagues.

> Did anyone see the last episode of Homeland?
> I can't stand that woman!
> Which woman?
> Her – the one!
> You mean Carrie? Oh, I *love* Carrie! *And* she[1] reminds me of my daughter!
> Oh! (laughs) – *that* must be a worry!

Popular culture remains a crucial forum for educating publics about identity, subjectivity, and who and what matters (Dyer 1997; Rowley 2015). Moreover, the 'box set' (whether a physical set or viewed online) is increasingly popular; a recent example is the television series *Homeland*. This is a much viewed programme in which the introductory plot revolves around US marine Sergeant Nicholas Brody, rescued by US soldiers after spending eight years in captivity in Iraq. Has he been 'turned' away from America, and toward terrorism? Carrie Mathison is the brilliant female CIA agent (played by Claire Danes) who 'knows' Brody has turned, though no-one believes her. She also harbours a secret; she has bipolar disorder, for which she is outed toward the end of the first series. The closing scenes of series one show Carrie on a hospital bed undergoing electroconvulsive therapy.

Series two of *Homeland* opens with scenes of Carrie gardening and grading night-school exams. A nascent gendered commentary might be ventured here, given the highly masculinised security profession she has been made to retreat from, and these more domesticated settings. Indeed, it was Carrie's feminised hyper-emotionality and her gender-fluid excessiveness that first drew me to her when thinking about this chapter. But a gendered narrative about Carrie is not easily reached, or perhaps too easily. A counter-intuitive comment, perhaps, but then emotion is like that, as the intertwining of violence and love indicates.

By the second episode, Carrie is back at work for the CIA. No-one else is able to do the work the CIA needs, though her return is otherwise not welcome. She even overhears her long-time mentor, close colleague and friend Saul Berenson, say that he never wanted her back in the first place. No-one trusts Carrie now; no-one except the informant who will speak only to her. Carrie's erratic and excessive behaviour is now comfortably categorised as a form of madness. Her temporary return takes her to Beirut, where a meeting is to be arranged with the wife of Abbas Ali, the Hezbollah district commander, though plans immediately go awry. Carrie is scheduled to meet Saul in a café, but he realises he is being watched and warns her on his cell phone not to stop, but to walk past.

A subsequent scene shows Carrie in a bedroom, sweating profusely and panicking. She can hardly breathe; she begins to crawl around the floor, crying and desperate. She drags herself onto the roof where Saul finds her. An intriguing scene follows. Carrie, working on her own initiative following the missed meeting with Saul, has located and met with her informant and garnered extremely important information, though the meeting took place unexpectedly without Saul and he is unhappy about this. He was not able to make his judgement about the informant's trustworthiness. And he doesn't trust Carrie. But then Carrie doesn't trust herself either.

***Beirut roof top scene***

CARRIE (EXTREMELY UPSET): It's not lost on me why people don't trust my judgement; it fucked me up being wrong about Brody. I have never been so sure and so wrong. That fact made me unable to trust my own thoughts. Every time I think I see something clearly it just disappears … I recruited her [wife of Abbas Ali], I helped her get through an abusive domestic situation. I remember knowing that one day she would be ready to leave here and she would be on my side. The way I am now I wouldn't trust me either. But the Carrie who recruited her, that one I believe.

Carrie's character might be superficially represented as emblematic of feminism's success, given she is one of a series of female leads in the genre of militarised, policing and security television dramas (for example, *The Killing, The Bridge, The Fall* and *Borgen*; also 'Hollywood movies' in the post (post)-9/11 era such as *Rendition* and *Zero Dark Thirty*). A woman in this kind of role is beginning to appear somewhat 'normal'. To be sure, Carrie is damaged in a range of ways (as are many of the other female leads), but I think Carrie opens up a particularly profound, if elusive, series of questions about boundaries, violence and the subject of woman. To help think about all of this, I want to move to the other Carrie – Carrie White, the central character in Stephen King's novel.

## Carrie White

Elspeth Probyn suggests that to work properly with affect, you have to follow through what different affects do, or the different ways they splinter. She also notices that 'sometimes you catch a whole worldview from a snippet of … talk' (2010: 75). This moved me to think more precisely about the snippet of everyday conversation that opened the previous section. What was so distasteful about Carrie Mathison? Why was the conversation discomforting, at least for me? Though I suppose I was a touch unnerved by the comment in response to my saying Carrie reminded me of my daughter. I laughed, of course, without saying anything, and the conversation turned to the business of the work-day meeting. But following it more, I was struck by the sticky and dense entanglement of love, popular culture, security, embarrassment, theory, identity, abhorrence and tension which seemed to linger. Moreover, given the intricate mix of gendered judgment and alienation gestured toward here, I judged it important to follow it around some more.

Carrie is not a common name, certainly not in Britain where I live. Though it is a name I know, given Stephen King's book *Carrie* (1974) and the iconic 1976 film of the same name with brilliant performances by Sissy Spacek and Piper Laurie. The tale's enduring popularity is illustrated by consistently high book sales and a recent remake of the film in 2013. Excess, violence, femininity, pain and blood – especially the blood – all of these drip and ooze through King's *Carrie.* In the introduction to the 1999 edition, King writes about one of the inspirations for his book, two girls he names Tina and Sandy. His introduction ends with this wish:

> Sometimes – quite often in fact – I wish that Tina and Sandy were alive to read it. Or their daughters.
>
> (King 1999: xviii)

Two of King's high school contemporaries, he recalls the relentless bullying of Tina and Sandy for being 'different', perhaps a little fat, or a little unwashed, or a little strange. Whatever the 'truth' of their difference, the 'something' that broadcast 'keep away, not like us!' was transmitted on a wavelength not quite discernible, perhaps not real at all, yet felt and acted upon. Their ghosts combined in King's imagination to become the Carrie of his novel, neatly obliterating the fake line between fact and fiction. As young women without children, Tina had committed suicide in her cellar and Sandy died of an epileptic seizure alone in her small apartment. King's recollection and the dedication of his book are deeply touching. They touch me as I imagine Tina and Sandy in their misery and recall the excruciating pain suffered by the real/fictitious Carrie. And King's imagined daughters for Tina and Sandy speak of generations of female lives lost; perhaps an allegory of feminism in its despairing and anticipatory hopes and promises. How were all these fleeting affective moments of pain and longing working to move some stories forward, or in some other direction? Ephemeral connections seemed to fade in and out, and I thought again about King's and *Homeland's* Carrie and perhaps also my own daughters.

> It's 1979 and Carrie White is taking a shower in the School locker room after gym class. She wished there were private showers. They stared. They always stared. Showers turned off one by one, girls stepping out, towelling, spraying deodorant, bras unhooked, underpants stepped into. Carrie stays a little longer in the heat and warmth. The girls begin to giggle. Carrie turns off the shower and notices the blood running down her leg. '*Per*-iod!'
>
> 'PER-iod!'
>
> '*PER*-iod, *PER*-iod, *PER*-iod!'[2]

It might seem unusual, even for the 1970s, that a girl of sixteen from the seemingly most developed country in the world knew nothing about menstruation.

Though the brutal, pious fervour exhibited by Carrie's mother perhaps explains why Carrie was oblivious to what de Beauvoir called the 'monthly curse', and thought she was bleeding to death. The girls continued with the chants – '*PER*-iod, *PER*-iod, *PER*-iod!' Carrie stood dumbly in the centre of a forming circle … aware that the joke was on her (as usual).' The incantations continued, tampons thrown sticking ungallantly to Carrie's dripping body, 'at sixteen, the elusive stamp of hurt was already marked clearly in her eyes', her pitiful snivelling drowned out by the jubilant howls of the other girls delighting in Carrie's pain. King's story ends dramatically and violently; Carrie's 'gift' of telekinesis eventually releasing her to wreak lethal devastation. A fictitious tale perhaps, but we can momentarily think about Carrie through the shape of the hopes of the era of feminism through which she lived, 'second-wave feminism', to help think a little more about the discomforts our twenty-first century Carrie throws up, and how any of this helps us to think more (deeply) about some of the things that continue to trouble us in regard to violence and women and the international.

'PER-iod, *PER*-iod, *PER*-iod!' The taboos around menstruation, though much dented in the contemporary western landscape, were very strong in the 1970s, perhaps especially the 'small-town-America' typical of King's novels. Distaste for the idea, sight and smell of menstrual blood was commonplace. Second-wave feminism vibrantly and insistently ushered in new (or revitalised) thinking and theorising about women's bodies. A raft of activism, publications and subsequent legislation extending and awarding women's previously curtailed or withheld rights, particularly over 'our bodies', littered the 1960s and 1970s. 1973 saw the publication of the iconic *Our Bodies Ourselves* by the Boston Women's Health Collective, and in the same year the infamous *Roe vs. Wade* court case in the USA resulted in radically changing women's access to abortion, as did the UK Abortion Act passed a few years earlier in 1967.

Though Carrie's ignorance about menstruation might seem at odds with all of this, the gendered script of her young life seems very time-typical; the promise and rewards of prettiness, and to be the prom date of the most popular boy at school, remain the prizes and are the things that entice Carrie to the final scene of destruction. Then she takes complete control. Though perhaps echoing conventional and persistent narratives about 'gender(ed) violence', she ends up being the ultimate violator through her exposure of the original violence; the fictionalised fact of her telekinesis only acting as a form of poetic licence in King's expert writer's imagination. Resisting, violent women still so regularly appear as *only* violent, and doubly blamed, given their gender.

## Affective connections

> A commitment to descriptive entanglement is hard to sustain for long and harder still to shape into something approaching academic conclusions.
>
> (Highmore 2010: 135)

My brief foray into questions about emotion began with an uncomfortable moment, one which I described as a sticky and dense entanglement of love, popular culture, security, embarrassment, theory, identity, abhorrence and tension. These rich and meaningful connections between seemingly unconnected things indicate we might be missing something in our theorising of the questions about violence in which we are interested as scholars of international politics. What has following the two Carries around subsequent to a fleeting affective moment disclosed? Do their performances, their excesses, their confusions, their unmissable gender usher us a little closer to some of the secrets of violence? I think they do, though this does not come with any answers about how to proceed subsequently in conventional academic and bureaucratic registers. Rather, it invites deeper methodological and affective absorption into the messy entanglements of feeling, matter and thoughts which are so central to our meaning-making in and with the world – we can't really avoid the disorder and untidiness of everyday life, though we persistently try. Let me offer some thoughts by way of explication.

There is what Ben Highmore terms a 'sensual pedagogy' (2010: 134) in the stories of the two Carries, about feminism, about violence, about the subject of woman, and about the unease that appears when the edges of some of our boundaries containing meaning flicker into our senses – when we walk into 'the atmosphere'. Over four decades of feminism stretch between the two Carries; their lives, in many ways, stand as allegories for feminism's journey, a journey which is saturated with constraining spatial and temporal narratives around failure, success and the journey still to come. Carrie Mathison seems entirely different from Carrie White. *Homeland*'s Carrie is a very modern woman, she earns her own (presumably high) salary, she has her own apartment, is excellent at her high-pressure and powerful job, and she looks for sexual encounters when and where she wants to, a perfect example of feminism's success, perhaps. To be sure there are costs, but there are costs for anyone in such a demanding, dangerous job. The potential consequences of her sexual encounters with men are conventional, and by the end of series two Carrie is pregnant. Nearing the end of series three, Carrie's pregnancy is well advanced and the sex of the baby known (a girl). I fleetingly imagine that Stephen King's wish for Tina and Sandy is poetically fulfilled; a daughter for Carrie. My thoughts are shamelessly emotive, indulging in a fantasy of Spielberg-esque heteronormatively secured generational resolution. My more enduring thoughts coalesce around the ways the very existence of emotion destabilises so many of our liberal, individualistic shibboleths. The more emotion surfaces and sticks, the more the sham of secure boundaries around identity, around violence, around reason, all might come too close to bear.

Though Carrie Mathison seems emblematic of the apparent freedoms of modern westernised woman, she also demonstrates the messy and disorderly assemblage that gender as concept and experience is. The unwieldy but visceral connections between gender, woman and feminism are also elicited – in her speaking of herself (as other) she proffers a beautiful metaphor for the workings of feminist knowledge, 'every time I think I see something clearly it just disappears'. This is perhaps most noticeable in the context of our theorising of violence; we know what and where it is, and then we don't – or we don't seem to, given its resilience. It is also suggestive of the corporeal theoretical and philosophical challenges birthed through feminism about the illusions and insecurities of boundaries. The boundaries containing women appear to have changed, evident through our two Carries, though the thing we hoped to (finally) control – gender – keeps appearing and re-appearing like an amorphous border guard, persistently materialising like a mirage or ghost, sometimes visibly violently.

We can glimpse some of this slipperiness further through the theatricality of their performances; the performativity of gender is not devoid of 'actual' performances. The feminised excessiveness of both Carries as emotional and 'leaky' women is fictionally explained and contained within frames of 'madness' (of a sort) – bipolarity for Carrie Mathison and telekinesis for Carrie White, constructing something of a safety net around the shaky fiction of secure subjecthood. Though the kaleidoscope of their identities is frequently illustrated by both Carries as both beside and outside of themselves, this is temporarily stabilised through their states of medicalised 'unreason'. Recall the Beirut rooftop scene where Carrie Mathison is stunningly beside herself – 'the way I am now I wouldn't trust me either. But the Carrie who recruited her, that one I believe'. This is an intriguing expression – and recognition – of the 'split-self' – Irigaray's sex which is not one (1985). Though the discomfort of how this feels, and what this might mean for our control over ourselves, and our access to and manipulation of the worlds we seek to manage and contain and re-deliver back to the world as useful knowledge, are too close to the surface. I think the intensities we feel with and from Carrie Mathison make this impossible to ignore, suggestive of good reasons for being wary of her, or even disliking her, giving force to Gregg and Seigworth's claim that emotions work as 'intensities' and 'resonances that circulate about, between and sometimes stick to bodies and worlds' (2010: 1).

For Carrie White, her state of 'besideness' or 'outside-ness' is painfully present in her knowing the joke will (always) be on her, like Tina and Sandy. And though the truth of the violence she suffers is known to readers/viewers, her particular form of mental instability or 'difference' (so often with a heavily gendered history) emerges in classically feminised ways (if extreme) of not knowing where the boundaries are, or where to stop, which so regularly incites 'reasoned' restraint from the 'sane' world; though too late in Carrie White's case. And for Carrie Mathison, the performative production of the excessively feminine and the failures/achievements of impossible and multiple subjectivities materialise forcibly through her, the messiness and feminised tension of this keenly felt by my colleague.

## Concluding thoughts

> Affect emerges out of muddy unmediated relatedness.
>
> (Seigworth and Gregg 2010: 4)

Affective moments, a feeling, a sense of discomfort – tracking how they splinter is not simple. Yet following some of the resonances which glint through the snippet of conversation I opened with – an imbroglio of a kind, though conventionally not worthy of such a description – unearths some interesting things, not least the circularity of the framing and shaping of women, if in changing forms. Perhaps more significantly, the lingering intensity of responses to those who, by virtue of their lurid presence at the edge of sense and reason like our two Carries, make a little clearer – if transiently – something about the hollow ground of knowledge on which we importantly make statements, policy and theory about violence, and yet so willingly continue to fail in the wake of their inadequacies. So often it is through the bodies of women, and the emotions that swirl oftentimes ungallantly around them, that this becomes apparent, even if 'only' felt.

The problems that haunt and blister the surface and depth of contemporary world politics, as Bleiker says, are far too serious and deadly not to employ the full register of human intelligence to access and perhaps better understand them (2009: 1). If our struggles around emotion do alert us further to some of the impossibilities of methodology and the ongoing challenges of formulating bits of knowing, feeling and sensing into useful and usable knowledge in a chaotic world, the over-inflated certainty which marks theory and policy production in contemporary International Politics/Relations may have to shift in a more humble direction in order to look more closely, if uncomfortably, at more of the ways in which our everyday and worlds are compressed so tightly together into an illusory whole, though what this promises is not clear or predictable. There may be strong desires to discover ways to make better sense of the ongoing 'blood-drenched' challenges staining the contemporary international landscape, and mobilising methods traditionally undermined or overlooked by hegemonic disciplinary conventions might provide this; though perhaps this is not the case at all. A dissensual energy infuses aesthetic approaches, at least those which draw inspiration from the work of Jacques Rancière (2004, see also Frost 2010). This infers that a more subversive imagination might be at work in our theorising emotion, one distanced from the urge to supply remedies for the shortcomings of hegemonic approaches which simply re-articulate specific configurations of power relations. Rather disrupting or indeed deranging the accepted order of things, and in particular the 'general distribution of making and doing', emerges as the important work to do.

## Notes

1 The 'she' here is probably a combination of Carrie and the actor Claire Danes.
2 This and the following extracts are from pp. 4–7 of King's book, abridged.

## Bibliography

Ahmed, S. (2004) *The Cultural Politics of Emotion*. Edinburgh: Edinburgh University Press.

Boston Women's Health Collective (1973) *Our Bodies Ourselves.* New York: Simon & Schuster.

Bleiker, R. (2009) *Aesthetics and World Politics.* Basingstoke: Palgrave Macmillan.

Brennan, T. (2004) *The Transmission of Affect.* Ithaca, NY and London: Cornell University Press.

Chan, S. (2010) 'The pain of Susan Sontag', *Global Society*, 24(3): 369–380.

Clough, P. T. (2007) *The Affective Turn: Theorizing the Social.* Durham, NC and London: Duke University Press.

Dyer, R. (1997) *White.* London and New York: Routledge.

Frost, L. (2010) 'Aesthetics and politics', *Global Society*, 24(3): 433–443.

Gregg, M. and Seigworth, G. J. (eds) (2010) *The Affect Theory Reader.* Durham, NC and London: Duke University Press.

Highmore, B. (2010) 'Bitter after taste: Affect, food and social aesthetics', in *The Affect Theory Reader*, Gregg and Seigworth (eds). Durham, NC and London: Duke University Press, 118–137.

Irigaray, L. (1985) *This Sex Which Is Not One.* Ithaca, NY: Cornell University Press.

King, S. (1999) *Carrie.* London: Hodder & Stoughton.

Probyn, E. (2010) 'Writing shame', in *The Affect Theory Reader*, Gregg and Seigworth (eds). Durham, NC and London: Duke University Press, 71–90.

Rancière, J. (2004) *The Politics of Aesthetics: The Distribution of the Sensible*, G. Rockhill (transl.). London: Continuum.

Rowley, C. (2015) 'Popular culture and the politics of the visual', in *Global Gender Matters*, second edition, Shepherd (ed.). London and New York: Routledge.

Sedgwick, E. K. (2004) *Touching Feeling: Affect, Pedagogy, Performativity.* Durham, NC and London: Duke University Press.

Zalewski, M. (2013) *Feminist International Relations: Exquisite Corpse.* London and New York: Routledge.

# 4 Human dignity, basal emotion and a global emotionology

*K. M. Fierke*

The language of human dignity was pervasive during the Arab Spring in Tunisia and Egypt. While both human dignity and the prohibition on humiliating treatment have, since the Universal Declaration of Human Rights (1948), been moral and legal principles of international law, I argue that the concepts of human dignity and humiliation have acquired a deep emotional resonance, against the backdrop of not only the Holocaust, but a history of imperialism, colonialism and racism. These terms are frequently expressed by groups resisting oppression (Fierke 2013) and are what I refer to as 'basal emotions', which relate to existential concerns about survival and value as a human being.

Three specific points underpin the argument that follows. First, in the international realm, emotions more often relate to group identity than to individuals per se, which highlights the social dimension of emotion. The question of the neurological basis of emotion or the cognitive processing of emotion by individuals, while important, is less central than the socio-political expression and consequences of emotion, particularly in relation to conflict and its resolution. Many psychologists and philosophers agree that emotions have both a social and an ethical function (Keltner and Haidt 1999; Schweder and Haidt 2000; Haidt 2001; Johnson 2007). Second, the varying ways in which emotion is expressed or experienced across culture suggest that emotion, and its appropriate expression, are shaped as much by context and socialisation as neurology. The stimulus for the neurological response is often socially and culturally defined, and in this respect the somatic response is a reaction to the evocation of socially meaningful categories that have emotional resonance. Third, the concepts of humiliation and dignity not only have acquired a legal status in international law but, in contexts of repression or conflict, have become the trigger for existential emotions about what it means to be human. The codification of human dignity and the prohibition on humiliating treatment in international law represents a significant change in the global context in the aftermath of World War II, and have since often become the focal point of emotions relating to contemporary struggles for recognition (Honneth 1995). The Arab Spring, while emerging from cultures of the Middle East, was also an expression of this more global culture of emotion, arising from 'basal emotions' relating to human value and worth.

## Emotions as social

Biologists, philosophers, anthropologists, sociologists and psychologists have found it difficult to come to an agreed definition of emotion or to specify which states qualify as emotions (Elster 1999: 241; Crawford 2000: 123–4; Rozin and Cohen 2003). Emotion is often assumed to be subjective and irrational. There has been considerable debate about whether the values that give rise to emotions are themselves derived from reason, or some combination of reason and emotion, or are in conflict with reason (Altieri 2003: 153–80). Martha Nussbaum (2003: 4) argues that emotion is a rational measure of value and that emotions are 'appraisals or value judgements which ascribe to things and persons outside the person's own control great importance for the person's own flourishing'. Emotions are thus expressions of our vulnerability to people and events that we don't control and, far from the opposite of rationality, involve a form of judgement about the importance of an object to one's survival and flourishing. Emotion expresses a relationship between feeling and value. Positive emotions, such as joy, relate to the presence or achievement of a valued subject or object, and agency in achieving one's objectives. Negative emotions, such as humiliation or betrayal, may arise from a loss of dignity, value, safety or agency, and a subsequent inability to flourish. Emotions are a response to things that matter. While emotion, at the individual level, may be a spontaneous response to an experience of injury or pain, the salience of an emotion is likely to be connected to a history, and thus memory, which gives it content and specificity. From this perspective, it is rational to experience emotion in response to a lowering of value.

The experience of emotion may be individual, but emotions have meaning within a social world and, if expressed, they are expressed in relation to others, and in a language understandable to them, particularly if an experience is shared. In this respect, the appraisal or value judgements discussed by Nussbaum are not purely cognitive; inner feelings connect to a social world. Individuals within a culture make appraisals and value judgements that draw on cultural knowledge and memory (Johnson 2007). Wittgenstein situates the self in a common world of language, where expressions of pain or joy, or other expressions of our inner life, are radically dependent on customs, uses and institutions (Wittgenstein 1958: para. 199). In this view, emotion finds expression only in a language and a culture, which is linked to a moral order and moral appraisal (Harre 1986; Levinson *et al.* 1992; and Schweder 1994), which helps to define when emotion is appropriate, how it is expressed, and how it is given meaning, whether in the ruminations of the self or in relation to others. Emotions do not stand alone, but are attached to further entailments by which various subjects, objects and acts have meaning. While the same basic emotions are experienced across cultures, culture defines the circumstances which should give rise to emotion, including what constitutes an injury to human dignity or a humiliation. The emotion alerts a person to the need to take action, change or continue with the present course of action; or, in the case of inappropriate action, may give rise to a reconsideration of action (Johnson 2007: 660).

The previous paragraphs made several points about the social nature of emotion. First, emotion is often a rational expression of value within a relationship. Anger, fear, joy, love, humiliation, betrayal are most often experienced in relation to other people. Second, emotion brings with it the weight of memory and social meaning. Third, emotion is social insofar as it arises from identification with a group, and thus may also be experienced by the group as a social whole. Neuhauser (in Kaufmann *et al.* 2011: 22–30) asks how it would be possible for humiliation to be experienced by a collective, as distinct from an individual. He argues that the humiliation of members of a group is humiliation 1) if the humiliation targets a collectively shared element of identity; 2) when this shared identity is constitutive of the self-respect of group members; and 3) if the humiliation is sanctioned on a social level or no measures are taken to respond appropriately to the humiliation.

Neuhauser identifies three clear cases of collective humiliation. The first is when individuals who belong to a group are subject to humiliation because every member of the group, if put in a certain situation, would be humiliated. He provides the example of airport controls for stopping and searching that target a particular group, for example, those who appear to be Muslims. The second is when whole groups of individuals are humiliated by the mistreatment of symbols of the group and when this mistreatment is associated with past humiliation as well as the threat of present humiliation. For instance, the defilement of Jewish graveyards both evokes a memory of the Holocaust and represents a threat in the present. The third point is that entire groups can be humiliated when one or more of its members are humiliated, and this is somehow sanctioned by society. In the past, some societies have, for instance, condoned spousal rape, based on arguments that women should not have control over their bodies as men do. It has become more common for societies to condemn spousal rape, in which case the woman is still 'humiliated in the normative sense, but…she does not need to feel humiliated in the psychological sense because society recognizes the way she was treated as a violation of her rights' (Neuhauser in Kaufmann *et al.* 2011: 30).

Systematic rape in warfare rests on an intention to humiliate the entire group, rather than victims as individuals. As Hague (in Lentin 1997: 54) notes in the context of Bosnia, 'by humiliating non-Serb persons through a systematic programme of raping women and girls, and by raping women, girls, men and boys as torture in prison camps, Bosnian Serb forces bolstered their own masculine national identity and, through the extreme humiliation of rape, eroded the identities of non-Serbs'. In this case, attributes of identity, which are not purely individual, were the central reason for being devalued. The women and men who were raped during the conflict in Bosnia were not attacked because of who they are as individuals, but because of the ethnic group with which they were identified.

## Emotionology and culture

The above discussion highlights the social foundations of emotion and its expression. There is, however, another element of this sociality that is more cultural insofar as it relates to the types of emotional expression allowed by a society, which Stearns and Stearns (1985) refer to as emotionology. Emotionology is about how the norms of different societies shape the appropriate expression of emotion. Through the process of socialisation, the emotionology of a culture influences how the individual experiences emotions. For instance, the degree to which people openly grieve following a death, or the extent to which autonomous action by women is a source of rage or even humiliation, varies from culture to culture. The emotionology of a culture can be said to have a social function in shaping public attitudes about violence towards others. Andrew Linklater (2011: 32) notes that all societies rely on emotions such as guilt, shame, embarrassment and remorse to ensure that people comply with prohibitions against harmful behaviour. Emotions such as indignation or disgust also play an important role when transgressions occur, as do pity or compassion towards the victims of unwarranted mental or physical harm. While the same emotions exist across cultures, they find culturally specific expression. Culture is not a bounded or static entity and, indeed, individuals may, through experience with more than one culture, acquire different and even competing elements of distinct emotionologies. Much like a Wittgensteinian (1958: para. 66) approach to language, this requires that we 'look and see' how emotion is expressed in the specific case.

There may also be an explicitly political dimension to a culture's emotionology. In a society that is under the thumb of a repressive regime or system, the gap between the individual emotional experience and the range of emotions that are allowed publicly may be far greater, and the scope for the public expression of emotion far more constrained. In this respect, a private/public distinction arises less from *properties* of emotion, that is, the assumption that they are inherently subjective and individual, than from the risk of punishment for public displays that are anything other than positive about the regime. Thus, in a society such as Communist Poland, where open criticism was repressed, economic shortages or frustrations of other kinds often erupted into an avalanche of rage, followed by violent repression. In a context dominated by fear, which silences and isolates, there is no public space for the direct expression of emotions. Inner fear in this case becomes the counterpart of external conformity.

The Polish example highlights the contrast between emotion that is repressed or denied, and emotion that may erupt subsequently in the public sphere. The denial or internalisation of emotion may be encouraged within a social space. This may take the more benign form of keeping emotions to oneself to avoid appearing to be irrational, which is common in some Western societies. The other is the authoritarian culture where x, y, a, b, c all feel humiliated, but the cost of expressing these emotions publicly is punishment. In this case, the internalisation of emotion is political, although potentially reinforced by cultural norms. The process of moving away from internalisation to the *externalisation* of political emotion was evident in the Arab Spring where, following the self-immolation of Mohamed Bouazizi, people took to the streets in large numbers, abandoning their fear. In abandoning their fear the protesters broke through the walls of this private/public divide, which then began to dissolve. The act of defiance was symbolic of the transition from isolation defined by fear, and lacking a public space for politically relevant emotion, to freely expressed emotions associated with autonomy, dignity and independence. In moving from internalisation to externalisation, emotions associated with humiliation, such as fear, shame or loss of self-respect, are transformed into emotions that accompany feelings of dignity and grounding in a positive social world.

Emotion is the glue that binds communities together. Indeed, a conception of emotion that is purely individual shares more in common with a concept of trauma, insofar as the latter is associated with isolation from others (Fierke 2004). We feel anger toward or love for someone; betrayed or humiliated by someone. These encounters at the individual level are interactions with an Other, one's environment or symbols of the past. The emotions are political insofar as they grow out of identification with a group or nation, or out of an injury that was inflicted because of this identification. The emotions express a desire for recognition of value in a world populated by others. The Arab Spring highlights a process of change within Middle Eastern culture, which links to the development of a more global emotionology.

## Global emotionology

The previous sections have analysed the social basis of emotion, pointing in particular to examples relating to humiliation or a lowering of value and its opposite counterpart, dignity. The latter section explored the idea that cultures have an emotionology, which individuals acquire through a process of socialisation, and which shapes their experience and expression of emotion. The third step is to argue that human dignity and the prohibition on humiliating behaviour have, since World War II, became part of a more global emotionology which has influenced the shape of many conflicts and the potential for their resolution.

Kamir (in Kretzmer and Klein 2002: 232) argues that a society may, at a historical turning point, choose to declare a certain value or set of values as its fundamental constitutional core, as was the case with the US claim to equality and liberty in 1776, or France in 1789, or (West) Germany's incorporation of human dignity in its constitution following World War II, or that of dignity and equality in South Africa in 1992. These dramatic moral and legal choices, she argues, typically coincide with times of revolution, when a society is faced with deep structural questions about the fundamental values that underpin it. The collective declaration of a new fundamental value indicates a major socio-cultural change. The codification of this value in a new constitution becomes a legal manifestation of the socio-cultural shift. The incorporation of human dignity, first in the UN Charter and a few years later in the 1948 Universal Declaration of Human Rights (UDHR), was a similar socio-cultural shift, but at the international level. This 'revolution' followed on the extreme degradation of human dignity represented by the Holocaust. The value of human dignity was codified in international law, but transcended any individual state, given its emphasis on the human, and thus could be seen as a rudimentary expression of a global society or culture.

While the first declarations of human rights go back to the eighteenth century, the UDHR was the first document in the history of declarations of rights to refer to human dignity as the *foundation* of human rights (Dicke in Kretzmer and Klein 2002: 112). This represents a departure from earlier periods or contexts where dignity presupposed neither human rights nor equality, and was related to privilege and honour or the status of a dignitary (Meeks in Moltman 1984: IX). Dignity consists of a set of human rights which must be afforded to all human beings by all other human beings as well as human social institutions. Dignity establishes the conditions by which humans can exercise their autonomy (Capps 2009: 108). The use of dignity in the UDHR drew on Christian, Jewish and Enlightenment concepts, which identify the source of human dignity, respectively, with God's creation, the god-like image of the person or the idea that human beings are endowed by nature with reason and, therefore, equality (Dicke in Kretzmer and Klein 2002: 112). While human rights have often been criticised as a specifically Western construct, human dignity has meaning across cultures, and is often a part of the conceptual language of repressed groups who seek change (Fierke 2013). In this respect, one could say that the meaning of human dignity travels between the global and the more local; it is translated into contextually specific uses that are buttressed by a more global shared understanding. Mohammad Kamali, a Professor of Law at the International Islamic University, Malaysia, argues:

> [W]hen human rights are seen as a manifestation of respect for human dignity, human rights are likely to have a more authentic basis across cultural traditions. As one commentator noted, "nothing could be more important than to underscore and defend the dignity of the human person." To take dignity as the goal and purpose of human rights would be to enrich the caliber and substance of these rights.
>
> (Kamali 2002: xv)

The UDHR refrained both from defining dignity and from identifying it with a particular tradition. It called for policies that establish the conditions to secure a life for all human beings in dignity, but was unclear about how an undefined concept could establish a norm from which human rights could be derived. According to Dicke (in Kretzmer and Klein 2002: 118–119), the ambiguity of human dignity is a function of its contextuality, that is, the historical, economic, political and cultural conditioning of societies in which the human rights claims are articulated, as well as the universality of human rights.

Margalit (1998) argued that we learn most about human dignity by looking at its violations and what it means for people to be degraded, humiliated and wronged. Rather than analysing abstract values or capacities, we can ask a question about why we care about dignity, or why it is a source of emotion. By approaching dignity from its negative opposite, we gain insight into some of its central features. If emotions are understood to belong to a relational field, where subjects are acting or being acted upon, then the problem is not a straightforward one of labelling particular emotions. In this case, we want to explore the relational field surrounding human dignity as it relates to its negative counterpart, that is, humiliation, and ask how this shapes the global emotionology of the twenty-first century. Humiliation can be a verb – to humiliate someone, which suggests intention on the part of an agent. To feel humiliated may be the emotional response of a subject to the action of an Other, which refers more to the impact of an Other's actions on one's sense of self-value or self-respect. As Statman notes, the relationship is complex:

> To humiliate a person is not only to provide her with a reason to feel humiliated but actually to produce this painful feeling … You can betray a person behind her back … By contrast, you cannot humiliate a person without her knowing it and, furthermore, without her accepting it, i.e., experiencing a loss in her self-respect and acknowledging you as its source.
>
> (Statman in Kretzmer and Klein 2002: 220)

Margalit (1998) argues that the humiliating act is intended to lower the value of the object; however, in order for the humiliation to be effective, the humiliated has to retain sufficient agency to recognise and acknowledge that they have been humiliated. It is this acknowledgement that substantiates the power of the humiliator. The acknowledgement doubles the voice of the authority insofar as their power is substantiated by the conformity of those who consent (Fierke 2013). In reclaiming their dignity in the face of humiliation and punishment by the respective regimes, the protesters in Tunisia and Egypt exercised agency in refusing to acknowledge this humiliation, even in the face of death.

When the behaviour of others communicates a message of subordination, rejection or exclusion, there are sound reasons for feelings of humiliation, and thus the emotional response can be said to be rational. Just as we may respond with fear to events that threaten our vital interests, feelings of humiliation are likely to arise in response to behaviours that injure or threaten to injure our self-respect (Statman in Kretzmer and Klein 2002: 218). This rational emotional response can be distinguished from a more irrational example. A traumatic experience, for instance, can predispose someone to treat events in the present as if they were a repeat of the past. In this case, a small family resemblance between two people or contexts can trigger a reaction that is based on this assumption of sameness, rather than understanding the present context in its own terms. For instance, a child's experience of abuse by a man with a hairy nose might later result in generalisation that all men with hairy noses are potential abusers, in which case the response would be irrational. An emotional response to a traumatic interaction may be rational, but the generalisation to all interactions based on a single attribute may be irrational. Parties to an ongoing political conflict, such as the Israelis and Palestinians, may have a tendency to interpret each new interaction as a repeat of the past, which then becomes a self-fulfilling prophecy. Insofar as there may be a tendency to see humiliation even when it is not intended, the emotional response may be disproportionate to the actual threat, or contribute to its constitution. Rather than an emotional condition that serves the end of survival, the traumatised reaction reproduces conflict.

Feelings of humiliation may be a rational emotional response to behaviour that excludes or denigrates; recognition of that humiliation, based on Margalit's argument, may not be. As already suggested, the refusal to acknowledge humiliation, and to instead reclaim one's dignity as an expression of autonomy, is a political alternative that found expression in the Arab Spring. Mohamed Bouazizi's act of setting himself on fire arose not only from the loss of his livelihood, but from feeling humiliated by authorities. His act touched the experience of so many others in his social environment that it unleashed a storm of emotion in the public realm which brought thousands into the street and emboldened them to engage in acts of resistance. The brutalisation by the state in response brought the everyday experience of humiliation into public view, while transforming it into an expression of dignity. The action of Bouazizi and others raises a question about the relationship between autonomy and dignity on one hand, and survival on the other. Bruno Bettelheim, a survivor of a Nazi concentration camp, articulated the relationship and the potential tension:

> [T]o survive as a man, not a walking corpse, as a debased and degraded, but still human being, one had first and foremost to remain informed and aware of what made up one's personal point of no return, the point beyond which one would never, under any circumstances, give in to the oppressor, even if it meant risking and losing one's life.
>
> Bettelheim (1961: 157)

## Autonomy and survival

The autonomy of the body is, I would argue, the focal point of 'basal' emotion at the international level. In this respect, human dignity and the prohibition on humiliating treatment are to the individual body what sovereignty and non-interference are to the 'body politic'. In both cases, while the boundaries of the body differ, autonomy and agency are central concerns. Interference in the state, like humiliation of the human body, is understood to be a violation that impacts on autonomy. The role of humiliation in warfare is a subject that has not received the attention it deserves. In the context of the attacks on 9/11, Osama Bin Laden, for instance, stated the intent to humiliate the US as Muslims and Arabs had been humiliated for 80 years. Or Hitler referred to the humiliation of Versailles as one of the reasons for his efforts to make Germany great again (Fierke 2004; Fattah and Fierke 2009).

Going back to Hobbes, the central problem of sovereignty has been articulated as one of survival. For the sovereign state, survival is the prior condition for autonomy and, in this respect, the two go hand in hand. A state has to survive to be a sovereign state. However, in regard to human dignity, the two are not necessarily linked. As the Bettelheim quote and the example of resisters in the Arab Spring highlight, there may be situations where an expression of autonomy is more important than individual survival, where an act of agency is undertaken with the recognition that it may result in death, but may also contribute to the restoration of community (Fierke 2013).

In one respect, survival is the necessary condition for autonomy and agency. One must exist as a sovereign entity or be alive, in the case of the human person, to act as an agent. But it is at this point that the problem of sovereignty and non-interference departs from that of human dignity and the prohibition on humiliating treatment. As already stated, the emotional problem is the same, whether we are talking about the body politic or the human body, that is, the problem of maintaining autonomy and value. Both involve a struggle for recognition, but one that is more or less complete in the two cases. Sovereignty is a form of social recognition that states extend to one another. It is the absence of recognition and agency by communities that lack sovereignty that has fuelled many post-World War II conflicts.

Why is this a problem of emotion rather than purely legal? What is the added value of approaching the problem in terms of emotion? One need only think of what is expressed in the images of starving men standing behind barbed wire in Auschwitz or Bosnia, or in images of Abu Ghraib or apartheid. The images of humiliation express a form of 'bare life', where life has been reduced to the management of bodies and where autonomy is absent (Agamben 1998). The claim to dignity in the Arab Spring or in countless nonviolent revolutions was a cry for autonomy and agency as part of a struggle for recognition as 'human'. Conflict or war often revolve around a struggle for recognition where the identity of a 'body politic' as sovereign is at stake (Scarry 1983).

Human dignity, like state sovereignty, is an existential value, where value or worth is imputed to the identity of the person or body politic. When existence is at stake the matter is existential. Kateb (2011: 12) distinguishes existential values relating to identity, such as autonomy, freedom, equality, and honour, from moral values. For many, he claims, morality has to do with human suffering, which is of course related to human dignity, but the latter, in its concern for status and stature, has to do with the proper recognition of the identity of every human being, as well as the identity of the human species. While the emotional motives for inflicting suffering or assaulting dignity may be the same, 'being made to suffer bodily and materially is not conceptually the same wrong as being treated as if one is not a human being' (Kateb 2011: 13). The existential consideration is the prior condition for the moral precept that no person should suffer needlessly. As Kateb (2011: 23) states, 'persons are to be treated in some ways and not in others. To cause them needless suffering is to treat them in a way that denies their dignity'.

The existential nature of human dignity relates to emotions that arise from what Robin Dillon (1997) refers to as 'basal self-respect'. Basal self-respect is the primordial interpretation of the self and self-worth, or the most profound valuing of ourselves. Systematic oppression and devaluation of, for instance, women or different ethnic groups is a social, political and cultural reality. As Wolf (2011) argues, questions of respect and dis-respect are at the heart of many international conflicts. One source of self-respect is social, given that self-respect depends at least in part on the respect or disrespect shown by others. Self-respect is vulnerable to injury by others, not least through humiliation. It is social insofar as it rests on identity as a member of a group rather than the individual per se. Damage at this level affects the lens through which reality is assessed, and points to the importance of social inclusion and the danger of exclusion. Humiliation alerts us to a threat of exclusion. It is precisely because humans are social beings that exclusion or lowering before others arouses the most painful of emotions.

Going back to Nussbaum's claim that emotion is a measure of value, it is a small further step to a notion of *basal emotions* as those emotions, both positive and negative, that circulate around our human dignity as individuals and members of groups. Emotions are a response to how and whether we are valued, which will be magnified by a loss of autonomy. The existence of global norms of human dignity becomes a part of the social designation of existential value, and a structure of meaning for undertaking a moral valuation regarding the nature of any injury that has occurred. Many international conflicts, in the context of emancipatory movements such as the Arab Spring, grow out of basal emotions associated with the absence of human dignity and autonomy. It is not surprising that the expression of basal emotions has increased since the incorporation of human dignity into the UDHR, and particularly since the end of the Cold War preoccupation with state and bloc security. As in the case of spousal rape or rape in warfare, the moral and legal codification of an ethical judgement provides a lens through which acts are interpreted, and which shapes the self-understanding of individual victims or of the groups with which they identify. The codification of these norms has provided social legitimacy for struggles of recognition in a world that has been divided into sovereign spaces. These sovereign spaces have often been uneven in recognising basic human dignity, often lowering value or excluding portions of the population who have suffered a loss of autonomy within state boundaries, imposed on the basis of artificial boundaries from a colonial or imperial era. One consequence is often that the state defines acts of resistance as a threat to its sovereignty, and a form of criminality or terrorism; from the perspective of excluded populations, resistance arises from a cry of injustice and a desire for autonomy (see Fierke 2013).

## Conclusions

The causes of conflict are often complex, and may be fanned by nationalism, ethnicity, religion or ideology. Participants may be motivated by the justice of their own cause, or may have been the victims of naked oppression, including marginalisation and exclusion within a particular society, or in response to dissent against an abuse of power or arbitrary rule. But, as Dicke (in Kretzmer and Klein 2002: 142) argues, these situations often hold in common the treatment of victims as persons of little worth, whose death or suffering is justified as necessary, often in response to the security needs of states. That the problem has increasingly been articulated as one of human dignity is a function of an assessment of core values of the international community in the aftermath of World War II and the experience of the Holocaust in Europe, although the logic has since been drawn on by groups to resist imperialism, colonialism and racism as well. This has provided a legitimating framework for resistance, as well as a social framework for judging violations of human dignity. The legal scaffolding that has since developed is a construction that obscures the core of the matter as fundamentally one of emotions relating to human vulnerability and our worth or value as human beings. The problem goes beyond a question of survival and highlights the crucial importance of autonomy to the dignity of human life.

Emotion relates to moral concerns about the suffering of human beings, and existential concerns about the basic survival and autonomy of either states or human beings. While the international legal scaffolding has provided a basis for judging violations against collective or individual victims, it has also provided an ethical and emotional framework for victims to understand the harm done to them, for moving the suffering out of a purely individual experience into a social world where humans are understood to have worth and value by virtue of their humanity. The moral and legal infrastructure can thus be said to constitute a more global emotionology, which facilitates the expression of basal emotions related to human dignity or its opposite, humiliation.

## Bibliography

Agamben, G. (1998) *Homo Sacer: Sovereign Power and Bare Life*. Stanford, CA: Stanford University Press.

Altieri, C. (2003) *The Particulars of Rapture: An Aesthetics of the Affects*. Ithaca, NY: Cornell University Press.

Bettelheim, B. (1961) *The Informed Heart: Autonomy in a Mass Age*. New York: Free Press.

Capps, P. (2010 [2009]) *Human Dignity and the Foundations of International Law.* Oxford: Hart Publishing.

Crawford, N. (2000) 'The passion of world politics: Propositions on emotion and emotional relationships', *International Security*, 24(4): 116–156.

Dillon, R. S. (1997) 'Self-respect: Moral, emotional, political', *Ethics* 107: 226–249.

Elster, J. (1999) *Alchemies of the Mind: Rationality and the Emotions.* Cambridge: Cambridge University Press.

Fattah, K. and Fierke, K. M. (2009) 'A clash of emotions: humiliation and political violence in the Middle East', *European Journal of International Relations*, 15(1): 67–93.

Fierke, K. M. (2004) 'Whereof we can speak, thereof we must not be silent: trauma, political solipcism and war', *Review of International Studies*, 30(4): 471–491.

Fierke, K. M. (2013) *Political Self-Sacrifice: Agency, Body and Emotion in International Relations.* Cambridge: Cambridge University Press.

Haidt, J. (2001) 'The emotional dog and its rational tail: A social institutionalist approach to moral judgement', *Psychological Review*, 108: 814–834.

Harre, R. (ed.) (1986) *The Social Construction of Emotions.* Oxford: Basil Blackwell.

Honneth, A. (1995) *The Struggle for Recognition: The Moral Grammar of Social Conflicts.* Cambridge: Polity Press.

Johnson, K. A. (2007) 'The social construction of emotions in the Bhagavad Gita: Locating ethics in a redacted text', *Journal of Religious Ethics*, 35(4): 655–679.

Kamali, M. H. (2002) *The Dignity of Man: An Islamic Perspective.* Cambridge: Cambridge University Press.

Kateb, G. (2011) *Human Dignity.* Cambridge, MA: Harvard University Press.

Kaufmann, P., Kuch, H., Neuhauser, C. and Webster, E. (eds) (2011) *Humiliation, Degradation, Dehumanization.* London: Springer.

Keltner, D. and Haidt, J. (1999) 'Social functions of emotion at four levels of analysis', *Cognition and Emotion*, 17(2): 294–314.

Kretzmer, D. and Klein, E. (eds) (2002) *The Concept of Human Dignity in Human Rights Discourse.* The Hague: Kluwer Law International.

Lentin, R. (ed.) (1997) *Gender and Catastrophe.* London: Zed Books.

Levinson, R. W., Ekman, P., Heider, K. and Friesen, W. V. (1992) 'Emotion and autonomic nervous system activity in the Minangkabau of West Sumatra', *Journal of Personality and Social Psychology*, 62: 972–988.

Linklater, A. (2011) *The Problem of Harm in World Politics: Theoretical Investigations.* Cambridge: Cambridge University Press.

Margalit, A. (1998) *The Decent Society.* Cambridge, MA: Harvard University Press.

Moltman, J. (1984) *On Human Dignity; Political Theology and Ethics.* London: SCM Press.

Nussbaum, M. (2003) *Upheavals of Thought: The Intelligence of Emotions.* Cambridge: Cambridge University Press.

Rozin, P. and Cohen, A. B. (2003) 'High frequency of facial expressions corresponding to confusion, concentration, and worry in an analysis of naturally occurring facial expressions in Americans', *Emotions*, 3: 68–75.

Scarry, E. (1983) *The Body in Pain: The Making and Unmaking of the World.* Oxford: Oxford University Press.

Schweder, R. A. (1994) '"You're not sick, you're just in love": Emotion as interpretive system', in *The Nature of Emotion: Fundamental Questions*, Ekman and Davidson (eds). New York: Oxford University Press, 32–44.

Schweder, R. A. and Haidt, J. (2000) 'The culture psychology of the emotions: Ancient and new', in *Handbook of Emotions*, second edition, Lewis and Haviland-Jones (eds). New York: Guilford Press.

Stearns, P. N. and Stearns, C. Z. (1985) 'Emotionology: Clarifying the history of emotions and emotional standards', *American Historical Review*, 90(1): 813–836.

Wittgenstein, L. (1958) *Philosophical Investigations.* Oxford: Basil Blackwell.

Wolf, R. (2011) 'Respect and dis-respect in international politics: The significance of status recognition', *International Theory*, 3(1): 105–142.

# 5 Embodiment, emotions, and materialism in International Relations

*Ty Solomon*

In March 2003, US General Tommy Franks held a press conference at Bagram Air Base in Afghanistan to report on the ongoing war efforts. Franks was asked a question about reports that US-led forces had killed large numbers of Taliban and enemy fighters, estimated at over 1,000 by some local reports. He responded that 'I don't believe you have heard me or anyone else in our leadership talk about the presence of 1,000 bodies out there, or in fact how many have been recovered. You know we don't do body counts' (quoted in Epstein 2002).

Franks' candid admission illustrates a number of issues surrounding contemporary warfare, such as the ethnocentrism of war, public debate about the costs of war, and so on. Yet it also raises more particular questions that International Relations (IR) scholars have yet to sufficiently probe. What is the role of the body in contemporary warfare? How should we think about the body in what has traditionally been a state-centric discipline? Moreover, how should we think about the interpenetrating roles of emotions and the body? Franks' assertion produces subjects that 'count' and others that do not. In this sense, interrogating the politics of language in boundary-drawing is necessary, but not sufficient if we want to come to grips with the more corporeal and embodied dimensions of war and security. Similarly, the passionate debate over the politics of whose bodies 'count' returning home is fundamentally a question over meaning – the meaning of the bodies themselves – and over the purposes and costs of the war. The urgency behind such debates is not, this chapter will argue, simply epiphenomenal to deeper underlying structures of anarchy, hegemony or conflict between nation-state actors. Rather, the heated nature of the debates themselves tells us something about the role of such factors that mainstream IR has largely neglected.

Following recent interest in IR in the role of emotions, this chapter makes two main arguments: first, that emotions and the body are not two separate analytical issues, but are rather bound together through the symbolic politics of discourse; and second, that the study of the body should become a focus in the IR emotions literature. These claims will be developed with respect to two observations regarding IR's recent interest in emotions. First, the recent IR interest in emotions has been remarkably *dis*embodied so far. This is somewhat surprising, for while this chapter leaves open the question of whether the study of emotions *necessarily* entails study of the body, the manner in which IR scholars have taken up the question of emotions has mostly led to a neglect of the body. This is illustrated in a recent trend of studies that focus on state-level emotions. Second, a focus on the body entails a much needed dialogue between studies of emotion and discourse-theoretic approaches in IR. Discourse-based approaches in IR – mainly poststructuralism – have focused on how meanings and subjectivities are produced in language. However, the focus on language often downplays the more affective and visceral dimensions of security and identity. This chapter draws upon a number of insights from recent work on 'new materialisms' in socio-political theory to suggest a shift of focus to the affective and visceral processes of materialisation and embodiment in the study of emotions and security in IR. Although following the insights of the linguistic turn, new materialists position themselves as taking a step beyond the study of discursive practices toward more thoroughly incorporating the role of materiality of social life without falling back into the old material determinism of classic approaches such as Marxism (Coole and Frost 2010: 6). As the body is often at the very nexus of the interweaving of collective discourses and affective dynamics, more comprehensive analyses should encompass all three phenomena as mutually entangled.

These ideas are developed in three sections. First, the chapter briefly surveys recent IR work on emotions and discourse. It argues that recent state-centric approaches to emotions miss vital dynamics that are necessary for more comprehensively understanding the visceral and embodied politics of security. Similarly, IR discourse theories well analyse key issues such as the production of difference through language, yet new materialists contend that these approaches still lack adequate means to account for the role of materiality. Second, the chapter offers an overview of key findings of the new materialisms literature, focusing on the body and understanding visceral processes of materialisation, corporeality and embodiment. Finally, it suggests a dialogue between studies of emotions, discourse and the body, and offers a new way to more comprehensively understand security practices in global politics.

## Emotions and discourse in IR

While IR research has so far examined a variety of emotions from a number of theoretical perspectives,[1] a recent trend in this literature has been to analyse the significance of emotions at the level of state actors. Although many of these studies nicely illustrate the contribution of bringing emotions into IR, they also tend to produce a trajectory that leads away from the more embodied and visceral aspects of emotions and politics. For instance, take Löwenheim and Heimann's (2008) excellent study on revenge, in which they argue that 'corporate actors can experience emotions through the individuals that compose them, identify with them, and are constituted by them'. Elites, acting as state agents, 'possess emotions that are distinct from their personal emotions because of their institutional capacity and embeddedness' (Löwenheim and Heimann 2008: 690). Similarly, Hall (2011) develops a state-level theory of diplomatic displays of anger. For him, 'state actors – ranging from top leaders, policymakers, officials, and diplomats, to low-ranking soldiers – can collectively project an image of anger through their discourse, symbolic gestures, and concrete actions' (Hall 2011: 532). Along parallel lines, Eznack (2011) argues that attributing emotions to state actors entails neither the claim that states themselves experience emotion, nor that emotions are subject to simply leaders. Instead, she argues that in the politics of emotional attachments to interstate alliances, one state being affectively attached to another state entails 'decision makers acting as the state' (Eznack 2011: 242). Hymans (2006) develops a sophisticated theory of why some states choose to pursue nuclear weapons while some do not, and traces this preference back to leaders' conceptions of national identity and their corresponding emotions. In a critique of some of these tendencies, Sasley (2011: 453–454) uses intergroup emotions theory to argue that focusing on the state as a monolithic actor does not account for the variety of emotional responses within a state, and focusing on individual leaders as representatives of the state, while useful, may be too specific to develop generalisable theories of emotion.

While each of these studies rigorously theorises (in different ways) the various relationships between states and emotions, their focus at the state level nevertheless downplays other vital ways and levels of analysis in which emotions and affects play integral roles in politics. First, while most of these studies recognise that there are various types of emotional dynamics within states, their focus at the state level nevertheless mostly neglects to incorporate these important domestic dynamics. Even Sasley's insightful critique downplays the question of emotions at the bodily level, and how these are co-constituted through more collective-level symbols. Second, a focus at the state level leaves open the question of how emotions are involved in contestations of discursive meaning in debates over war and security. As many discursive approaches (discussed below) have emphasised, the politics of security often constitutes the politics of identity and contestations over the meaning(s) thereof. While a state-level analysis is apt to capture this process between nation-states, it is largely unable to address these issues at other levels of analysis. Third, focusing on the state level does not address how collective circulations of emotions 'gain traction' with audiences and are *felt* in regard to the body. For it is through the body that collective politics is experienced, and it is this nexus between emotions and the body which should be more thoroughly investigated.

Some of the same kinds of shortcomings are also seen in how many IR scholars have conceptualised the role of discourse in global politics. As Hansen (2006: 6) explains, such an approach to the study of identity entails conceptualising identity as discursive, political, relational and social. To think about identities and subjectivity as discursive and political is to argue that 'there are no objective identities located in some extra-discursive realm', and it only therefore exists as a phenomenon that is continually contested (Hansen 2006: 6).

To conceptualise identity as relational and social is to argue that it is always defined through difference (e.g. by what it is not), and that identity is always established through intersubjective understandings rather than being the sole 'property' of single individuals (Hansen 2006: 6). Yet such approaches often lack the analytical lenses necessary to more fully grasp the embodied and corporeal dimensions of subjectivity. This is not to say that some IR scholars have not been cognisant of these kinds of shortcomings of discourse analysis. Neumann (2002) argued that, although the analysis of discourse helps to reconstruct the conditions of possibility for certain practices, such analyses often neglect to examine the lived experiences of material practices themselves. Yet, as discussed below, new materialist research contends that 'the dominant constructivist orientation to social analysis is inadequate for thinking about matter, materiality, and politics' in light of current pressing concerns in biopolitics and the global political economy (Coole and Frost 2010: 6).

From another direction, feminist work has long focused on the gendered practices that work to produce bodies as 'masculine' or 'feminine.' As Shepherd (2010: 6) explains, the body is not a fixed referent that can be known objectively or neutrally, but is instead socially constituted as having particularly gendered meaning which influences how different peoples' bodies are differentiated, legitimated, oppressed or marginalised. How particular bodies are socially produced as 'masculine' or 'feminine' is key since 'attending to the positioning and marking of bodies, both male and female' matters greatly for understanding deeply embedded practices that traditional theories of IR ignore (Shepherd 2010: 7). Moreover, even understanding 'sex' as the base biological factor upon which cultural constructions are overlaid neglects to interrogate how the conventional binary of 'sex' (male/female) itself is a discourse that produces particular understandings of materiality (Shepherd 2010). In this sense, this work excels in analysing the myriad of gendered global practices, and this chapter builds upon this work to suggest that IR emotions research follow Connolly's (2013: 400) imperative 'to stretch prevailing modes of subjectivity in a new direction'. Moreover, while there has been some recent work on the body in IR, much of it neglects to more fully develop the interconnections between emotions and bodies. Shinko (2010), for example, critiques contemporary IR's relative neglect of the body and argues that IR's legacy of liberalism has led to conceptualising agents as autonomous and rational, rather than relational and embodied beings. Two recent works by Mavelli (2012) and Puumala (2013) pick up on these themes in studies of the role of the body in resistance practices. Both, in different empirical contexts, demonstrate how the body can spark and enact resistance to sovereign power which escapes other frameworks, yet the potential emotional underpinnings of bodily agency remain under-examined.

Overall, a more comprehensive analytical framework of the interweaving politics of emotion, materiality and the body remains to be more fully developed in IR. Building upon the insights of these existing works would go some way towards advancing a theoretical accounting of how these issues are mutually constitutive and how they may offer new insights into embodied emotional experiences of security politics. The following section develops insights from the new materialisms literature to argue for the significance of the corporeal embodied experiences of collective emotions. The subsequent section develops these ideas within the context of contemporary IR understandings of the politics of security.

## Materialism and embodiment

A turn towards the interweaving politics of emotions, discourse and the body follows a few recent trajectories in socio-political theory. The first comes from recent calls that political analyses bring in the body as an object of study. As it has been absent from most mainstream political science research, some argue that incorporating the body into social analysis offers a much richer account of lived experiences of collective politics. Much of this neglect stems from the tradition separating 'reason' from 'passion' and the mind from the body. As Jenkins (2005: 2) argues, social action takes place not merely through individuals as rational actors, but 'takes place with reference to feelings and/or physical qualities and from an embodied subject position'. Not only does a focus on bodies break down these dualisms, but doing so also helps us to better see that 'in an embodied state of being where the ideational and material are intimately linked … there is no meaning which is not embodied, and no matter which is not meaningful' (Jenkins 2005: 8). Similarly, Coole (2007: 416) contends that thinking through politics solely as the interactions of rational, disembodied agents effectively denies the agency of the body whereby it 'exerts power in its own right and according to its own visceral talents and experiences'.

In addition to the neglect of the body, two other related and interlocking trajectories are first, that the concept of 'materialism' itself must be rethought; and second, that poststructuralism largely neglects to fully capture the affective and material flows that characterise contemporary political life. In an overview of 'new materialist' research, Coole and Frost (2010) argue that the dominant frameworks associated with the linguistic turn are largely inadequate for thinking about the complex ways in which materiality affects political life. Such approaches, 'where overtures to material reality are dismissed as an insidious foundationalism – [have] had the consequence of dissuading critical inquirers from the more empirical kinds of investigation that material processes and structures require' (Coole and Frost 2010: 6). In contrast, while new materialist approaches do not deny the centrality of language, they do contend that addressing new challenges requires more nuanced ways of thinking about the interweaving of social construction and materiality.

Poststructuralism has a complex relationship with materiality, which can be usefully viewed through the debate between Judith Butler and her new materialist critics such as Brian Massumi. Earlier research argued that what is denied in this work is not 'material' objects, but 'rather the different assertion that they could constitute themselves as object outside of any discursive condition of emergence' (Laclau and Mouffe 1985: 108). However, Butler has attempted to rethink the relationship between discourse and materiality through a critique of the sex/gender binary. She argues that understanding 'sex' as materiality which is then overlaid with cultural constructs of 'gender' downplays how the body itself is materialised through practices. Once '"sex" itself is understood in its normativity, the materiality of the body will not be thinkable apart from the materialization of that regulatory norm' (Butler 1993: 2). The meaning of 'sex' and 'materiality' itself is produced through the significations that allege to describe it. Massumi, however, argues that Butler's effort (and poststructuralism more generally) ultimately reverts back to an emphasis on discourse rather than taking materiality on its own terms. For him (2002: 2), poststructuralism fixes the body within 'positions on a grid' of culture that effectively denies the inherent liveliness of the body which escapes such positioning. The problem as Massumi (2002: 4) sees it is that, even in accounts that claim to take the body seriously, starting with the role of cultural constructs/positions in this manner means that matter, 'bodily or otherwise, never figures into the account *as such*'. Emphasising the cultural positioning/construction of materiality (of 'sex' etc.) neglects the *movements* of materiality; 'the emphasis is on process before signification or coding' (Massumi 2002: 7).

One of the many virtues of Massumi's critique is to point out notable weaknesses in some forms of poststructuralism in accounting for the corporeal dimensions of materiality. Yet Massumi arguably swings too far back in the other direction, bracketing off the likely much more complex relationship between discourse and the materiality of affect. For him (Massumi 2002: 26–9), the body's potential as excess that escapes signification plays a much greater role in social life than Butler and poststructuralism concede, and at the same time affect in this view is pre-personal and pre-discursive. While this no doubt captures many experiences which can escape description, Massumi's parsing affect, materiality and discourse in this manner is likely inadequate to capture how affect and discourse can *infuse* each other through meaningful social effects (Hemmings 2005; Wetherell 2012). In this sense, an engagement between notions of materiality, affect and discourse would likely go some way towards reversing the separation that has tended to occur in research on each.

There are a number of themes that characterise much of this work on materialism which are relevant here. One is the notion that in re-thinking materialism, we must also re-conceptualise corresponding classical notions of mind/body and causality. As Coole and Frost (2010: 8) explain, a key theme of this research is an 'insistence on describing active processes of materialization of which embodied humans are an integral part, rather than the monotonous repetitions of dead matter from which human subjects are apart'. Rethinking matter as having a significant role in the construction of the human subject not only takes a step beyond the relatively limited ways in which IR constructivists have discussed 'rump materialism' (Wendt 1999). More importantly, it conceives of matter as much more ambiguously interwoven with 'ideas', discourse, the social field, etc. than most traditional approaches concede.

> Conceiving matter as possessing its own modes of self-transformation, self-organization, and directedness, and thus no longer as simply passive or inert, disturbs the conventional sense that agents are exclusively humans … Instead, the human species is being relocated within a natural environment whose material forces themselves manifest certain agentic capacities.
>
> (Coole and Frost 2010: 10)

Given these interpenetrating fields of matter, the human subject and agency leads to a conception of causality as non-linear. Materiality 'is not causally determining or determined, nor are its future forms teleologically prefigured' (Coole 2013: 453). Rather, causation here is thought by way of different forces coming together in complex assemblages in which matter's effect are inseparable from other elements, agencies and subjects (Cudworth and Hobden 2013).

Re-thinking materialism thus involves considering the lively materiality of the body in ways that political science and IR largely neglect. Thinking more thoroughly about the body in this manner entails overturning the mind/body dualism that has traditionally structured social inquiry. As Jenkins (2005: 5) reminds us, this distinction is rooted in Descartes' argument that the mind cannot be reduced to the body, since the body can be altered yet our awareness of our own consciousness or sense of self remains the same. What this perspective side-steps, however, is the notion of how the mind and body interact – indeed, posing the issue in this way posits two separate entities and then proceeds to ask about their 'interactions', instead of beginning with their interactions (Jenkins 2005: 6). This dualism, then, is a way of shortcutting the issue of ontologically reflecting on the body as an object of legitimate analysis (Jenkins 2005: 6). Moreover, the materiality of the body offers an opportunity to unfold not only how the body itself is embedded within natural and social surroundings, but also how its efficacy stretches our thinking about its involvement in social practices. Bodies 'exhibit agentic capacities in the way they structure or stylize their perceptual milieu, where they discover, organize, and respond to patterns that are corporeally significant' (Coole and Frost 2010: 19–20).

Thinking about agency in this way has been another key theme of new materialist work. In traditional frameworks, materialism usually precluded a complex view of agency – if material reality determined agents' actions, then little room was left for the agent to act on his/her own accord independently of material determinism. However, such views are arguably not up to the task of critically inquiring into the complex nature of agency, given that matter can no longer be said to exert merely linear causal effects. This complicates views of bodies by introducing notions of agency which move beyond conventional notions of rationality and cognition. As Orlie (2010: 121–122) argues, the 'stuff of which selves are made is impersonal because the matter of which they are born and made does not begin with us nor is it ever possessed or controlled by us'. Or, as put by Connolly (2013: 400), new materialists 'project variable *degrees* of subjectivity and agency well beyond the human estate, far into the biosphere'. To take seriously, then, a renewed focus on the materiality of the body is to render extant modes of agency inadequate. It is through the body's embedding in both the social and material world, and through its manipulations of and interactions with that world, that agency is enacted (rather than through the unified rational actor of traditional approaches).

Such perspectives offer a few suggestions of how to think through the main issue posed in this chapter: how should we think about the body in what has traditionally been a state-centric field? And how should we think about the overlapping and interpenetrating roles of emotions, discourse and the body? The final section discusses these links and suggests a few potential routes for continued research on emotions and security in IR.

## Embodied subjectivity, emotion and security

New materialism holds some suggestive possibilities for staging a productive dialogue between the IR emotions and discourse literatures, and interweaving both concerns with studies of the body and materiality. In particular, there are at least two key issues that are drawn into a sharper focus: first, a more visceral conceptualisation of the power of sub-state emotions; and second, the corporeal and embodied aspects of identity/difference dynamics.

As discussed above, there has been a recent trend in IR emotions research to analyse emotions at the state level. A virtue of examining emotions at the state level, as Sasley (2011: 453–454) explains, is that it offers new analytic leverage over the field's traditional unit of analysis. However, emotional analyses must also delve below the state level in order to more thoroughly explore societal flows of emotions and how bodies become affectively inscribed via collective symbolic processes. Some of this work could productively interlace work on actor-network theory (Barry 2013) or complexity theory (Cudworth and Hobden 2013) with work on affective flows and bodies. For instance, Marlin-Bennett's (2013) insightful study on information flows and bodies in the digital age suggests how such dynamics 'below' the state level are crucial for more fully grasping contemporary politics. Ross's (2006: 199) notion of 'circulations of affect' also points in this direction, with such affective flows helping to constitute collective identities to which subjects become attached.

Such a move to emotions and the body at the sub-state level parallels Sylvester's (2012) call for IR theory to bring emotions back into the study of world politics. 'What if we think of war as experience, as something ordinary people observe and suffer physically and emotionally depending on their locations?' (Sylvester 2012: 483). In her view, mainstream IR security studies 'is not addressing one of the key elements of war: its actual mission of injuring human bodies and destroying normal patterns of social relations' (Sylvester 2012: 484). Indeed, as Scarry (1985: 12) notes, 'while the central fact of war is to out-injure the opponent, the fact of injuring tends to be absent from strategic and political descriptions of war'. Adopting such an analytical perspective would entail putting bodies at the centre of attention along the lines suggested here. Even at a micro-perspective of soldiers and combatants, a focus on the embodiment of emotions would likely open new possibilities of thinking about the drawing of boundaries between 'us' and 'them'. As McSorley (2012: 7) contends, 'it is when corporeal co-presence occurs that the boundaries of enmity and friendship may blur, and an alternative empathetic recognition of humanity, often rooted in bodily frailty and mutual vulnerability, may emerge'. The key point here is that state-level studies of emotion are largely unable to capture these more intricate emotional and embodied dynamics. Yet it is at these more embodied levels that citizens experience the forces of collective symbolic politics. How the materiality of the body exerts forms of agency that co-constitute rational agency, and how this bodily agency is embedded in wider ideational-material assemblages of nationalism, militarism and technologies, open up questions that state-centric frameworks downplay or neglect altogether.

The question of how citizens experience collective political forces raises the issue of language and discourse, and it is at the nexus of collective discourse and emotions that the body is located. The fleshy materiality of the body becomes meaningful through language, yet the body's very corporeality exhibits forms of agency that often escape linguistic capture. In this sense, IR emotions researchers would do well to more thoroughly investigate the intersections of emotions, discourse and the body. Specifically, the conceptualisation of security as the discursive production of identity/difference would likely prove fertile analytical ground in this regard. For example, Hansen's (2006) arguments about the production of identity as discursive, relational, political and social emphasises the linguistic aspects of subjectivity – how its constitution through discourse exposes its ultimate contingency and therefore contestability. Yet such approaches have nevertheless tended to downplay the more visceral and embodied aspects of these productions of (in)security. Building off feminist research that investigates the power implications of representations of identity/difference (Gatens 1999; Shepherd 2010), an approach to the embodiment and emotional significance of discursive productions of difference entails both a recognition of the complexity of the identity/difference performance and an acknowledgement of its embedding in materiality. As Seigworth and Gregg (2010: 2) argue, affect 'marks a body's *belonging* to a world of encounters or; a world's belonging to a body of encounters but also, in *non-belonging*, through all those far sadder (de)compositions of mutual in-compossibilities'. The affective effects of discourses producing identity/difference resonate as linguistic categories that, however contingent, are nevertheless often felt by adherents to express some inner 'essence'. Moreover, the body's materiality is socially co-constituted as meaningful in the interlacing of affect, encounter, and representations of such encounters.

Another way to approach this issue is to pose the question: how do discourses of identity/difference resonate with the materiality of bodies? The issue of resonance is one that has been taken up recently by a number of IR scholars, all of whom (in one way or another) are concerned with how discourses of security appeal to target audiences. For instance, Barnett (1999: 8–9) argues that 'actors are constantly attempting to guide political mobilization toward a particular outcome and for a particular goal by using symbols, metaphors, and cognitive cues to organize experience and fix meaning to events'. Similarly, Balzacq (2005: 185) notes that leaders often 'cloak security arguments in the semantic repertoire of the national audience in order to win support'. Holland (2011: 6) argues that rarely 'do foreign policy practitioners attempt to hail an entire population, but rather isolate and target key imagined constituencies' (see also Solomon 2012). While these authors are indeed correct to emphasise the linguistic nature of resonance, they nevertheless tend to downplay the more visceral dimensions of what factors make resonance 'work'. Adding a focus on materiality and the body would supplement these studies of discursive resonance with a view to how such discourses are felt and 'lived' by the audiences which are hailed as subjects by them.

Connolly's (2002) work is helpful here in conceptualising what a bodily/material perspective would contribute. For him, discourses of difference resonate not only on a linguistic/rhetorical level, but on several registers of experience often neglected in IR security research. On one level, difference is indeed registered in the linguistic intersubjective production of identity. However, this register shades into another:

> … in which surpluses, traces, noises, and charges in and around the concepts and beliefs of embodied agents express proto-thoughts and judgments too crude to be conceptualized in a refined way but still intensive and effective enough to make a difference to the selective way judgments are formed, porous arguments are received, and alternatives are weighted.
> (Connolly 2002: 43)

Drawing upon work in neuroscience, Connolly reminds us that political judgment is often far from the rational disembodied agents of mainstream political science. Instead, symbolic performances and judgments inevitably 'require complex biological brain systems in which they are set' (Connolly 2002: 63). Because human activity is both symbolic and mixed with the materiality of natural surroundings, traditional categories of 'nature' and 'culture' mix into a 'zone of indiscernibility' where common categories of agency become blurred (Connolly 2002: 63–4). Attention to such features regarding the production and wider resonance of security discourses of identity/difference could lead to a framework for analysing the 'micropolitics' of security. For Connolly, micropolitics involves the myriad ordinary and everyday affective relations, material interactions, feelings, habits and emotions that shape our intersubjective relations and judgments, and which typically reside in levels of experience 'below' rational or immediately cognitive processing. As Connolly (2002: 9) argues, attempts 'to give singular priority to the highest and conceptually most sophisticated brain nodules in thinking and judgment may encourage those invested in these theories to underestimate the importance of body image, unconscious motor memory, and thought-imbued affect'. A micropolitics of security that approached the issue of resonance from this perspective would necessarily draw together new thinking about bodies, materialism and discourse in a manner that would draw out the co-constitution of each, and would suggest new ways to conceptualise the wider resonance and political success of discourses of (in)security.

## Conclusion

General Tommy Franks' 'we don't do body counts' offers a useful juxtaposition to illustrate the claims of this chapter. That is, rather than investigating only how discursive boundaries are drawn around some bodies which excludes others, IR scholars should more frequently consider the material and corporeal experiences of security issues. The mutual interconnections between bodily materiality, the symbolic politics of discourse, and the power of affect are ripe for further interrogation. Specifically, the study of emotions and IR should investigate the links between emotions, the materiality of the body and discourses of security. The body is often – if not always – at the nexus of emotional experience and collective discourses of security producing subjectivities of 'us' and 'them'. Turning away from the recent tendency in IR to study emotions at the nation-state level of analysis, this chapter argues that, despite the insights of such an approach, a shift of focus to the materiality of the body offers a new way to think about the effects and resonance of discourses of (in)security. In this sense, this chapter is a call for IR emotions researchers to give serious consideration to the role of the lived experience and materialisations of meaning that constitute the felt effects of emotions and discourses of (in)security.

## Note

1 For a sample of the increasing number of emotions studies in IR, see Ross (2006); Leep (2010); Mercer (2010); Steele (2010); Hall (2011); Solomon (2012, 2013).

## Bibliography

Balzacq, T. (2005) 'Three faces of securitization: Political agency, audience, and context', *European Journal of International Relations*, 11(2): 171–201.

Barnett, M. (1999) 'Culture, strategy, and foreign policy change: Israel's Road to Oslo', *European Journal of International Relations*, 5(1): 5–36.

Barry, A. (2013) 'The translation zone: Between actor-network theory and international relations', *Millennium: Journal of International Studies*, 41(3): 413–429.

Butler, J. (1993) *Bodies That Matter: On the Discursive Limits of 'Sex'*. New York: Routledge.

Connolly, W. (2002) *Neuropolitics: Thinking, Culture, Speed*. Minneapolis, MN: University of Minnesota Press.

Connolly, W. E. (2013) 'The 'new materialisms' and the fragility of things', *Millennium: Journal of International Studies*, 41(3): 399–412.

Coole, D. (2007) 'Experiencing discourse: Corporeal communicators and the embodiment of power', *British Journal of Politics and International Relations*, 9(3): 413–433.

Coole, D. and Frost, S. (2010) 'Introducing the new materialisms' in *New Materialisms: Agency, Ontology, Politics*, Coole and Frost (eds). Durham, NC: Duke University Press, 1–46.

Cudworth, E. and Hobden, S. (2013) 'Of parts and wholes: International relations beyond the human', *Millennium: Journal of International Studies*, 41(3): 430–450.

Epstein, E. (2002) 'Success in Afghan War hard to gauge', *San Francisco Chronicle*, March 23. Available online at: www.globalsecurity.org/org/news/2002/020323-attack01.htm (accessed October 2013).

Eznack, L. (2011) 'Crises as signals of strength: The significance of affect in close allies' relationships', *Security Studies*, 20(2): 238–265.

Gatens, M. (1999) 'Power, bodies, and difference', in *Feminist Theory and the Body: A Reader*, Price and Shildrick (eds). Edinburgh: Edinburgh University Press, 227–234.

Hall, T. (2011) 'We will not swallow this bitter fruit: Theorizing a diplomacy of anger', *Security Studies*, 20(4): 521–555.

Hansen, L. (2006) *Security as Practice: Discourse Analysis and the Bosnian War*. New York: Routledge.

Hemmings, C. (2005) 'Invoking affect: Cultural theory and the ontological turn', *Cultural Studies*, 19(5): 548–567.

Holland, J. (2011) 'Foreign policy and political possibility', *European Journal of International Relations*, 19(1): 49–68.

Hymans, J. (2006) *The Psychology of Nuclear Proliferation: Identity, Emotions, and Foreign Policy*. Cambridge: Cambridge University Press.

Jenkins, L. (2005) 'Corporeal ontology: Beyond mind-body dualism?', *Politics*, 25(1): 1–11.

Laclau, E. and Mouffe, C. (1985) *Hegemony and Socialist Strategy: Towards a Radical Democratic Politics*. London: Verso.

Leep, M. C. (2010) 'The affective production of others: United States policy toward the Israeli–Palestinian conflict', *Cooperation and Conflict*, 45(3): 331–352.

Löwenheim, O. and Heimann, G. (2008) 'Revenge in international politics', *Security Studies*, 17(4): 685–724.

Marlin-Bennett, R. (2013) 'Embodied information, knowing bodies, and power', *Millennium: Journal of International Studies*, 41(3): 601–622.

Massumi, B. (2002) *Parables of the Virtual: Movement, Affect, Sensation*. Durham, NC and London: Duke University Press.

Mavelli, L. (2012) 'Postsecular resistance, the body, and the 2011 Egyptian Uprising', *Review of International Studies*, 38(5): 1057–1078.

McSorley, K. (2012) 'War and the body', in *War and the Body: Militarization, Practice, and Experience*, McSorley (ed.). New York: Routledge: 1–31.

Mercer, J. (2010) 'Emotional beliefs' *International Organization*, 64(1): 1–31.

Milliken, J. (1999) 'The study of discourse in International Relations', *European Journal of International Relations*, 5(2): 225–254.

Neumann, I. B. (2002) 'Returning practice to the linguistic turn: The case of diplomacy', *Millennium: Journal of International Studies*, 31(3): 627–651.

Orlie, M. (2010) 'Impersonal matter', in *New Materialisms: Agency, Ontology, Politics*, Coole and Frost (eds). Durham, NC: Duke University Press, 116–136.

Puumala, E. (2013) 'Political life beyond accommodation and return: Rethinking international relations between the political, the international, and the body', *Review of International Studies*, 39(4): 949–968.

Ross, A. A. G. (2006) 'Coming in from the cold: Constructivism and emotions', *European Journal of International Relations*, 12(2): 197–222.

Sasley, B. E. (2011) 'Theorizing states' emotions', *International Studies Review*, 13(3): 452–476.

Scarry, E. (1985) *The Body in Pain: The Making and Unmaking of the World*. Oxford: Oxford University Press.

Seigworth, G. J. and Gregg, M. (2010) 'An inventory of shimmers', in *The Affect Theory Reader*, Gregg and Seigworth (eds). Durham, NC and London: Duke University Press, 1–25.

Shepherd, L. J. (ed.) (2010) *Gender Matters in Global Politics: A Feminist Introduction to International Relations*. London and New York: Routledge.

Shinko, R. (2010) 'Ethics after liberalism: Why (autonomous) bodies matter', *Millennium: Journal of International Studies*, 38(3): 723–745.

Solomon, T. (2012) '"I wasn't angry, because I couldn't believe it was happening": Affect and discourse in responses to 9/11', *Review of International Studies*, 38(4): 907–928.

Solomon, T. (2013) 'Resonances of neoconservatism', *Cooperation and Conflict*, 48(1): 100–121.

Steele, B. J. (2010) 'Irony, emotions, and critical distance', *Millennium: Journal of International Studies*, 39(1): 89–107.

Sylvester, C. (2012) 'War experiences/war practices/war theory', *Millennium: Journal of International Studies*, 40(3): 483–503.

Wendt, A. (1999) *Social Theory of International Politics*. Cambridge: Cambridge University Press.

Wetherell, M. (2012) *Affect and Emotion: A New Social Science Understanding*. Los Angeles, CA: Sage.

# 6 Anger, war and feminist storytelling

*Swati Parashar*

For a student of South Asian history, two inherited stories about wars and the celebration of 'militarised masculinity' point towards the centrality of emotions in the construction of 'nation' and in the conduct of international relations. Both stories have as their main protagonists two women artists who eulogised soldiers and their bravery in their songs. Indian legendary icon Lata Mangeshkar sang '*aye mere watan ke logon*'[1] at the National Stadium in New Delhi on 27 January 1963, in the presence of Prime Minister Jawaharlal Nehru. The emotional patriotic song about the courage of Indian soldiers, who died in the Sino-Indian war of 1962, famously moved Prime Minister Nehru and fellow Indians to tears.[2] The song was 50 years old in 2013 and continues to evoke an emotional patriotism among the new generation of Indians, who have also witnessed the changing nature of 'enemy' identity.[3]

During the 1965 India–Pakistan war, the legendary singer from Pakistan Madam Noor Jahan produced patriotic songs which are still highly popular today.[4] It is common knowledge that Noor Jahan camped at the Lahore radio station for 17 days and recorded songs when her infant daughters were ill. She not only procured a curfew pass, but also organised other musicians to accompany her in Lahore, and her songs won her great admiration from the public and soldiers at the front. Her contributions to the war efforts, for which she did not charge any money, earned her the 'Pride of Performance' on the next Pakistan Day, on 23 March 1966. General Ayub Khan, President of Pakistan, even credited Noor Jahan for what was perceived as a successful military campaign, and it is arguable that her songs remain the high point of the war from a Pakistani perspective.[5]

In both these cases, patriotic emotions were stirred through songs that were acknowledged even by the heads of states, and helped in the war efforts as well as in healing the 'nation'. However, both Lata Mangeshkar and Noor Jahan have never featured in the study of war in the Indian subcontinent. International Relations (IR) in particular has not held a conversation with these artists and the emotions they invoke among the civilians and fighting forces. I have previously argued that IR's preoccupation with the causes and impacts of war leaves out important human experiences that shape individual and community relations as sites of knowledge (Parashar 2013). Emotions are an important part of the human experience of war and, contrary to the view that they distract, becoming hazards and obstacles (Ure and Frost 2014: 2), they have a positive engagement with politics. In that spirit of acknowledging the 'everyday' life within wars and the emotional experiences it involves, this chapter pays attention to the politics of 'anger'.

Dominant emotions (positive and negative) exist and acquire collective dimension, shaping political and social processes in the international system. Expressing an emotion itself constitutes a political act, and emotions shape geopolitics (Crawford 2000; Marcus 2000; Moisi 2009). 'Beliefs fuelled by emotions stimulate people to action, or allow them to approve of the actions of others in political contexts' (Frijda et al. 2000). International relations are centred on the 'clash of emotions' (Moisi 2009). *Jihadis* cite humiliation, terrorism generates fear and anger, feminists rely on pain and anger, while globalisation causes desperation and excitement as well as hope. Nationalism, ideologies, wars, conflicts and peace, truth and reconciliation, are all important concepts in IR, which capture a range of emotions. Communities (ethnic, religious, sectarian, national and international) are also fostered around emotions. If the 9/11 attacks were a calculated but emotional response to American hegemony, the global war on terror was launched from an emotional platform of outrage and anger (see Cheung-Blunden and Blunden 2008).[6] Public display of tears and emotions (especially by politicians and sportsmen)[7] has become a trend and is considered important and legitimate to bring out the 'real' self. It is important to point out here that, if women in public life are unappreciated for displaying tears or other forms of emotion, which are 'naturally' attributed to them as a gender trait (which they must actually overcome), men demonstrating emotions are highly appreciated for challenging the dominant norm around unemotional masculinity.

While history is rife with examples of reason's triumph over emotions (that being the eternal human dilemma) and over the display of appropriate emotions at different times (like patriotism in times of war; grief and mourning in times of loss; anger and revenge in times of war; forgiveness in times of reconciliation), Sara Ahmed reminds us that emotions are not psychological states, but social and political practices. 'Emotions are not "in" either the individual and the social, but produce the very surfaces and boundaries that allow the individual and the social to be delineated as if they are objects' (Ahmed 2004: 10). This becomes all the more evident as one studies the performance of emotions in wars, and how war bodies are constructed through affective understandings of the 'self' and 'other'.

Women have traditionally been associated with emotions, and in the hierarchy between emotion and reason, their lower status has also meant that women's emotions have been seen as inferior. Their affective presence in wars is either (re)presented in stereotypical ways (wailing and mourning mothers and wives whose pictures dominate war propaganda), or denied in cases where women support the war or take up arms (Parashar 2014). More importantly, recognising their supporting roles in wars generates emotional responses of negativity and later even anger towards what is perceived as cultural deviance. Feminists, who remain committed to the idea of 'the personal being the political', and who study bodies as sites of discursive practices of sex and gender (Shepherd 2015), have started paying attention to the 'emotional' (Sylvester 2011). The interest in the 'personal' inadvertently negotiates interests in bodily experiences and emotional responses, very often by default. In that sense, the 'move' to analyse emotions isn't really that 'new' or distanced for feminists who reject the emotional/rational divide anyway. Feminist storytelling, scholarship and activism are increasingly accounting for the emotional experiences of women and men and how they shape the constructions of masculinity and femininity.

Elsewhere, I have contributed to a forum on emotions and feminist IR, where participants discussed the emotional journeys of feminist IR researchers who engage in challenging and confronting research (see Sylvester 2011). The contributors to the forum recognised and debated the ways in which emotions can be written into feminist scholarly works and the extent to which such an exercise could circumvent any accusations of self-aggrandisement and self-indulgence (Inayatullah 2011). In this chapter, I expand on the discussions at that forum and focus on two aspects: first, the centrality of anger as a powerful emotion in war projects that attract women participants, supporters and combatants; and second, the emotional encounters between the researcher and researched that result in anger being both reflected and suppressed, which eventually affects the research in both data gathering and writing. Before understanding the role of anger in the lives of militant and warring women, it is worthwhile to discuss how anger, a deeply experienced individual and social emotion, acquires a political character and inspires collective action, and especially violent resistance.

## Anger and collective action

A Poison Tree
I was angry with my friend:
I told my wrath, my wrath did end.
I was angry with my foe:
I told it not, my wrath did grow.

And I watered it in fears,
Night and morning with my tears;
And I sunned it with smiles,
And with soft deceitful wiles.

And it grew both day and night,
Till it bore an apple bright.
And my foe beheld it shine.
And he knew that it was mine,

And into my garden stole
When the night had veiled the pole;
In the morning glad I see
My foe outstretched beneath the tree.
William Blake, *Songs of Experience*

The English poet William Blake's 'A Poison Tree' captures the self-transformation that occurs due to 'anger'. The poem emphasises the view that giving an outlet to anger is important to reduce the need for vengeance. Blake's poem has been analysed by many authors and literary critics in the contexts of the French Revolution (where anger either motivated rational action or prevented reason from prevailing) and the prevalent British Christian ideas of suppression and self-denial.[8] Blake believed that anger needed to be expressed, in the absence of which it would lead to violent excesses. A significant aspect of this poem is also the manner in which the poet describes the easy expression of anger with a friend, and suppression of it with a foe.

As Blake seems to suggest, addressing anger with the 'enemy' is far more challenging. Left simmering inside, anger can do much more than simply harm, as it could implode and take on gargantuan proportions. Faulkner (2014) argues that anger motivates two kinds of action: it enables us to confront the harm-doer; and inspires concrete action to mitigate the suffering. In that sense, Faulkner invokes the compassionate healing that anger can engender (if it is allowed to be expressed), and perhaps Blake was alluding to that. My concern here is that the anger inspired confrontation with the harm-doer, which does not inspire compassionate healing, but provokes collective violence. What is an individual's experience in Blake's poem takes on a collective dimension when the 'enemy' is commonly identified and injustice appears to be the norm.

Nandini Sundar, who has studied the civil war between the Maoist guerrillas and the Indian government for several years, argues that the war is about how 'emotions are mobilised, conscripted and engendered by both sides'. She is concerned about the denial of emotional citizenship to the *adivasis* (indigenous people) while the state performs 'outrage, hurt and fear-inducing domination, as part of its battle for legitimacy' (Sundar 2012: 701).

> Intrinsic to this is the privileging of certain kinds of emotions – fear, anger, grief – and the emotions of certain kinds of people over others. Subject populations are distinguished from citizens by the differential public acknowledgement of their emotional claim.
>
> (Sundar 2012: 701)

Sundar persuasively conveys that emotion is an important ingredient in the civil war in India and outrage and righteous anger are invoked by the state, while the Maoist guerrillas embrace martyrdom and heroism. Even winning hearts and minds, which is considered essential in the counter-insurgency operation, conveys that this conflict is an armed contest about public emotions (ibid.). I can confirm Sundar's findings with regard to the other insurgent wars I have studied. Individual experiences of oppression and injustice result in collective public anger that is targeted against those perceived as the 'other' (representatives of the state, such as security forces).

It is collective anger that finds various outlets in an armed insurgency, and its excesses may appear to be less terrifying if located within the context of the material conditions that produce such strong and collective emotional responses. Humiliation, pain and grief experienced over time can cause angry outrage. Thus it could be argued that:

> [C]ollective action frames not only provide an intellectual account of the injustice of certain situations but they also legitimate the expression of moral indignation and righteous anger directed towards the source of injustice. The centrality of anger to collective action stems from its link with action.
>
> (Hercus 1999: 36; Faulkner 2014)

Anger in the case of militant wars that I have studied does not lead to individual violent revenge straightaway, but as an emotion it influences belief: '[Anger] may give rise to beliefs where none existed, or change existing beliefs; and they may enhance or decrease the strength with which a belief is held' (Frijda and Mesquita 2000: 45). In the case of Kashmir, anger gave rise to a political belief in Kashmiri militant nationalism and the centrality of armed resistance within that; in Sri Lanka, anger against the discriminatory practices of the state strengthened the belief that armed resistance by the Tamil militant groups was the only way to counter a belligerent state that did not respond to non-violent protests. Sara Ahmed's point that 'emotions accumulate over time, as a form of affective value' (2004: 11) is reflected in considerations of anger and how it may not be impulsive, building an argument for violent resistance over a period of time. Cultural norms decide the role that women would play in that resistance and the 'legitimate' expressions of anger, which would restrain or silence any socially deviant behavior. In the next section, I discuss the relationship between anger and women's collective political action in support of wars and armed conflicts.

## Angry women make war

There is a certain paradox when we think about women and emotions. On one hand, they are considered to be naturally inclined towards emotional responses, and the public–private dichotomy is firmly entrenched in the duality of reason/emotions; on the other, certain kinds of emotions are denied to them.

In that sense we are talking about a hierarchy of emotions where some emotions are more legitimate than others, more powerful and more acceptable than others (Ahmed 2004: 3). Angry women challenge gender norms and disrupt the image of the submissive/docile woman. Shibles suggests, 'if women encourage anger it contradicts their claim to be nurturing. But clearly, women do get angry and feminists have drawn on anger in acting politically' (1991: 209). Anger is not only considered a negative and deviant emotion, but is also gendered and, as we know, even racialised in who is allowed to have access to it and how. Cheryl Hercus (1999) points out that, despite the notable and rapid achievements of feminists in the western world, anger is not an emotion attributed to them, even though anger is instrumental in shaping identity and feminist collective action. Holmes (2004) concedes, 'shifting sets of conventions have had some continuity in discouraging women in western nations (particularly white and middle-class women) from showing anger'.

On the other hand, feminist (not just women's) anger has been represented and understood in stereotypical ways, especially 'anger' that has featured in the works of race feminists (e.g. see hooks 1995). In giving voice to concerns about racism, misogyny and intersectionality, anger is an effective tool, but the response to it often serves to silence and delegitimise, as if anger is an inherent trait (of certain racialised bodies) instead of being targeted at a harm-doer. Thus the negative argument about anger and its extreme irrationality become a tool to delegitimise challenge to the existing power dynamics. Black feminists have articulated this extensively in their works and activism, and have drawn attention to how they have been labelled angry (and therefore irrational).[9] Anger, therefore, is not only gendered but has a deeply racial connotation in feminist theorising.

I am again drawn to Sara Ahmed's argument about how feminism navigates through pain and anger (Ahmed 2004). Experiences of pain constitute the self, community and the 'other', but pain alone does not engender the feminist movement; anger is the response to pain that emerges out of a need for action (ibid.: 174). In that sense, Ahmed believes that feminism is a reactive politics and 'there is no pure or originary action, which is outside such a history of "reaction", whereby bodies come to be "impressed upon" by the surfaces of others' (ibid.). Ahmed opens up discursive spaces to understand what anger means to collective identities of women, and to feminism in particular. If anger is the response to what one is against, the against-ness is not mitigated and the history of injuries remains. Anger does not lead to revenge, which is just one of the many outcomes it can generate. It is also important to consider that the different outcomes of anger depend on how the 'other', the 'against-ness' is viewed (ibid.). 'Feminism, as a response to pain and as a form of anger directed against that pain, is dependent then on acts of translation that are moving' (ibid.: 175). That is how the lives of militant women and the choices they make must be viewed. While pain and anger are instrumental in their participation in political violence and in resisting the 'against-ness' through violent methods, it is a choice embedded in experiences of pain, humiliation and injury.

While studying and analysing women's support to militant wars in South Asia, I concluded that anger was instrumental in shaping their responses. By no stretch of imagination am I making the claim that women in militant wars are feminists (interested in emancipatory politics and gender equality),[10] drawing on their personal anger to justify and participate in political violence. However, their actions, sometimes full of emancipatory desires, are driven by a deeply motivating anger towards injustices against their families, communities and selves. A desire to understand what motivates women to participate in insurgent wars has drawn me towards fieldwork in Sri Lanka, Kashmir and the Maoist conflict-affected regions of India. The overwhelming participation of women in these conflicts is driven by different aspirations, circumstances and ideologies, but underlying all this is deep-rooted anger and a perception of injustice and dehumanisation that can eventually be mitigated only through violent and revengeful acts (see Parashar 2014). My field interviews, in Sri Lanka and Jammu and Kashmir in 2008, and in the Maoist insurgency-affected states of Jharkhand, Bihar and Chhattisgarh in 2011 and 2013, have emphatically suggested that insurgent wars are fought on an emotional plane, but that does not necessarily imply irrational and impulsive decision-making by warring sides. The choices made by women in these conflicts, to support and participate in political violence and direct combat, are well considered, strategised and ideologically framed (ibid.).

In Sri Lanka, the conflict between the LTTE[11] and government forces had plunged the country into a bloody civil war between 1983 and 2009. The interviews I carried out in Colombo and in the eastern towns of Trincomalee and Batticaloa confirmed the overwhelming presence of anger on all sides. The LTTE was the subject of anger among the Sinhalese, who blamed the militant group for unleashing the war on innocent civilians. The Tamil women in Colombo were also angry with the LTTE for the undue suffering caused to Tamil civilians in the war. However, some claimed that their anger was also a mark of frustration, fear and anxiety, as news kept pouring in that the LTTE would lose the war eventually. As one interviewee said, 'I don't agree with the LTTE's violent methods but I also know that if it hadn't been for the LTTE, I wouldn't have walked around in Colombo, so freely wearing my *pottu*'[12] (Parashar, interview 2008).

The former LTTE women I met expressed unequivocal anger at the Sinhala state and its policies that had disempowered the Tamils and caused many of them to take up arms. Daya Somasundaram, Tamil psychiatrist and author, said in an interview, 'They might have seen their fathers or brothers or somebody killed so they have a strong burning anger or revenge' (Parashar, interview 2008). Thrushna was a 16-year-old Tamil teenager travelling to a nearby town (from Batticaloa) when the security forces carried out a detailed and harassing inspection of a wound on her leg. 'They were suspicious that the wound was inflicted in battle and that I was an LTTE fighter. They questioned me for more than two hours. I was angry and disappointed because the government was torturing innocent people like me' (Parashar, interview 2008). Thrushna's decision was made after this incident: she left without informing her family and joined the LTTE, serving in their wireless communications division. Rudra expressed anger at the LTTE chief Prabhakaran, whose stubborn belief in the war and demands of his female combatants, she believed, had caused immense hardship and suffering. 'There are many checkpoints and there are no women forces. Men check the breasts of women. Black Tigers [suicide bomb unit of the LTTE] put the bomb into their bra and also there have been pregnant ladies [as Black Tigers or suicide bombers]. Prabhakaran is insulting women, choosing strategies that are torturing women', she said (Parashar, interview 2008).

The Muslim women in Kashmir also cited anger at the Indian 'occupation' as the reason why they supported the militancy against the Indian state and security forces. The euphoria of the insurgency that broke out in 1989 captured the imagination of the women, who saw greater public roles for themselves and an opportunity to voice their anger (Parashar 2014). The important consideration in the case of Kashmir is that not only are women's stories of supporting and participating in the militancy silenced, but their emotional involvement is reduced to their roles as benign mothers and wives who sacrifice for the nation. The centrality of anger to collective resistance was recognised in Kashmir, but the legitimacy of anger would still not permit women to adopt more deviant roles as militants and combatants. The anger in the case of men was accorded legitimacy, and men who picked up arms became heroes and martyrs; women's anger was not considered emotional deviance, but was channelled into support roles for the militancy, and even then it would be written out of public narratives (Parashar 2014).

Whereas the politics of war-making is deeply embedded in physical and emotional narratives, these experiential narratives are the result of a certain kind of 'politics of injury' (see Sylvester 2011; Parashar 2014) that women experience much more intimately. Elaine Scarry was one of the first scholars to realise the 'relation between the interior content of war and what stands outside it' (1985: 63). She argues 'In participating in war, one participates not simply in an act of injury, but in the activity of reciprocal injuring where the goal is to out-injure the opponent' (ibid.). Scarry's interest in war pain can be extended to the analysis of war anger, where both kinds of emotion (pain and anger) endorse and engender each other (also see Ahmed 2004). Against popular belief that anger is an immature and negative emotion that directs violent revenge, I would argue that, while anger is instrumental in war-making and in causing injury to another who is the cause of that anger, the costs are well calculated, the pain well integrated.

Asiya Andrabi, founding leader of the women's militant group in Kashmir, the *Dukhtaran-e-Millat* (Daughters of Faith), articulated the measured response of anger in her interview with me. Andrabi conceded that women in Kashmir were very 'angry' at the military 'occupation' by India, but while they supported the armed resistance and provided assistance to the mujahideen, women did not take up arms themselves. That would not be culturally appropriate, as it would cause social upheaval (Parashar, interview 2008). Women's anger and emotional responses thus get recognised in acceptable political outcomes of protests and non-violent resistance, while their war efforts are silenced. As an angry feminist myself, I have tried to articulate how women's stories are written out of war narratives; their violent politics are almost always attributed to personality disorders and personal situations (Parashar 2014).[13]

## Anger and feminist storytelling

There is an important aspect of feminist storytelling about wars: the feminist researcher constructed by those that s/he researches and the emotional landscape on which the research journey is mapped. Anger shared or suppressed by the researcher and the researched becomes the site of knowledge production and aids in the construction of war subjectivities. I have written about the continuous emotional performances during my fieldwork in Indian Kashmir and Sri Lanka, where I was seen as the credible 'outsider' but also the representative of the 'occupier' and the 'bully' state (see Parashar 2014). Kashmiri Muslim women expressed deep anger at India's role in the militarisation of the Valley and the apathy of the Indian people; Hindu Pandit women angrily narrated stories of violence against their families by Islamic militants, and apathy and abandonment extended to them by the Indian state. Women and men in Sri Lanka looked at India's involvement in the ethnic conflict as dubious and that of a bully. The anger they felt while narrating their stories acquired personal dimensions as they often used words such as 'you', 'your country', 'your people', 'your army' while addressing me. As an Indian researcher, I became for them an embodiment of the difficult relationship they have with India.

The gendered, national, caste, class and racial constructions of the researcher by the research subjects could result in emotional encounters of a specific nature (see also Jauhola, Chapter 7 in this volume). Yamuna Sangarasivam captures the suppressed anger and angst of the researcher in war-affected Sri Lanka in her autobiographical reflection. During her stay in Colombo, she was detained, interrogated and body-searched, and her belongings were ransacked. She writes:

> I was questioned, as a Tamil, by Sinhalese soldiers who addressed me not only with the authority of their voice and their language (Sinhala) but also with the brandished authority of their weapons: AK47S, M16s, grenades, pistols, and batons. This was my ethnographic reality. It was the reality of war, and I, a Tamil, was marked as an enemy. In this everyday ethnographic moment I conducted my research. Such an experience in the field is ethnographic data. The suspicion and violence mapped onto me

> as a Tamil woman were material realities of my fieldwork; through them I analyze my 'ethnographic data'.
>
> (Sangarasivam 2001: 97)

The anger and frustration thus deflected by field subjects onto researchers potentially influences research outcomes, as the narratives that the researcher is able to access are laden with emotional references and hyperbole (Parashar 2011). After her return from fieldwork in the LTTE-controlled Jaffna, Sangarasivam worked at the International Centre for Ethnic Studies in Colombo, where regular taunts, jokes and prejudiced opinions made her angry and fearful. On one occasion she was flippantly referred to as a suicide bomber, kidnapped and trained by the LTTE (Sangarisivam 2001: 101). She mentions suppressing her anger and emotions, even as she wondered how these strong opinions from intellectuals contributed to the prejudiced environment in Colombo, where Tamils were regularly detained and tortured for being LTTE sympathisers.

I experienced similar anger and alienation during my research: some Sri Lankans labelled me as an Indian intelligence agent, while an Indian colleague believed that I had been brainwashed by the LTTE. In Kashmir, Pandit interviewees scolded/yelled at me as I brought up the issue of Kashmiri 'nationalism' (they only wanted to talk about Muslim fundamentalism), and Kashmiri Muslims who had no love left for the country (India) I belonged to. Like Sangarasivam and others who have carried out research in war zones, I also preferred to keep my political views and my emotional anger to myself, without engaging with my research participants in more meaningful ways. The suppressing of anger and other negative emotions by the researcher occurs in an environment where anger is stripped of any moral legitimacy. By choosing to remain silent, we enact a certain non-negotiable 'otherness' and 'difference' in the absence of critical self-reflection in our research. As Debbie Horsfall says, 'knowing the "self" and knowing "about" the subject are intertwined' (2008: 2; also see Parashar 2014).

Negotiating 'difference' (between the researcher and the researched) is possible only when emotional and angry encounters are acknowledged not just as influencing research, but as part of research data itself. Without trying to appear overtly antagonistic, acrimonious and disrespectful, if I had expressed my feelings and views, it might have enriched my research in various ways. As Bloom suggests, the possibilities of unlearning silences, prejudices and fears of conflict are enhanced when:

> [W]omen's differences are accepted as the foundation of feminist research, rather than a disturbing problem of it; when researchers and respondents are placed on the same critical plane; and when reciprocal, negotiated, honest, and realistic inter-subjective relationships are fostered.
>
> (Bloom 1997: 119)

Feminist storytelling about war not only will have to consider anger as an important emotion that drives women to support and participate in the violence of wars, but also influences the complex relationship between the researcher and the researched.

## Conclusion

As someone who has studied political violence, war and terrorism for over a decade now, anger has always appealed to me as an emotion that has its own moral legitimacy and imagination. Like Paul Muldoon, I would be cautious about understating the negative impact and excesses of anger. He says, 'it would be foolish (and critically irresponsible) to slight fears about the collapse of social trust and the perpetuation of cycles of violence' (2008: 309). In this chapter, I want to draw attention to anger, not as just a negative emotion, but as one that creates and inspires a belief system that allows women to rationalise political violence against the 'other'. Women's participation especially in insurgent wars, is not a random, impulsive reaction nor simply at the behest of, or instigated by, men. In many cases women channel anger in a well articulated plan to support and participate in the violence of wars. Angry women in Kashmir carefully delineated their roles as logistical and ideological supporters of the militant campaign against the Indian security forces; in Sri Lanka, Tamil women found that their anger and fears could only be assuaged by joining ranks with the LTTE and participating in all levels of violent resistance, including direct combat against the Sinhala state. Women in the Maoist movement in India also see armed resistance as a way to express anger at the state that chooses to be apathetic in the midst of growing inequalities and the untold exploitation and suffering that marginalised *dalits* (caste untouchables) and *adivasis* (indigenous people) experience at the hands of the Indian state.

I have also tried to demonstrate that the relationship between the researched and the researcher is on a complex emotional plane, and the anger that is either expressed by the former or suppressed by the latter affects the perception and scholarly analysis of war. This is anger that does not necessarily lead to excesses. There is merit in recognising that anger does not always evoke the same kind of reaction (either from individuals or communities) that descends into violent chaos. It is 'possible to be angry without succumbing to a violent rage that wreaks havoc in an entirely disproportionate and indiscriminate fashion' (ibid.: 310). This is the anger that is part of self-reflection, which emerges in feminist research conversations/interviews, and it is possible to engage with it through mutual respect, compassion and empathy. More importantly, this is the kind of anger that draws attention to the material conditions, to the injustices and negative experiences that lead to that deeply subjective (although socially and culturally constituted) and political reactions among people whose stories we include in our feminist storytelling (see Faulkner 2014 for compassionate anger). Recognising our own emotional subjectivities and the emotional citizenship of those we study would enrich critical war studies and allow the emergence of nuanced gender stories.

Feminists are more equipped to understand and relate to anger because the struggles of feminism are rooted in outrage and in offending societal norms and patriarchy.[14] Feminism offers spirited resistance to the patriarchal status quo, rejecting and raging against its treatment of women and other gender minorities. Feminism as a 'politics of anger' itself is capable of identifying the factors that propel angry women (and men) towards certain kinds of violent politics (see Shibles 1991; Ahmed 2004; Holmes 2004). In fact, it should be part of feminist scholarly responsibilities, as we expand knowledge in the field of conflict and war studies, to pay attention to the overwhelming sense of injustices and grievances that drives anger towards violent excesses and wars. There is never a better time for doing this than now, when we are beginning to understand and theorise emotions in world politics. Paying attention to anger that others experience involves a creative rethinking of our own selves, politics and research commitments. As Muldoon argues (although in the different context of the privileging of forgiveness over experiential anger in Truth Commissions):

> The point is rather that anger should not be regarded as something antithetical to the cultivation of humanity which should be eradicated at any cost .... To become indifferent to the worldly attachments that lead to anger would be to simultaneously take away the basis for compassion and this, perhaps more certainly than any of the excesses of anger, would certainly put an end to the hope of reconciliation.
>
> (Muldoon 2008: 310–3011)

It would be most appropriate to conclude this analysis with the following words of the feminist political scientist Nivedita Menon:

> To be a feminist is to feel part of the history that has produced us; it is to insert oneself into two centuries of thick, textured narratives of struggles and celebrations that transcend national boundaries; to hear the strains of songs of anger and sorrow and militancy in many tongues; to remember our heroines, our foremothers; and, above all, to feel an enormous sense of continuing responsibility.
>
> (Menon 2012: ix)

## Notes

1 *Aye mere watan ke logon. zara aankh mein bhar lo pani; jo shaheed hue hain unki zara yaad karo kurbani.* O people of my country, fill your eyes with tears. Those who have been martyred, remember their sacrifice. Author's translation. The full song with English translation can be found here. http://en.wikipedia.org/wiki/Aye_Mere_Watan_Ke_Logo (accessed 23 January 2014)

2 Significance of the song: http://articles.timesofindia.indiatimes.com/2013-01-25/india/36547127_1_kavi-pradeep-pandit-nehru-lata-mangeshkar (accessed 21 January 2013)

3 The 'enemy' now in India is not just the neighboring state of Pakistan and the jihadi terrorism associated with it. The ongoing Maoist insurgency in northern and central parts (which originated in the 1960s) and the conflict in the north-eastern states of India has demonstrated that states can marginalise their own citizens, who can pick up arms in a brutal internal war.

4 *Aey Watan Kay Sajeelay Jawaano*; *Merya Dhol Sipahiya*; *Mahi Chhael Chhabeela*; *Yeh Hawaoun Kay Musafir*; *Meray Ser Bakaf Mujahid*; *Rang Laey Ga Shaheedoun Ka Lahoo*. All these are martial songs in praise of the soldier at the war front, telling them that their sacrifices would not go in vain. The singer Noor Jahan also dedicates her songs to the soldiers in her renditions.

5 See http://herald.dawn.com/tag/ayub-khan; http://zaainbokhari.wordpress.com/2011/06/01/madam-noor-jahan-and-the-shattered-memories-of-pakistan's-'better-days' (accessed 15 December 2013)

6 Both George Bush and Osama Bin Laden made several emotional appeals to their constituencies in their speeches. Both whipped up frenzied nationalism (American secular, liberal, democratic and modern in the case of the former; Islamic radical, fundamentalist version of religion in the case of the latter.) Both play on the same set of emotions (nationalism and identity) and a similar kind of politics of ' us versus them', yet they have different objectives.

7 For example, in February 2010 the British media reported how a former media advisor to Tony Blair, Alastair Campbell, broke down on live television defending Tony Blair's 'honour' over the Iraq war. On the BBC's *Andrew Marr Show*, Campbell struggled to contain his emotions when it was put to him that Blair had misled parliament about the case for war, and had to take a series of deep breaths while trying to compose himself. Former British Prime Minister Gordon Brown wept in public in February 2010, when he talked of the death of his daughter Jennifer and spoke of facing up to the possible premature death of his son Fraser, who has cystic fibrosis. Mr Brown's wife Sarah, who was present, also sobbed in an extraordinary display of emotion when the Prime Minister was interviewed by Piers Morgan for a TV programme. Indian Home Minister P. Chidambaram became emotional while paying his respects to the 76 policemen who were killed by the Maoist insurgents in an attack on 6 April 2010. Politicians are only exceeded by sportsmen and women, whose display of emotions has been accepted as natural and real. Tennis star Roger Federer's tears after losing the Australian open finals in 2009 are still remembered by many. In 1993 a distraught Jana Novotná burst into tears and cried on the Duchess of Kent's shoulder after losing in the finals of the Wimbledon to Steffi Graf. Cricket, largely a non-contact sport, has several emotional moments now, and the practice of sledging (on-field verbal abuse or 'mental disintegration') is increasingly being adopted to emotionally unsettle the opponents.

8 I gratefully acknowledge the inputs of Janet Andrew-Shah, professor of English at Nirmala College, Ranchi, India, who drew my attention to this poem about anger and its possible meanings and impact.

9 Apart from bell hooks, I am also thinking of black and queer feminist Mia McKenzie's blog, *Black Girl Dangerous*, which captures the 'voices, experiences and expressions of queer and trans* people of colour'. See www.blackgirldangerous.org/about-bgd; Also, *The Angry Feminism Blog*, http://theangriestfeminist.tumblr.com (accessed 21 April 2014)

10 In fact, quite the contrary, in many cases women push their aspirations behind the national aspirations. The intellectual and emotional cohesiveness of a militant project is retained at the cost of preventing women's issues and concerns from being an 'unnecessary' distraction (Parashar 2014).

11 Liberation Tigers of Tamil Eelam (LTTE) was a militant guerrilla group that waged a civil war against the Sri Lankan state. The LTTE was eventually militarily defeated in 2009.

12 Red dot on the forehead that Tamil women wear in Sri Lanka.

13 For example, some authors argue that women involved in suicide bombings usually do so to redeem personal, family or community honour or are coerced by male members of their family. I have discussed the works of some of these authors, such as Mia Bloom and Barbara Victor, in my recent book. See Parashar 2014.

14 See www.theguardian.com/commentisfree/2013/feb/26/feminists-sexy-funny-anger-changes-world (accessed 21 April 2014)

## Bibliography


Ahmed, S. (2004) *The Cultural Politics of Emotion*. Edinburgh: Edinburgh University Press and New York: Routledge.

Bloom, L. R. (1997), 'Locked in uneasy sisterhood: Reflections on feminist methodology and research relations', *Anthropology & Education Quarterly*, 28(1): 111–122.

Cheung-Blunden, V. and Blunden, B. (2008) 'The emotional construal of war: Anger, fear, and other negative emotions', *Peace and Conflict: Journal of Peace Psychology*, 14(2): 123–150.

Crawford, N. C. (2000) 'The passion of world politics: Propositions on emotion and emotional relationships', *International Security*, 24(4): 116–156.

Faulkner, N. (2014) 'Guilt, anger and compassionate helping', in *The Politics of Compassion*, Ure and Frost (eds). London: Routledge, 107–120.

Frijda, N. H. and Mesquita, B. (2000) 'Beliefs through emotions', in *Emotions and Beliefs: How Feelings Influence Thoughts*, Frijda, Manstead and Bem (eds). Cambridge: Cambridge University Press, 45–77.

Frijda, N. H., Manstead, A. S. R. and Bem, S. (eds) (2000) *Emotions and Beliefs: How Feelings Influence Thoughts*. Cambridge: Cambridge University Press.

Hercus, C. (1999) 'Identity, emotion, and feminist collective action', *Gender & Society*, 13(1): 34–55.

Holmes, M. (2004) 'Feeling beyond rules: Politicizing the sociology of emotion and anger in feminist politics', *European Journal of Social Theory* 7: 209.

hooks, bell (1995) *Killing Rage: Ending Racism*. New York: Henry Holt.

Horsfall, D. (2008) 'Bearing witness: toward a pedagogical practice of love?', *Reflective Practice*, 9: 1–10.

Inayatullah, N. (ed.) (2011) *Autobiographical International Relations: I, IR*. London: Routledge.

Lyman, P. (1981) 'The politics of anger', *Socialist Review*, 11: 55–74.

Marcus, G. E. (2000) 'Emotions in politics', *Annual Review of Political Science*, 3: 221–250.

Menon, N. (2012) *Seeing Like a Feminist*. New Delhi: Zubaan/Penguin.

Moisi, D. (2009) *The Geopolitics of Emotion: How Cultures of Fear, Humiliation and Hope are Reshaping the World*. London: The Bodley Head.

Muldoon, P. (2008) 'The moral legitimacy of anger', *European Journal of Social Theory*, 11: 299.

Parashar, S. (2011) 'Embodied 'Otherness' and negotiations of difference: A critical self reflection on the politics of emotions in researching militant women', *International Studies Review*, 13(4): 687–708.

Parashar, S. (2013) 'What wars and "war bodies" know about International Relations', *Cambridge Review of International Affairs*, 26(4): 615–630.

Parashar, S. (2014) *Women and Militant Wars: The Politics of Injury*. London: Routledge.

Sangarasivam, Y. (2001) 'Researcher, informant, "assassin", me', *Geographical Review*, 91: 95–104.

Scarry, E. (1985) *The Body in Pain: The Making and Unmaking of the World*. Oxford: Oxford University Press.

Shepherd, L. J. (ed.) (2015) *Gender Matters in Global Politics*, second edition. New York: Routledge.

Shibles, W. (1991) 'Feminism and the cognitive theory of emotion: Anger, blame and humor', *Women & Health*, 17(1): 57–69.

Sundar, N. (2012) '"Winning hearts and minds": Emotional wars and the construction of difference', *Third World Quarterly*, 33(4): 701–717.

Sylvester, C. (ed.) (2011) 'Forum: Emotion and the feminist IR researcher', *International Studies Review*, 40(4): 687–708.

Ure, M. and Frost, M. (eds) (2014) *The Politics of Compassion*. London: Routledge.

# 7 On 'being bored'

## Street ethnography on emotions in Banda Aceh after the tsunami and conflict[1]

*Marjaana Jauhola*

This chapter draws on the initial insights gained from my street ethnography of the lived experiences in the provincial capital of Banda Aceh in Indonesia.[2] It focuses on the embodied experience of 'boredom' and how it offers affective maps of a gendered/ing city, and challenges the government practices that aim at totalising the 'political presence'. By focusing simultaneously on 'being bored' as a research method and 'punk boredom' as a focus of ethnographic study, I suggest that these affective research encounters – at times smelly, dirty, gross and hallucinatory – offer insights into the modes of political engagement with the aesthetic ordering and disordering of the city.

I approach the city of Banda Aceh and the ideal of 'civilised city'[3] from the perspective of everyday lived experience – as social practices that function as sites of struggle over legitimate subjectivities. Understood in this way, Banda Aceh is formed through social practices and multitudes; it breathes life, and is fluid rather than stable and unchanging.

As the closest major city to the epicentre of the Indian Ocean earthquake and tsunami in 2004, Banda Aceh made it onto the mental disaster maps of most people globally. However, the tsunami and its aftermath is just one way in which the Banda Acehnese narrate their stories, as the city is also rebuilding itself after a three-decade-long armed conflict between the Indonesian army and the Free Aceh Movement (GAM). Thus 'war' in this text refers specifically to how narratives of 'now' in Banda Aceh are built through the experiences of political violence, conflict and militarisation. The focus on the experiential and lived everyday also illustrates the absurdity of dividing analysis into separate spheres of 'conflict' or 'natural disaster', or even assumptions that post-conflict stands for 'after', or 'end of' violence.

Stressing the Islamic identity and history of Aceh is part and parcel of the wider project of strengthening the provincial self-governance, stipulated in the peace agreement signed in 2005 between the Free Aceh Movement and the Government of Indonesia, and in the Law on Governance of Aceh approved in 2006 (Feener 2012; Miller and Feener 2010). Since 2006, Banda Aceh's mayoral leadership have taken several steps to execute their formal duties as guardians of Shari'a Islam implementation. One of the key ideological concepts used is *kota madani* (civilised city), which has specifically focused on public guidance of adolescents and young adults, emphasising the importance of building their *ahklah dan aqidah* (morality and belief).[4] In my previous research I argued that emphasising gender difference with rhetoric on religion, morality and piousness has become part of disciplining post-disaster subjectivities and attempts to re-establish 'normalcy' in the aftermath of disasters, in particular through the policing of bodies and behaviours of adolescents and young adults (Jauhola 2013). However, focusing on ritual performances and everyday practices of Islam, anthropological research has attempted to challenge approaches that are limited to the 'governmentality' of Islamic jurisprudence, and rather focus on the varied ways in which Muslims orient themselves towards normative codes and expectations of piousness (Dupret *et al.* 2012).

The chapter is structured as follows: first, I discuss some of the conceptual and methodological debates that currently drive my research. I then move on to the ethnographic encounters of being bored, in order to focus on 'punk boredom' in Banda Aceh. I conclude by arguing that an analytical focus on the experienced post-disaster and post-conflict city benefits from the practices of academic unlearning and ethnographic orientation towards mindful research practice.

## Ethnography as mindful research practice

> Materialistic slaves
> Fixed ideology and idealism
> So be prepared!
> His/her brain is imprisoned
> Prison of thoughts
> Flow of indoctrination
> (Totaliter: 'Prison of thoughts')[5]

The initial postmodern and postcolonial critique of ethnographic methods in the 1980s and 1990s, also described as the crisis in anthropology, has since produced reflexive debate upon the possibilities and restrictions of ethnographic endeavours with lived experience: focus on power, exploitation and colonial reproduction, on the one hand, and possibilities of resisting the Enlightenment-driven ontologies without having to discard the method altogether, on the other: 'the desire was not to know the other as other, or to study the other as a way of knowing oneself, but to understand how previously marginalised groups existed in the circuits of meaning, cultural formation and structural location' (Skeggs 1999: 36).

Further, instead of assuming that positionalities and hierarchies are identifiable, knowable and communicable prior to the research encounter, I draw on the works of scholars who suggest that positionalities and differences in research gain their meaning 'right here and now' through social practice (Elliston 2000: 178; Skeggs 2001: 432; Penttinen 2013: 35; Puumala 2013: 126): we are produced through our experience (Skeggs 1999: 39, 42) and this experience has to be translated into a perspective before it can become a standpoint (Skeggs 2001: 432). The method of 'here and now' is an active stand against 'mindlessness', i.e. conducting research through an automatic pilot function and using preconceived beliefs, categories and frames (Penttinen 2013: 37).

As the lyrics of the song 'Prison of thoughts' by Banda Acehnese punk band Totaliter (engl. Totalitarian) suggest, the focus on 'here and now' is a call for understanding of concepts as accomplishments at the *end* of an investigation, rather than before, with the aim of creating possibility for imagining alternative worlds and political imaginaries (Shapiro 2013: xii, xiv). Thus, instead of producing the researcher's 'Me self' through 'navel-gazing' reflexivity and confessing potential positionalities, this approach rather focuses on the experiences of states of temporal becoming through intersubjectivity and relational forms of being that are not restricted to the physical bodies, but form connectedness to and resonance[6] with bodies, materiality, space, and how the body and affects move within that space (see also Solomon, Chapter 5 in this volume).

What does it mean concretely? Instead of identifying and verbalising the researcher's encounter with the researched as always already dichotomous and hierarchical, I draw on a body of literature that understands such research encounters as active processes of becoming, of being touched and moved (Puumala 2013: 126). Or, that gender is a process of becoming relationally, rather than a state of being of a sovereign gender-specific embodied subject (Skeggs 1999: 42). Mindful research practice thus deconstructs the constructed illusions of a researcher-subjectivity that is a whole, autonomous and sovereign entity (see e.g. Jackson 2007).

For example, Eeva Puumala explores 'exposure', or 'being exposed' as a method as well as an analytical focus on the governmental practices of migration policies. 'Being exposed' as an ethnographical research method requires perceptive focus on presence in 'here and now' and being through shared encounters, it reactivates the connectedness of self into a sense of temporality and spatiality of politics, understanding political communities as experiential and touching – in which bodies are in flux, open, and form through corporeal junctures (Puumala 2013: 125–126). To Puumala, this creates a tension between politics and acts that insist ontologically upon sovereign subjectivity, distinctions between inside/outside, and self/other (ibid.: 127–128). Furthermore, Hanna Väätäinen (2003, 2009) proposes an ethnographic methodology that connects affects to engaged and embodied practice – ethnographic orientation that is aligned with changes and transformation. Ethnographic improvisation requires both careful planning and preparedness, yet is combined with the ability to discard those plans, willingness to let go. Improvisation does not mean acting without any frames or boundaries, but rather, accepting permeability and inability to know what happens next (Väätäinen 2009: 43). This requires openness to intuition, immediate experience, which according to Elizabeth Grosz allows us to get closer to movement, resonation and transformation that resides the outside of all senses. Intuition is creativity, ability to see and do things that elude everyday need, or use-value (Grosz 2005: 136).

However, understanding ethnographic encounters taking shape 'here and now' does not refer to endless possibilities or freedom opening up in all possible directions. Rather, it refers to studying connectedness consisting of dimensions of ethics and responsibility relating to 'our receptivity to others … the voices to which we listen and the experiences we account for – and in how we craft our explanations: whether our analytics remain attuned to the intricacy, openness, and unpredictability of individual and collective lives' (Biehl and Locke 2010: 318). The task for the researcher is to problematise conceptualisations that insist upon the sovereign subjectivity and its independence, and recognition that the researcher's body is connected to unseen forces and flows (Väätäinen 2009: 47).

What does a mindful researcher do during ethnographic encounters? Experience of conducting street ethnography in Banda Aceh has been a major process, personally, of undoing and unlearning the practices of a neoliberal university geared towards mindless multitasking, and the inherent goal of output orientation of being a scholar. It has resulted in dealing with the feelings of being frustrated and bored in the face of not being able to evaluate the usefulness of certain daily research practices, such as walking in the rain, taking shelter, and waiting for hours. The attempt to observe events non-judgementally opens up possibilities to move beyond the predetermined concepts, analytical frameworks and explanatory models. The possibility to seize moments such as 'being stuck' for hours because of the rain allowed me to challenge my pre-set ideas of what was to happen next, and refocus on 'non-events', mundane activities 'imperceptible events … that are outside the great events of history' (Bhabha 1994: 243 quoted in Löfgren and Ehn 2010: 229, n3). It was through the initial feelings of frustration that I gained an appreciation of 'going along' as a method (Kusenbach 2003) and of exploring extended 'time-space paths' (Tani and Surma-aho 2012): squatting or sitting still for hours, walking, and following flows of objects, texts and bodies – both online and offline. Similarly to how Unni Wikan explored silence in her research, I 'gave in' to boredom: focused on the experience of boredom 'not as a void or an absence but as a space full and pregnant with meaning' (Wikan 1992: 470).

## *'Street as my teacher'*[7] *– searching for the punk Banda Aceh*

The Banda Acehnese punk community became part of the global media circuit two years ago when 65 punks (62 males and three females) were arrested on the evening of 11 December in 2011 at Taman Budaya, a stage and event venue administered by the municipality of Banda Aceh. The event was followed by tens of punks and metal fans from different parts of Aceh, but also Northern Sumatra and Jakarta. All in all, some 15 bands were planned to perform, and formal permission for the event was applied for and granted by the municipality administration and the Ulama Consultative Assembly (MPU). Using a commonly known strategy to get official permission for such a public event (Idria 2013: 189); it was explicitly advertised by the local organisers, punk and metal rock bands as a charity event aiming to support orphanages in Aceh.

The arrests led to three days of detention at the police station and then a further ten days of 're-education camp' or 'moral rehabilitation' at the police academy compound. It was not the first punk arrest in the city. Rather, it took place after the local police had officially banned twelve local punk communities by publishing a list of banned groups in the local media (Idria 2013: 195). As the arrest and detention coincided with the campaigning period for the 2013 mayoral elections, the December 2011 arrests were narrated by the members of one banned group, Museum Street Punks, not as a coincidental arrest, but rather as a carefully planned intervention to discipline 'out of control' bodies and practices that were claimed to be incompatible with Acehnese and Islamic culture (Idria 2013: 185; see also Syam and Hasan 2013).

Both the global English-speaking media and the rhetoric by the local government portray the events of December 2011 in a well rehearsed binary of the implementation of Shari'a law in Aceh. The international media narrated the story as a threat of Shari'a law, a crackdown on punks in the name of Islam. The local media and authorities repeated the story of punks being a Western phenomenon, inherently alien to Islam, and thus to Islamic and Acehnese way of life and culture (for a more general discussion on punk and Islam see e.g. Fiscella 2012). Authorities further constructed their and the state's responsibility to speak the language of concerned parents. For example, the police chief reasoned: 'they are our nation's children[8] who need to be saved' (Anon. 2011), and Deputy Mayor Illiza specifically elaborated her motherly feelings to express her concern and firm action: 'as a mother I feel very bad to see a child behave like that' (Jinnmonkey 2012). By expressing her emotions, she made a direct connection between maternal emotions, her mayoral position and the gendered state ideology of 'state momism' (Suryakusuma 1996) and its normative assumptions of women's roles and duties as mothers: bearers of the future generations of Acehnese citizens, and her moral duty to act. State power, embodied and vocalised through a concerned and motherly caring executive power, did not formally fulfil any of the legal requirements of arrest, nor of detention. Instead, it was framed as an act of affection.

Once the punks were arrested and detained, journalists were let in to document the spectacle of their re-education on *akhlak* (Islamic character). Furthermore, the arrest and the re-education camp became a performance of state violence and authority, illustrating a contestation of political and legal power in Aceh (Kloos 2013: 225–226, 234): negotiation between the multiple legal and moral realms, and moving the responsibility of dealing with breaking of social norms from internally within family and within the village or neighbourhood structure (*adat*) to mayoral power assisted by formal military and civilian state security – parties that are formally mandated to maintain the order and mainstream implementation of Shari'a law (for a similar case of 'restoring moral order' see Kloos 2013: 220–223).

After my arrival in Banda Aceh, however, I became more interested in exploring the kinds of experiential maps of Banda Aceh created and enabled by the retelling of the December 2011 arrests – to journalists and researchers alike – or the repetitious watching of YouTube videos of the demonstrations and other expressions of solidarity, the media coverage of their re-education camp, and the release ceremony. What kinds of stories do the singing of well known Indonesian anarchist and punk songs in the streets of Banda Aceh repeatedly every evening after evening prayer, DIY patches and T-shirts, and daily routines tell of the complexities and precariousness, gendered and embodied politicisation of urban post-conflict and post-disaster urban space, in a (post)-colonial yet also a global imaginary? (For previous analyses of punks in the Indonesian context – Jakarta, Bandung and Bali – see Wallach 2005, 2008; Baulch 2007; Pickles 2007; Martin-Iverson and Ryan 2011).

A year after the arrest, finding the punks was not an easy task, although I knew the city centre quite well; it was after all my fifth visit to Banda Aceh since 2006. Despite walking the streets of Banda Aceh in September 2012 and asking around for help, I wasn't able to find a single punk in town. Just tags, graffiti and litter left on the riverbank. I returned to the city in June 2013, and it was when I gave up walking one day that our time-space paths collided and I found their rhythm in the streets. I was handed a flyer advertising a 'food not bombs' event, by a group of punks walking towards the tsunami museum. Once I introduced myself as a social movement activist and researcher, they welcomed me with open arms. Connecting with the outside world, mostly journalists, has been their strategy since December 2011 in order to get their stories heard and to raise solidarity outside the province. During the time I spent with the community, I slept a few nights at a deserted house used as their night shelter. However, due to regulation on gender segregation and Shari'a police raids at night, it would have been too risky to stay overnight on the street with a community consisting of mostly male punks. We would meet before noon, and I would leave when I received several hints that it might not be safe for a female at night-time. So when the male street punks explored the city until dawn, I returned to my room to write, and thus slowly adapted myself to their waking hours.

This meant literally adjusting my body, sense of temporality and spatiality into punk time and space, which consisted mostly of spending hours and hours at the museum. The initial feelings of anxiety and feeling bored, combined with an aching body from sitting on the tiled floor for hours, retrospectively opened up a possibility for practice of sensing and listening to emotions; to reflect upon what 'being bored' tells me, and to focus on the awareness that arises from this reflection. Here, a basic meditation technique of 'stopping'/'praise of non-doing' became useful. I let go of the idea that something will be gained, or something new revealed. I just watched the moment unfold, without trying to change it. In stopping, I reflected upon the following questions: What is happening, what do you feel? What do you see? What do you hear? It is important to note, however, that stopping is not a passive act: 'There is nothing passive about it [stopping]…[it] makes going more vivid, richer, more textured' (Kabat-Zinn 1994: 12). Stopping does lead to a change of rhythm, though. For someone raised in the world of hyper-activeness – making oneself busy and useful – stopping can be frightening, an experience that offers reconnecting with the consciousness of one's body and emotions. When the body stops, the mind keeps on wondering and travelling. Only by 'stopping doing' can one become aware of the present moment, as a researcher, for example. As with mindfulness, adjusting oneself into the 'new' embodied temporality and spatiality of punks required repetition and effort. Thus it was only once I let go of my pre-planned ideas of what street ethnography consists of, such as walking and conducting life-history interviews, that I was able to find myself in the microcosmos of the street punks.

Once the analytical focus is on the details, they become so talkative and noisy that they can no longer be sidelined as unimportant (Palin 2004: 46). Thus, whilst practicing the idea of 'stopping', I turned my focus onto the ways the punks occupy the urban space and use their bodies to form resistance towards the attempts to govern urban adolescence. I discovered how they form new kinds of intimate and caring relationships through bodily practices; establish 'home' rhizomatically, with their belongings hidden across the town; and establish friendships across the Indonesian archipelago and the rest of the globe using social media and visitors from outside, such as researchers, documentarists, journalists, punk rockers and anarchist tourists, who would retell these stories outside Aceh.

### *'Being bored' at the museum*

Each day, between five to ten punks, mostly males in their twenties, would gather at the tsunami museum after just a few hours of sleep in the streets, parks and abandoned houses. The raised ground floor of the museum provided shelter both from the hot sun and from the rain, and thus was ideal for hanging around. Leaning on the pillars, smoking, watching cars go by, checking out motorbikers and museum visitors, flirting with giggling and shy teenage girls, checking and mocking the Shari'a police patrols passing by. Other hanging around activities included making DIY (do-it-yourself) T-shirts, patches, bracelets, earrings and necklaces, shining boots, regulating the punk street political economy by punishing those stealing money, sharing and debating punk and anarchist ideology, squatting, sleeping, daydreaming, playing guitar and self-made drums – described as *bosan* (boring) – in anticipation of eventfulness, destruction of the routine. Yet the fact that most of the 'being bored' time was spent at the tsunami museum can be read to signify multiple things. As one of the punks explained to me, hanging around at the museum was their way of becoming visible.

The same visibility, however, also made them vulnerable to the violence of museum security staff and military police. In fact, hanging around at the museum was a result of having been evicted from the nearby recreation park owned by the military. Some of the punks slept under the counter of an unused cafeteria space, however they were warned not to use the premises outside the museum's opening hours. After a violent attack by civilian-clothed military police at the end of June, punks were forbidden to enter the museum premises. A few weeks later, however, once the situation had cooled down, they made their return. Forbidden or otherwise risky locations were commonly referred to as *panas* (hot), signalling a potential confrontation with the state apparatus, be it military, regular police, or civil service and Shari'a police.

This has meant periodic nomadism from one locale to another, leading to extended periods of chronic sleep deprivation. It is thus no surprise that mixed substance use formed, at least for some of the punks, a way to regulate affects: slowing and toning down fears and anxiety and replacing them with utopian euphoria and hallucinations, out-of-body experience and detachment, feelings of losing oneself, and being united with the surrounding environment with boundless and bodiless consciousness, as described to me. However, moments of euphoria and clarity were followed by days of confusion and agony, potentially a result of a bad 'mixture', or withdrawal symptoms. Confusion and agony were accompanied with loss of items, such as needle and thread used to stich patches, unrealised plans to hire a car and go to the beach, or problems that seemed trivial becoming multiplied and causing enormous stress. Thus what I was observing as 'boredom' was potentially also partially a result of trying to deal with it: 'It [drugs] is just such an easy way to cope with boredom (bosan)'.

Without wanting to romanticise or demonise such experiences, let alone support the common claim that all punks in Aceh use drugs, I argue that being bored and being high construct alternative ways to occupy the city, and provide a means to deconstruct the 'self' and normative temporality that results from embodied governmental practices, such as being beaten up or arrested for several days. In fact, these acts and experiences, I would argue, can also be seen as a resistance to post-disaster governmentality and a simultaneous reconstruction of utopian punkness, an escape from boredom, anxiety and negative thoughts, instead seeking punk aesthetic creativity such as writing lyrics and drawing.

Confrontation with the police and security apparatus, such as the arrest of three punks for three days in June, was echoed on the grounds of the museum through the repeated singing of anarchist songs[9], sometimes by altering the original lyrics, as in the band Sosial Sosial's song 'Difference is not a war':

> learning is not the enemy
> respect it, do not abuse/scold it
> clear observation, it's totally clear:
> of course there are differences
> yea, your narrow thinking
> does not accept difference
> I am proud of my principles
> DIY guides me
> difference is not a war, when he was born it was there already
> difference is not a war, yea, we do exist
> (Sosial Sosial: 'Difference is not a war')

Becoming an eyewitness to the punk everyday was an invitation to pay attention to the silent marks of physical violence: the residues of pain and

*Figure 7.1* 'Upgrade your senses': motto at the local internet café
Source: Photo by Marjaana Jauhola

suffering and the bruises left on bodies functioning as visual markers of their identity and politics as male punk bodies. As one person explained to me: 'our bruises are a reminder of the ongoing violence and discrimination in Aceh. Punks are here because of that violence.'

Punks have gained more visibility in urban spaces since the 2005 peace process, as occupying streets at night-time was nearly impossible during the conflict. However, it does not mean that this invisibility meant 'non-existence'. In fact, many told of the vibrant punk scene in Aceh that has existed at least since the early 1990s, and which shares an ideological collective history with the punk and anarchist communities within the rest of the Indonesian archipelago: opposing the authoritarian regime of President Suharto, militarism, neoliberalist economic reforms and corruption, but also reflecting upon Aceh's specific situation, i.e. the armed conflict and political disputes (Aiyub 2011; Idria 2013: 194; see also e.g. Wallach 2008).

Being openly against militarism in Aceh (both the army and the ex-combatants of the independence movement), in addition to hanging around in highly militarised locations in the city, pose a visible threat to dominant forms of masculinity in the post-conflict context of Aceh (Jauhola 2013). The punks' inaction and boredom actively mediated and negotiated their masculinities vis-à-vis the dominant forms of militarised hyper-masculinity in post-conflict Aceh, and more widely *babak* masculinity, through which senior men of a family have authority over everyone else and might thereby subject younger men and females to forms of control and subordination (Boellstorff 2004: 470; Nilan 2009: 333); the family orientation of the overall Indonesian, and Acehnese, society (Beazley 2003); and the collective norm of *malu* (shame or embarrassment) (Boellstorff 2004: 474–475; Lindquist 2004: 487–490).

Girlfriends of male punks reiterated these forms of hyper-masculinity and heteronormativity in the public sphere. Girls provided the punks with cash and other material resources, lending their mobile phones and motorbikes; supplied T-shirts for DIY; but also offered emotional and physical intimacy. As the Shari'a policing and raids in Banda Aceh specifically control female clothing and behaviour, few girlfriends would use visual signs of being a punk or hang out late in the evenings. This, in turn, facilitated other heterosexual hyper-masculine practices such as flirting with waiters and teenage girls hanging out in the alleys, as well as the consuming of pornographic materials on mobile phones.

Interestingly, these periods of socialising also included moments of homosociality; not necessarily explicitly expressed eroticism, but rather touching and caring. The focus on details allowed me to see how the male punks constructed alternative ways of intimacy, familial relations and, importantly, care of the self. The streets became their home, and punk friends in Aceh and elsewhere their immediate family – although most Banda Acehnese punks would return to their parents and formal guardians regularly to eat, wash up and change clothes. Items kept in hidden storage around the city provided a sense of belonging, of community and of 'home', but also allowed, very concretely, practices of self-care such as sewing, tattooing, bathing, brushing teeth and so on.

Leander and McKim suggest that space-time (or social space) 'is not simply a static background "upon" which human activity is played out, but rather on-going production of space-time is a rich process that draws upon multiple material and discursive resources, is imbued with relations of power, and is malleable through individual agency and imagination' (Leander and McKim 2003: 212). Thus hanging around at the museum and appropriation of public places through wrongly positioned bodies, for example laying on the ground and thereby breaking the Shari'a regulation of separating space according to female and male spaces, formed 'geographies of resistance' (Beazley 2003: 182) and constructed 'punk spatiality' in the sense that it provided space for the construction of social identity and forming of 'hidden transcripts' (Scott 1990) of the city: 'critique of power spoken behind the back of the dominant' (ibid.: xii).

## Conclusions

This chapter has suggested that in order to find oneself tuned into studying emotions, affects and landscapes of political violence and disaster, researchers would benefit from unlearning to plan, project and imagine their research outputs. By introducing ethnographic orientation towards the 'here and now' through mindful research practice, I argue that one is more capable of connecting with the experienced post-disaster and post-conflict city. Using the example of 'being bored', the chapter explores how the lived and embodied experiences of museum street punks contest and rupture the 'political present' in Aceh. It also shows how ethnographic encounters that are thickly embodied, at times violent, gross, embarrassing, and sometimes, with traces of hallucinations, provide ways of seeing the practice of politics, utopian punk temporality and spatiality being formed in the grounds of the tsunami museum.

## Notes

1 I would like to thank the editors and Ferdiansyah Thajib for their valuable comments of the draft versions of this chapter. Earlier versions presented at ECPR General Conference in Bordeaux, September 2013 and Indonesia Research Network Seminar in Helsinki, November 2013.

2 The focus of the street ethnography (2012–14) is anchored on the urban neighbourhoods of Banda Aceh around the riverbank of *Krueng Aceh* that cuts through the centre of the city, less than a square kilometre in size.

3 '*Madani*': Indonesian concept deriving from Arabic, translates into 'civil', but also 'sophisticated' or 'refined'. The widened use of the concept '*masyarakat madani*', often translated into 'civil society' or 'civilised society', emerged during the early 1990s, the final years of authoritarian regime of President Suharto. It has been specifically used in debates calling for democracy, yet debating the role of religion and the state, and offered as an alternative for '*sipil*', antonym of '*militer*' (military).

For a detailed analysis, see e.g. Bakti 2005. The concept '*madani*' also refers specifically to the city-state of Medina and Muhammad's role in building the city after having departed from Mecca in the seventh century. In the Banda Acehnese urban governance usage, however, it seems to be harnessed more directly to be used for conceptualisation of full implementation of Shari'a law. See also the uses of '*madani*' in relation to the Arab Spring in Hill 2013.

4 For the analysis of gendered adolescence, Indonesian/Acehnese nationalism, religion and neoliberalism, the discourse of moral and successful self see e.g. (Jauhola 2013; Parker and Nilan 2013)

5 For a video of the song made with my audiovisual data, see www.youtube.com/watch?v=xbJfFljc9vU.

6 See further e.g. Unni Wikan's exploration of the concept 'resonance' by which she refers to 'a willingness to engage with another world, life, or idea: an ability to use one's experience … to try to grasp, or convey, meanings that reside neither in words, "facts," nor text but are evoked in the meeting of one experiencing subject with another' (Wikan 1992: 463).

7 Detail that most punks in Aceh give as their formal education in Facebook (*alam raya sekolahku*). *Alam raya* translates literally as the great nature, or universe.

8 It is common in Indonesia to call punks as *anak punk*, punk kids or children, although their age varies from twelve to mid-twenties and beyond.

9 The songs that the street punks perform in the streets are popular anarchist and punk songs by well known Jakartan bands such as Marjinal, Romi & the JAHAT, Bunga Hitam, Sosial Sosial, and Toni Rastafara adapted to ukuleles and self-made drums, and thus not necessarily recognisable by their music genre as punk songs, but rather as folk.

## Bibliography

Aiyub, A. (2011) 'Saya azhari, saya punker: apa ada masalah besar?', *Acehkita.com*, 15 December. Available online at: www.acehkita.com/berita/saya-azhari-saya-punker-apa-ada-masalah-besar (accessed 9 January 2014).

Anon. (2011) 'Punk rockers sent to rehab in Indonesian province', *McClatchy-Tribune Business News*, 14 December.

Bakti, A. F. (2005) 'Islam and modernity: Nurcholish Madjid's interpretation of civil society, pluralism, secularization, and democracy', *Asian Journal of Social Science*, 33(3): 486–505.

Baulch, E. (2007) *Making Scenes: Reggae, Punk and Death Metal in 1990s Bali*. London: Duke University Press.

Beazley, H. (2003) 'Voices from the margins: Street children's subcultures in Indonesia', *Children's Geographies*, 1(2): 181.

Biehl, J. and Locke, P. (2010) 'Deleuze and the anthropology of becoming', *Current Anthropology*, 51(3): 317–351.

Boellstorff, T. (2004) 'The emergence of political homophobia in Indonesia: Masculinity and national belonging', *Ethnos: Journal of Anthropology*, 69(4): 465–486.

Dupret, B., Pierret, T., Pinto, P. and Spellman-Poots, K. (2012) 'Introduction', in *Ethnographies of Islam: Ritual Performances and Everyday Practices*, Dupret, Pierret, Pinto and Spellman-Poots (eds). Edinburgh: Edinburgh University Press, 1–10.

Elliston, D. A. (2000) 'Geographies of gender and politics: The place of difference in Polynesian nationalism', *Cultural Anthropology*, 15(2): 171–216.

Feener, R. M. (2012) 'Social engineering through Shari'a: Islamic law and state-directed Da'Wa in contemporary Aceh', *Islamic Law and Society*, 19(3): 275–311.

Fiscella, A. T. (2012) ‘From Muslim punks to taqwacore: An incomplete history of punk Islam’, *Contemporary Islam*, 6(3): 255–281.
Grosz, E. (2005) *Time Travels: Feminism, Nature, Power*. Crows Nest: Allen & Unwin.
Hill, P. (2013) ‘“The civil” and “the secular” in contemporary Arab Politics’. Available online at: http://muftah.org/the-civil-and-the-secular-in-contemporary-arab-politics/#.U1McoseoV5U (accessed 20 April 2014).
Idria, R. (2013) ‘Cultural resistance to Shariatism in Aceh’, in *Regime Change, Democracy and Islam: The Case of Indonesia*. Leiden: University of Leiden, 180–201. Available online at: www.hum.leiden.edu/lias/research/news/march-2013-final-irp-report.html.
Jackson, M. (2007) ‘Intersubjective ambiquities’, *Medische Antropologie*, 19(1): 147–161.
Jauhola, M. (2013) *Post-Tsunami Reconstruction in Indonesia: Negotiating Normativity through Gender Mainstreaming Initiatives in Aceh*. London: Routledge.
Jinnmonkey (2012) ‘Aceh Punks Arrested & Sent to Re-Education Camps’ [Video file 10 February] Available online at: www.youtube.com/watch?v=6HS8cci2T0M%3E (accessed 9 January 2014).
Kabat-Zinn, J. (1994) *Wherever You Go, There You Are: Mindfulness Meditation for Everyday Life*. London: Piatkus Books.
Kloos, D. (2013) ‘Strengthening local leadership. Sharia, customs, and the dynamics of vigilante violence in Aceh’, in *Regime Change, Democracy and Islam: The Case of Indonesia*. Leiden: Universiteit Leiden, 202–236. Available online at: www.hum.leiden.edu/lias/research/news/march-2013-final-irp-report.html.
Kusenbach, M. (2003) ‘Street phenomenology: The go-along as ethnographic research tool’, *Ethnography*, 4(3): 455–485.
Leander, K. M. and McKim, K. K. (2003) ‘Tracing of everyday ‘sitings’ of adolescents on the internet: A strategic adaptation of ethnography across online and offline spaces’, *Education, Communication & Information*, 3(2): 211–240.
Lindquist, J. (2004) ‘Veils and ecstasy: Negotiating shame in the Indonesian Borderlands’, *Ethnos: Journal of Anthropology*, 69(4): 487–508.
Löfgren, O. and Ehn, B. (2010) *The Secret World of Doing Nothing*. Berkeley, CA: University of California Press.
Martin-Iverson, S. R. (2011) ‘The politics of cultural production in the DIY hardcore scene in Bandung, Indonesia’, PhD thesis. School of Social and Cultural Studies, University of Western Australia.
Miller, M. A. and Feener, R. M. (2010) ‘Emergency and Islamic law in Aceh’, in *Emergency Powers in Asia: Exploring the Limits of Legality*, Ramraj and Thiruvengadam (eds). New York: Cambridge University Press, 213–236.
Nilan, P. (2009) ‘Contemporary masculinities and young men in Indonesia.’ *Indonesia & the Malay World*, 37(109): 327–344.
Palin, T. (2004) *Oireileva miljöömuotokuva. Yksityiskohdat sukupuoli-ja säätyhierarkian haastajina*. Helsinki: Kustannus Oy Taide.
Parker, L. and Nilan, P. (2013) *Adolescents in Contemporary Indonesia*. London: Routledge.
Penttinen, E. (2013) *Joy and International Relations: A New Methodology*. Abingdon: Routledge.
Pickles, J. (2007) ‘Punk, pop and protest: The birth and decline of political punk in Bandung’, *RIMA: Review of Indonesian and Malaysian Affairs*, 41(2): 223–246.
Puumala, E. (2013) ‘Politiikan tuntu, mieli ja merkitys: tapahtuva yhteisö ja poliitisen kokemus kehollisissa kohtaamisissa’, *Tiede & Edistys*, 2: 125–138.

Scott, J. C. (1990) *Domination and the Arts of Resistance: Hidden Transcripts*. New Haven, CT: Yale University Press.
Shapiro, M. J. (2013) *Studies in Trans-Disciplinary Method: After the Aesthetic Turn*. Abingdon: Routledge.
Skeggs, B. (1999) 'Matter out of place: visibility and sexualities in leisure spaces', *Leisure Studies*, 18(3): 213–232.
Skeggs, B. (2001) 'Feminist ethnography', in *Handbook of Ethnography*, Atkinson, Coffey, Delamont, Lofland and Lofland (eds). London: Sage, 426–442.
Suryakusuma, J. I. (1996) 'The state and sexuality in new order Indonesia', in *Fantasizing the Feminine in Indonesia*, Sears (ed.). London: Duke University Press, 92–119.
Syam, H. M. and Hasan, E. (2013) 'Perkembangan komunitas anak punk di kota Banda Aceh: pandangan masyarakat dan kebijakan pemerintah kota', *Jurnal Pendidikan Sains Sosial dan Kemanusiaan*, 6(2): 159–168.
Tani, S. and Surma-aho, O. (2012) 'Young people and the hidden meanings of the everyday: Time-space path as a methodological opportunity', *International Research in Geographical and Environmental Education*, 21(3): 187–203.
Väätäinen, H. (2003) *Rumbasta rampaan: Vammaisen naistanssijan ruumiillisuus pyörätuolikilpatanssissa*. Åbo: Åbo Akademi University Press.
Väätäinen, H. (2009) *Liikkeessä pysymisen taika: Etnografisia kokeiluja yhteisötanssiryhmässä*. Turku: Eetos.
Wallach, J. (2005) 'Underground rock music and democratization in Indonesia', *World Literature Today: A Literary Quarterly of the University of Oklahoma*, 79(3/4): 16.
Wallach, J. (2008) 'Living the punk lifestyle in Jakarta', *Ethnomusicology*, 52(1): 98–116.
Wikan, U. (1992) 'Beyond the words: The power of resonance', *American Ethnologist*, 19(3): 460–482.

# 8 Experimenting with emotions

*Rose McDermott*

A lot of traditional work in International Relations, especially work focused on the state as a primary actor, tends to ignore the role of individuals, and thus of personal emotions, in instigating and maintaining important phenomena such as war. However, any aficionado of war movies or memoirs immediately recognises the critical importance of emotions ranging from fear to anger, and especially revenge and vengeance, in prompting at least immediate actions in combat. Yet remarkably little systematic work has been done on the role of such emotions in stimulating and sustaining conflict and war, despite its prevalence in popular discussions and media punditry, which often revolve around representations of outrage and appropriate responses to such ostensible violations. Part of the reason for this may be precisely because most discussions of these phenomena emerge from anecdotal evidence, or from within narrative, experiential or qualitative traditions which deeply explore particular events, experiences and individuals.

Certainly, emotion can prove tricky to examine in any systematic way, particularly under conditions of extreme stress and urgent time pressure, such as combat. However, psychologists have a long and esteemed tradition of systematically investigating the manifestation and function of emotion across a wide variety of individuals in many circumstances through the use of experimental methods. Political scientists and scholars of IR can adapt these methods to novel avenues of inquiry in productive ways. Such methods can provide new insights into the emotional mechanisms and motivations which infiltrate decisions about conflict on the part of leaders, and the conduct of war on the part of combatants.

This chapter begins with a discussion of how experiments involving emotional phenomena have been, and can be, conducted, privileging previous work examining politically oriented topics. It remains noteworthy at this point that such work primarily involves the role of emotion in voting behaviour, with relatively little exploring the role of emotion in conflict settings, probably because of the conceptual difficulty of designing such studies in a laboratory setting and the logistical challenges of attempting to undertake such work in a field setting. Second, strategies for employing experimental methods to achieve a clearer and deeper understanding of the nature and role of emotion in structured conflict will be outlined. Emotion can be analysed as either an independent or dependent variable, and these topics will be treated independently.

There are many valid ways to study emotion, and experiments provide one powerful method by which to do so, although by no means the only one. However, experiments can provide useful traction and insight where other methods have more limited utility. Experiments allow observers to make generalisations about those aspects of human behaviour which may represent patterns of behaviour common to many, although certainly not all, people. Such regularities give us insight into the ways in which we all share a common humanity and have universal cognitive mechanisms, similar to the way that all healthy people can see and hear (Brown 2004); although each individual may see and hear different things in different ways, the process of how sensation translates into perception works remarkably similarly in most healthy people. Other methods, especially those derived from and espousing narrative and qualitative forms, offer unique insights into individual experience and provide critical information about the ways people differ. But both aspects of human nature are important to understand: how we are the same, and how we are different. While experiments provide unparalleled value in examining the more universal aspects of human behaviour, they can also provide insight into the ways in which each individual provides a unique contribution to, and perspective on, the world. Thus, in many ways, this chapter is intended as both an introduction to and a defence of the value of including experiments as one of many potential methods for studying the importance of emotion in generating and sustaining conflict.

## Previous experimental work with emotion in politics

As noted above, most work on the role of emotion in politics has not employed experimental methods, and has engaged more qualitative and case study kinds of investigations (Marcus 2002; Petersen 2002; Goodwin *et al.* 2009). Of course, this fact in no ways detracts from the value and importance of this work. Goodwin *et al.* (2009) provide insight into the role of emotion in social movements, and Petersen offers a brilliant and original analysis into the critical function of emotion in ethnic conflict in the Balkans. Such studies are very valuable in understanding how particular individuals or groups respond to specific circumstances or stresses. However, they do not always provide a basis for understanding the most general patterns of human emotional response, mentioned above. Some researchers may not find the pursuit of such tendencies to be valuable, while others do. But one of the values of understanding such general patterns resides in the ability to begin to understand and analyse the relationships between particular institutions, such as democracy, capitalism or authoritarianism, and people's emotional welfare under such conditions. Such recognition can begin to help establish a baseline for comparisons across political structures and institutions, and hopefully can eventually help guide strategies for intervention and remediation to help alleviate suffering caused, at least in part, and social ills and political structures that are not conducive to human welfare. Research that focuses on a particular place or phenomenon can be more difficult to generalise into such patterns because it remains so specific to a particular time, place or instigating circumstance. But such work remains essential for generating ideas about which emotions tend to arise in most people under particular circumstances. Sometimes such insights may seem obvious, as for example observers might note that those subject to oppression and discrimination may become angry and depressed. But further investigation may help uncover which particular precipitating circumstances make certain kinds of people more likely to react in one way as opposed to another. For example, those without power may be more likely to react with fear in the face of threat, while those with wealth may be more likely to react with anger. Once certain relationships suggest themselves through systematic observation, those basic mechanisms underlying emotional reactions to conflict can then be further interrogated, using various methodologies investigating different kinds of people in different kinds of circumstances. Yet often the study of emotion in war and other conflict studies skips over the analysis of patterns and seeks primarily the interpretation of individual and anecdotal experience. While essential to help describe and understand personal experience, such research is not able to tell us as much about how people in general respond to such experiences, and thus offers us very little in the way of policy prescriptions that might prove appropriate for broad swatches of people in conflict-ridden societies. Indeed, one of the benefits of employing experimental methodology is that it allows investigators to investigate exactly which aspect of emotion they believe might be driving certain outcomes, and through careful specification and operationalisation, experimentalists can begin to identify some of the emotional regularities that help shape human responses to various conditions and circumstances.

With this goal in mind, some experimental work involving the role of emotion in politics has been conducted. Early work in this area examined voter reactions to non-verbal aspects of candidates. Sullivan and Masters (1988), for example, used videotapes of candidates in the 1984 presidential election to study the role of candidates' facial expressions in voters' responses. They found that voters were more affected by candidates' facial expressions than more standard variables such as party identification or issue position.

Additional work revolved primarily around the role of emotion in campaign advertising and mass voting behaviour. For example, Ted Brader (2005) conducted a series of experiments to explore how music and images in political ads elicited particular emotions in voters. Specifically, he argued that evoking enthusiasm increased voter participation and reinforced existing loyalties, while stimulating fear increased voter vigilance, thus making persuasion more possible. Further experimental exploration of the role of these emotions in voting was conducted by Valentino *et al.* (2008). Their study showed that people did not really understand how emotions affected themselves very well at all; while claiming that anxiety, enthusiasm and anger all increased their attention, anger actually decreased the amount of information that voters sought. In a second experiment, they found that while political threats triggered many emotions, only anxiety increased the amount of information voters sought.

While most experimental investigations of the role of emotion in politics have concentrated on voting behaviour, two national field experiments conducted by psychologists have examined the influence of fear and anger on attitudes toward terrorism (Lerner *et al.* 2003; Small *et al.* 2006). In the first of these provocative and important studies, Lerner *et al.* (2003) experimentally primed the specific emotions of fear and anger in almost 1,000 people in a nationally representative sample. They found that fear increased people's perceived sense of risk and their plans for taking precautionary measures in the wake of those perceptions, while anger induced the opposite response. In addition, they noted that differences in emotional responses accounted for between 60 and 80% of the sex differences, showing that men had lower perceptions of risk than women. In addition, they demonstrated that emotional responses predicted public policy preferences. Later work (Small *et al.* 2006) found that triggering anger produced more causal attributions regarding the terrorist attacks on 11 September 2001 than priming sadness (see also Holland, Chapter 13 in this volume).

Druckman and McDermott (2008) conducted a more conceptual experiment to explore the role of specific emotions on the framing of risk choices. They found that specific emotions significantly influenced an individual's likelihood of taking risks and, depending on the emotion, acted to either enhance or suppress the influence of gains and losses framing on risky choices. In addition, they found that the context of choice, whether the individual was making a choice about money or life-and-death decisions, affected the influence of emotion as well.

Interesting and important work exploring the role of emotion in political phenomena has also taken place outside the realm of political science, but is worth mentioning for the promise it provides regarding the possibilities for both interdisciplinary collaboration and the employment of novel new technologies and methodologies to explore emotional phenomena of interest. Two examples suffice to demonstrate some of the significant new areas of inquiry in this regard. First, using ultimatum games derived from behavioral economics experiments, Xiao and Houser (2005) found that the ability to express negative emotions significantly reduced the likelihood that a responder would pay to punish a proposer who offered an unfair split. These findings are significant because they demonstrate that one of the functions of sanctions and punishments is to convey emotional information; if political and social structures can be devised which would allow for the expression of such emotions, the consequences of such negative consequences might be reduced. Indeed, the function of truth and reconciliation commissions following genocides and other forms of discrimination may provide such an outlet, although it appears likely that such expression may harm individuals by re-traumatising them through testimony, just as it may help heal larger societal fissures.

Westen *et al.* (2006) used MRI technology to explore the reactions of 30 committed political partisans in the 2004 US presidential election to information that threatened their own candidate, the opposing candidate or a neutral control. By demonstrating that different parts of the brain are activated in so-called motivated reasoning tasks, they showed that judgements involving strong emotional elements are qualitatively distinct from other kinds of reasoning and judgement.

## Strategies for experimenting with emotions

Various strategies exist for experimenting with emotion, but it is critically important first to theoretically differentiate whether emotions are being explored as an independent or a dependent variable. In addition, while some early work on the role of emotion tended to explore emotion in a valenced manner, meaning whether emotions are simply positive or negative in a general or global sense, the bulk of evidence clearly suggests that the investigation of discrete emotions, meaning the investigation of specific emotions such as anger or fear, provides greater specificity and traction in understanding the role and function of emotion in judgement, information processing, perception and other critical evaluative tasks (for a comprehensive review see Clore and Huntsinger 2007).

When emotions are being investigated as an independent variable, scholars seek to examine the particular impact of a specific emotion, for example fear or anger, on some particular outcome, such as vote choice or the endorsement of a particular public policy. In order to do so, psychologists often try to induce, prime or otherwise manipulate the emotion or mood of interest in subjects in order to examine its effects on outcomes of interest. Early work in this tradition used emotionally laden movies to examine the effect of emotion on interpersonal attraction (Gouaux 1971).

There are a variety of strategies the psychologists currently employ in order to manipulate emotion in subjects (Coan and Allen 2007). These can be roughly divided into those which utilise introspective techniques and those which involve reactive techniques. Introspective techniques often ask subjects to write in detail about an event from their past life that made them feel a certain way (e.g. really angry), encouraging them to recall as much detail about the circumstances and event as possible. Other introspective techniques include asking subjects to describe how a particular object or person makes them feel, or the use of hypnosis. Reactive techniques include exposing subjects to various stimuli, such as movies, images or music, or giving them gifts or food, or having confederates interact with them in a particular way designed to elicit a specific emotion. One of the complications of reactive techniques is that they often elicit numerous or blended emotions, such as fear *and* anger, so it can be difficult to elicit clear and specific emotions for interrogation.

The most common or useful strategy may depend on the emotion desired. For example, candy seems to work well to induce happiness, whereas music and movies tend to work better for eliciting sadness, fear or anger. Studies have examined which movies or music work best to manipulate certain emotions, and helpful lists can provide experimenters with various options (Coan and Allen 2007).

If scholars are interested in investigating emotion as a dependent variable, then the goal is to examine the influence of other variables, such as campaign advertisements, on particular emotional responses. So, for example, an experiment might examine the influence of particular images or music on vote choice in a hypothetical election. Under these conditions, experimenters need careful measures of emotional states. Some investigators use feeling thermometers to measure how positive (warm) or negative (cold) a particular stimulus makes a respondent feel. Some of these indications can take place in real time, as subjects turn a knob up or down while watching video feed, for example. In experiments where specific emotions become the dependent variable, it is critical for experimenters to obtain careful emotion ratings from subjects so that effects can be analysed in response to the specific independent variable being examined.

Regardless of whether emotions are being examined as independent or dependent variables, manipulation checks remain crucial in order to measure the effects properly. Some subjects may be more dispositionally inclined than others toward experiencing a particular emotion, such as fear, as a basic trait state, and thus may be more strongly reactive than others to threat-based stimuli (Hatemi *et al.* 2013). Because of this possibility, it is critically important that scholars control for baseline levels of emotional response, so that those with high levels of some emotion are not treated the same as those with low levels of reactivity; such conflation can hide significant findings by making overall effects wash out in analysis. Baseline levels simply refer to those individual differences in the underlying propensity a given person has to experience a particular emotion, for example. In many, although certainly not all, cases there are indications that such tendencies are genetically influenced (Hatemi and McDermott 2012). This process is similar to what might colloquially be considered 'temperament', for example, if someone is considered 'highly strung', although its aspects are explored in much greater specificity in genetic studies. For experimental purposes, it is simply important to realise that it will take much less of some particular stimuli, such as threat, for certain individuals to react than others. This can be controlled for in the analysis as long as measures that assess such baseline levels for the relevant outcome are ascertained prior to the manipulation in the experiment.

## Experimenting with emotions in war

So how can scholars of IR and basic conflict processes traction these methods to investigate phenomena of interest in a way that might generalise more broadly than the valuable studies of individual experiences and events which tend to dominate the existing literature on the role of emotion in, for example, combat? And why would experimentalists want to undertake such a task?

To be absolutely clear, there are as many ways to design an experiment properly as there are well trained experimentalists. There is no single right or best way to undertake experimental design. In many ways, it is up to the experimenter to design a study that investigates the particular relationships and dynamics they are most interested in understanding. Although it may be difficult to design studies of large phenomena in a laboratory setting, it is important to keep in mind that no single study demonstrates the entirety of any given phenomenon. Rather, replication across populations and domains provides the context and boundary conditions for any experimental demonstration, regardless of substantive area of inquiry. In addition, experimental methods both allow and encourage the exploration of micro-foundational processes whose effect can be aggregated over time across experimental conditions and designs. Calving off parts of a given phenomenon does not make their experimental demonstration any less important or significant, even if on first glance they may appear more sterile. What is important is psychologically engaging subjects in a meaningful manner so that investigators can uncover the underlying psychological mechanisms driving a particular outcome or process.

When such experiments are conducted in field settings, logistical, ethical and practical constraints may limit the ability of investigators to explore all the phenomena of interest. However, it may be possible to examine one particular area of interest at a time. As with laboratory experiments, for effective and clear results to be achieved, it is critically important for experimenters to start small, and build from areas of experience and knowledge to develop simple and clean designs which can explore a central dynamic of interest. In studying the influence of emotion on war and combat, it may be necessary, over time, to establish relationships with relevant governmental or military contacts and organisations in order to gain access to the populations of interest, as well as the most relevant conditions of investigation. Not everyone will be able to do this, or want to undertake such a challenge, but that does not mean such avenues are impossible or necessarily illegitimate. For example, if one wants to study the effect of combat exposure on the development of post-traumatic stress disorder, and to investigate the relative efficacy of various strategies designed to treat such trauma, then it becomes important to investigate those symptoms among people who are suffering either as a result of combat or as victims of war, rather than simply employing college sophomores as subjects.

In addition, whether experiments are conducted in a laboratory or field setting, human subjects' constraints clearly can and should constrain the intensity of emotion that investigators can elicit from them. However, this does not mean that carefully and cleverly designed experiments cannot explore the dynamics involved in eliciting emotions and observing their consequences.

## Trade-offs in the design of real-world experiments

One of the first questions in designing an experiment investigating the role of various emotions in conflict settings inquires whether a laboratory or a field experiment would be most conducive to discovering or investigating a proposed relationship. Each kind of study carries with it associated expected costs and benefits, which are described below.

In a laboratory setting, it is possible to obtain great control, at the typical cost of external validity. For example, if someone is studying the role of combat in the development of post-traumatic stress disorder, it becomes extremely important to recognise that the population who self-select into the military may differ in important ways from the civilian population, making generalisability to populations that suffer trauma for other reasons, such as the result of sexual assault, much less likely. This does not mean that general patterns do not exist or cannot be discovered, but rather indicates that researchers must be especially sensitive to the boundary conditions to which any given phenomenon is assumed to be relevant. While some may argue that this recognition highlights the importance of individual experience, this insight does not mitigate against the reality that public health and public policy demands often require that best practices be instituted in a cost-effective way. Uncovering treatment options that work best for most people suffering from a particular kind of trauma has real-world value, both for the individual who is suffering, as well as for the society responsible for their care which must nonetheless meet other social obligations under conditions of limited resources.

Experiments conducted in the field offer more real-world ecological validity, which is to say that some experiments do a better job than others of mirroring the phenomena that individuals encounter in their everyday life. One of the issues in experimental design relates to how well the experiment looks like the real world. However, such aspects of so-called mundane realism are much less important than might appear at first blush. Instead, what matters is creating an experimental environment that genuinely engages subjects psychologically in ways that mimic their experience of similar dynamics in other parts of their life. Establishing experimental realism in this way is much more important for investigating the psychological processes by which individuals perceive, interpret and respond to their world. For example, Shanto Iyengar tells the evocative story of conducting some of his early experiments on the effect of negative advertising on voter choice. He worked diligently to create realistic living rooms in malls in southern California, complete with couches, coffee tables and remote controls for the televisions that were going to show the advertisements whose effects he wanted to evaluate. But, because his experiment was so effective in creating mundane realism, people did what they do in real life: when the ads came on, they used the remote to change the channel, thus making it impossible to examine the effect of the negative ads. It was only by creating an environment with slightly less mundane realism that he was able to truly create experimental realism to see how subjects responded when they did engage with negative advertising. In this way, it is important to try and create an experimental environment that is valid to the local cultural and social ecology in which it takes place; this is the goal and value of striving to achieve ecological validity in experimental design. However, field experiments often risk losing control over the specific areas of inquiry, so that someone studying the effect of fear on the development of trauma may have a hard time separating out its effect from that of anger, which may often co-exist in conflict situations in real-world populations. That does not mean such studies should not be conducted, but rather that researchers need to remain sensitive to the specific mechanisms they hope to investigate so that contamination does not threaten their ability to discern any meaningful findings.

## Conclusions

Emotions infuse our lives with richness, texture and great complexity. From a psychological perspective, most studies in political contexts have been largely restricted to the role of emotions in voting behaviour, although some limited anecdotal work has also examined how emotion can affect leaders' choices in IR. Barbara Farnham's study of Franklin Roosevelt's decision to side with the British in World War II following the Munich Crisis is one such example (Farnham 2000). Although qualitative and case study examinations of the role of emotion in politics prove invaluable for understanding particular events and for generating hypotheses about the causal nature of those relationships, they prove limited in their ability to provide systematic evidence designed to uncover the specific mechanisms at play in such dynamics.

Experiments offer the possibility of examining the causal relationships between emotions and both the precipitating and sequential factors involved in war and combat. In this way, experiments involving emotions can situate them as either independent or dependent variables for investigation. Although challenging, careful design can allow investigators to explore what events produce particular emotions, such as how particular classes of grievance generate the desire for vengeance and revenge; or how specific emotions, such as fear or anger, can produce predictable effects, making compromise and negotiation more or less likely. In addition, such work can help explore related phenomena, such as dispositional differences in baseline emotions, and how these levels relate to particular choices, judgements or evaluations. Even if people behave differently in the face of fear, each individual enters the world with a very different proclivity for experiencing it; it may take very little to frighten some people and a lot to scare someone else. Such baseline differences in propensity can exert meaningful and significant differences in the political positions people espouse. For example, Hatemi *et al.* (2013) find that genetically informed differences in fear disposition significantly affect individuals' attitudes toward outgroups as measured by their feelings toward immigration policy. Extensions might also explore how sex differences in fear and anger produce predictable differences in policy positions not only regarding war and peace, but also regarding other public policy positions, for example those related to such topics as capital punishment. While such notions clearly remain gendered, and feminist literature has important critiques of this (Enloe 2000), earlier research showing that women are more likely to experience fear while men are more likely to experience anger may help explain higher support for war among men (Shapiro and Maharjan 1986), at least in part (Gault and Sabini 2000). Precisely because anger leads to optimism in ways that fear does not, angry people may be more confident of victory in the face of conflict (Lerner and Keltner 2001).

Experiments may not have been, nor are they likely to become, a dominant method of inquiry in the study of emotions. That fact, however, does not vanquish their utility for investigating deep and important emotional phenomena, even in those issues related to conflict, combat and trauma. The value of experiments lies in their ability to uncover and demonstrate systematic causal relationships which may transcend particular populations, areas or circumstances. Of course, not every response will show such a pattern, but that is part of the value of experimentation. Observers can begin to uncover which patterns appear more general and which seem to be more unique. Both recognitions are important depending on one's goal, and certainly very different types of research strategy can complement each other in examining diverse aspects of the same phenomena, or by approaching similar topics from divergent methodological perspectives. But where larger-scale public policy intervention is desired, large-scale data on efficacy are often required to justify expense, and this is where experiments can shine. Certainly, experiments cannot demonstrate every unique aspect of experience, but neither can unique individuals allow us to generalise experiences in ways that provide insight into those aspects of common humanity we all share. Because experiments traction control and manipulation to isolate influential factors, findings can produce generalisable regularities in human behaviour as well as determine the boundary conditions for their operation by domain or population. They can help identify the micro-foundational mechanisms and processes which serve to support and sustain the larger behaviour we witness and observe. By offering a technique by which it becomes possible to break down complex phenomena into component parts, experiments allow investigators to begin to discover the psychological factors that undergird the political outcomes we seek to understand. And, hopefully, such understanding can help provide a foundation for the kind of effective change which can help alleviate suffering and promote human wellbeing.

## Bibliography

Brader, T. (2005) 'Striking a responsive chord: How political ads motivate and persuade voters by appealing to emotions', *American Journal of Political Science*, 49(2): 388–405.

Brown, D. E. (2004) 'Human universals, human nature and human culture', *Daedalus*, 133(4): 47–54.

Clore, G. L. and Huntsinger, J. R. (2007) 'How emotions inform judgment and regulate thought', *Trends in Cognitive Sciences*, 11(9): 393–399.

Coan, J. A. and Allen, J. J. B. (eds) (2007) *Handbook of Emotion Elicitation and Assessment*. New York: Oxford.

Druckman, J. N. and McDermott, R. (2008) 'Emotion and the framing of risky choice', *Political Behavior*, 30(3): 297–321.

Enloe, C. H. (2000) *Bananas, Beaches and Bases: Making Feminist Sense of International Politics*. Berkeley, CA: University of California Press.

Farnham, B. (2000) *Roosevelt and the Munich Crisis*. Princeton, NJ: Princeton University Press.

Gault, B. A. and Sabini, J. (2000) 'The roles of empathy, anger, and gender in predicting attitudes toward punitive, reparative, and preventative public policies', *Cognition and Emotion*, 14(4): 495–520.

Gouaux, C. (1971) 'Induced affective states and interpersonal attraction', *Journal of Personality and Social Psychology*, 20: 37–43.

Goodwin, J., Jasper, J. M. and Polletta, F. (eds) (2009) *Passionate Politics: Emotions and Social Movements*. Chicago, IL: University of Chicago Press.

Hatemi, P. K. and McDermott, R. (2012) 'The genetics of politics: discovery, challenges, and progress', *Trends in Genetics*, 28(10): 525–533.

Hatemi, P., McDermott, R., Eaves, L., Kendler, K., Neale, M. and Hatemi, P. K. (2013) 'Fear dispositions, attachment and out-group political preferences', *American Journal of Political Science*, 57(2): 279–293.

Lerner, J. S. and Keltner, D. (2001) 'Fear, anger, and risk', *Journal of Personality and Social Psychology*, 81(1): 146.

Lerner, J. S., Gonzalez, R. M., Small, D. A. and Fischhoff, B. (2003) 'Effects of fear and anger on perceived risks of terrorism: A national field experiment', *Psychological Science*, 14(2): 144–150.

Marcus, G. E. (2002) *The Sentimental Citizen: Emotion in Democratic Politics*. University Park, PA: Penn State University Press.

Petersen, M. B. (2010) 'Distinct emotions, distinct domains: Anger, anxiety and perceptions of intentionality', *Journal of Politics*, 72(2): 357–365.

Petersen, R. D. (2002) *Understanding Ethnic Violence: Fear, Hatred, and Resentment in Twentieth-Century Eastern Europe*. Cambridge: Cambridge University Press.

Small, D. A., Lerner, J. S. and Fischhoff, B. (2006) 'Emotion priming and attributions for terrorism: Americans' reactions in a national field experiment', *Political Psychology*, 27(2): 289–298.

Shapiro, R. Y. and Mahajan, H. (1986) 'Gender differences in policy preferences: A summary of trends from the 1960s to the 1980s', *Public Opinion Quarterly*, 50(1): 42–61.

Sullivan, D. G. and Masters, R. D. (1988) '"Happy warriors": Leaders' facial displays, viewers' emotions, and political support', *American Journal of Political Science*, 32: 345–368.

Valentino, N. A., Hutchings, V. L., Banks, A. J. and Davis, A. K. (2008) 'Is a worried citizen a good citizen? Emotions, political information seeking, and learning via the Internet', *Political Psychology*, 29(2): 247–273.

Wagner, J. D., Flinn, M. V. and England, B. G. (2002) 'Hormonal response to competition among male coalitions', *Evolution and Human Behavior*, 23(6): 437–442.

Westen, D., Blagov, P. S., Harenski, K., Kilts, C. and Hamann, S. (2006) 'Neural bases of motivated reasoning: An fMRI study of emotional constraints on partisan political judgment in the 2004 US presidential election', *Journal of Cognitive Neuroscience*, 18(11): 1947–1958.

Xiao, E. and Houser, D. (2005) 'Emotion expression in human punishment behavior', *Proceedings of the National Academy of Sciences, USA*, 102(20): 7398–7401.

# Part II

# Emotionality and War

# 9 Compassionate soldiering and comfort

*Julia Welland*

Compassion is an emotion that opens up the one who experiences it to another's suffering. It is an emotion that positions the experiencer in direct relation with another and gives rise to a desire to alleviate that suffering, to engage in what Carol Gilligan (1982) might call an 'ethic of care'. As a sentiment that entails a revelation of vulnerability, an opening up of subjectivity, and an engagement in empathetic relations, feminists and non-feminists alike have aligned compassion as a distinctly 'feminine' emotion. Elided with experiences of nurturing and care-giving associated with motherhood (for example see Ruddick 1983), such relational emotions and practices are understood as anathema to the more autonomous, rational and reasoning masculine subject. As an emotion, therefore, compassion is productive of, and enters into, relations that are profoundly 'unmasculine'. It is an emotion that, for these reasons, has been conventionally understood as 'outside' the (assumed masculine) soldiering experience.[1] In order for soldiers to effectively fight wars and engage in the bloody and brutal violence that combat entails, soldiers dehumanise the enemy – they make him (and it is nearly always a 'him') an object, a thing, that they have no connection with, no relation to – and, along Cartesian lines, disassociate their emotional selves from their physical enactments. This is seen in the linguistic turning of people into 'targets',[2] obscenely in the dismembering and collecting of killed enemy body parts,[3] and in soldiers' attestations in the aftermath of a battle 'that training took over'; that their physical body went through the motions of combat, while their mind, their emotional self, was disconnected from the events.[4]

However, as counterinsurgency – 'COIN' – was initiated as the formal military doctrine for all International Security Assistance Force (ISAF)[5] troops in Afghanistan, soldiering underwent something of a shift. One described by Patrick Hennessey, a former officer in the British Army, as a shift from a way of fighting wars that sought to 'DESTROY and NEUTRALIZE' (2012: 12) the enemy, to one that wins local 'hearts and minds'. Taking place against a background of an imperilled local population – in particular, an imperilled *female* population – victimised by the Taliban, COIN represents a strategic and tactical shift that no longer views military destruction of the enemy as a goal in its own right. Instead, soldiers are required to live amongst the local population, to engage in dialogue with them, and to be capable of 'see[ing] issues and actions from the perspective of the domestic population' (Aylwin-Foster 2005: 4). In short, soldiers are now expected to engage in empathetic and, as we will see, compassionate relations with those they have been sent to protect. Claire Duncanson, writing about British militarised masculinities in Iraq and Afghanistan, points to instances of a 'peacebuilding masculinity' being constructed: a masculinity enacted through interactions with Iraqi and Afghan allied soldiers and civilians, and 'through relations of equality, empathy, care, respect and recognition of similarities and shared experiences' (2013: 148–9) – a compassionate militarised masculinity. Meanwhile, a cursory glance through the proliferation of 'TiC-lit' (troops-in-combat literature), which has appeared in recent years, reveals compassion as a central framing device for soldiers' reasoning and desire for involvement in Afghanistan and their experiences while there. Speaking to journalist Sean Rayment about the UK's military involvement in Afghanistan, Guardsman David Walton states: 'It's not often in life that you really get a chance to help people and defend the country, and that's what I think we are doing here' (cited in Rayment 2011: 108). Sergeant Doug Beattie, in his first memoir of his time in Afghanistan, writes that it is the 'idea that you are doing what is right, that you are helping people' that keeps you going during battle (2009: 180). Have we then witnessed the onset of compassionate war? Not only war that seeks to alleviate the suffering of others as humanitarian intervention and 'Responsibility to Protect' does, but the continuation or 'next step' in the waging of liberal war: war enacted not only for compassionate *reasons*, but enacted through compassionate *actions*. Wars where it is not guns and bullets that are deployed, but empathetic relations. Wars where soldiers wearing the ISAF badge open themselves up and share the vulnerability and suffering of others.

I want to critically engage with this idea of a soldier as a compassionate actor, and detail what happens to war when we read it through a discourse of compassion. Following Lauren Berlant, I do not engage in a critique of compassion to befoul it, rather, 'the project of critique seeks not to destroy its object but to explain the dynamics of its [operations,] optimism and exclusions' (2004: 5). This chapter 'works against the desire for the good to feel simple'. For 'there is nothing simple about compassion apart from the desire for it to be taken as simple' (ibid.: 7). Compassion, as will be revealed, is an emotion that can obscure, it is an emotion that can divert attention, and despite implying social relations and connections between the spectator and sufferer, compassion can separate, divide and redraw boundaries. The first section of this chapter addresses the ways in which an announcement of compassion can work to conceal the ongoing violence and obscenity of war. The tension between soldiers' proclamations of wanting to help others and the centrality of violence and kinetic operations to counterinsurgency is explored via the contrast between individual acts of compassion ISAF soldiers show towards the enemy they are fighting, and the unremitting use of airpower against enemy positions. The section ends with a discussion on how an assertion of compassion can work to interpellate the asserter as a 'good' and virtuous political subject. The second section shifts from focusing on the operation of compassion as an emotion felt on behalf of another, to the operation of compassion as suffering alongside another. Through this operation, attention is redirected, both towards the feelings and sensations of compassion itself, and through the appropriation of another's suffering, in order to make sense of a soldier's own. In both these operations, compassion functions as a comforting device; comfort, however, not for those it is proclaimed to be directed towards, but a device of comfort for those who profess to experience it on behalf or in tandem with another.

## Compassion as concealment

When military intervention comes to be understood through the prism of compassion, it elicits something of a 'writing out', or at least an obscuring, of the simultaneous presence of weaponry, violence and death. For while Afghanistan may have been framed as a conflict that was, in the words of Richard Dannatt[6], about 'help[ing] people less fortunate than ourselves' (Dannatt 2011: 14), it remains a conflict that at least partially took place through the firing of bullets, the dropping of bombs, and the killing and maiming of enemy others. Thus, alongside soldiers' desires to 'do good' and their attempts to empathise with the local population, the Afghan security forces, and even the Taliban enemy, are references to the brutality of combat, the continued use of airstrikes, and the sheer amount of firepower deployed. For despite the 2006 hopes of former Secretary of State for Defence John Reid that British troops would leave Helmand, southern Afghanistan 'without a single shot being fired' (cited in Harding 2008), this was a conflict that witnessed the disgorging of an immense amount of bullets, bombs and other ordnance. In the year following John Reid's statement of hope for a peaceful, non-violent tour of duty, British troops expelled 2,020,000 SA80 assault rifle rounds, 1,830,000 general-purpose machine gun rounds, and 25,000 artillery shells alone (Harding 2008). 'TiC-lit', too, tells story after story of intense gun battles, with empty bullet magazines falling around the soldiers involved and numerous airstrikes enacted on enemy positions. Leo Docherty, a former captain in the British Army, recalls an American Forward Operating Base calling in a total of thirteen 500 lb bombs after being caught in enemy fire and suffering two fatalities. Docherty describes this display of firepower as 'an incredible amount of destructive ordnance' (2007: 74). Beattie meanwhile writes, in a memoir dominated by recollections of airstrikes, that '[t]he ability to call in such destructive [air]power was something I had been doing regularly since day one' (2009: 187).

One specific way this tension between soldiers' compassionate rhetoric and the continuing violent (re)enactment of war is rendered visible is in the relations soldiers have with enemy fighters who they come into direct contact with and fight with from afar. Claire Duncanson (2013) draws attention to the ways in which enemy soldiers are not always simply dehumanised, noting that most British soldiers who have penned memoirs of their time spent fighting in Afghanistan 'express admiration and respect for the insurgents they are fighting' (2013: 108) at least some of the time. Corporeal Dean Fisher exclaims, 'They've got bigger balls than what I have … The amount of firepower we put down, we completely blitzed on them, but they still kept coming' (cited in Duncanson 2013: 108), while Lieutenant Colonel Stuart Tootal, watching a Taliban fighter receiving medical treatment on badly shot legs, is reminded of 'what hard bastards these people are' (Tootal 2009: 74). There are also attempts to situate and contextualise why some Afghan men may choose to fight alongside the Taliban. As Duncanson states:

> Some soldiers grasp that fighters are not always evil incarnate or Islamic fundamentalists, but often just ordinary people, fighting because there are few alternative ways of making a living, because of a sense of a need to defend their land and livelihoods, or out of a sense of revenge.
>
> (Duncanson 2013: 108)

Seeing enemy fighters as brave soldiers, and thus how British soldiers themselves would like to be viewed, or seeing the enemy as 'ordinary people', is a crucial step in being able to experience empathy for them, and it is through these perspectives that compassionate acts take place. Compassionate acts such as the injured Taliban fighter treated by a British military medic witnessed by Tootal, above; or Beattie removing the plastic cuffs from a captured and dying member of the Taliban: 'If he was going to die in a strange place, surrounded by the faces of his enemy, then at least he was going to have a degree of dignity' (Beattie 2009: 142).[7]

However, this compassion experienced and demonstrated towards individual enemy fighters with whom soldiers come into contact – recognition of their bravery, contextualising their reasons for fighting, and treating them with respect and dignity – is seemingly absent in both the sheer amount of airpower called in and soldiers' jubilation, even pleasure, in the destruction wrought by 'direct hits'. What compassion is there in the continued dropping of 500 lb, 1,000 lb and 2,000 lb bombs on enemy targets? What compassion is there in the 'sense of exhilaration and power' (ibid.: 119) experienced in the aftermath of an airstrike, or in '[t]otting up the limbs' to count the number of dead insurgents: 'The more the better' (ibid.: 267)? When soldiers proclaim themselves as compassionate actors, and simultaneously engage or take pleasure in the wreaking of such destructive power, compassion can be understood as having two interrelated functions.

Firstly, and as authors such as Derek Gregory have pointed out, when soldiers and soldiering are 'softened' and presented as a caring profession – 'armed social work' (Gregory 2010: 165) – the continuing reliance on and centrality of kinetic force and physical violence to counterinsurgency practices is concealed. In presentations of COIN, the focus tends to be the rhetoric of 'hearts and minds', tales of senior military figures engaging in *shuras* [8] with village elders, and individual soldiers' desires to 'do good' and help those understood as less fortunate than themselves. That the underside of hearts and minds doctrine is destructive and obscene violence, that engagement with the local population may amount to intelligence gathering which will later be used to launch strikes and plan attacks, and that 'doing good' may involve the dropping of bombs, is rarely considered for any length of time. Secondly, and connected, continued and seemingly contradictory proclamations of compassion by soldiers who also kill and wound may also work to remap and rearticulate a soldier as innocent; to reiterate him or her as a caring, ethical and compassionate actor. There appears something of a desire for the compassion proclaimed to be felt by soldiers to smooth over the tensions that emerge between a soldier's empathetic assertions, and their violent and destructive actions. As Berlant has written, 'we like our positive emotions to feel well intentioned and we like our good intentions to constitute the meaning of our acts' (2004: 5–6). In short, it matters not so much what soldiers *do*, but that they *mean* to do well and to not cause harm. Compassion, a 'positive, world-building social relation' (ibid.: 7), is a seductive emotion. It is an emotion that feels good to unthinkingly engage with, and to proclaim to feel.

To profess compassion, to declare the empathy you feel for others, is to announce your own virtue, your own engagement with and connection to a positive social relation. It is not only to assume to do good, but to feel good. However, to identify as compassionate is also to utter an interpellative performative statement. Drawing on Judith Butler's theoretical appropriation of Louis Althusser's (2001 [1971]) use of interpellation as the 'hailing' of an individual into a subject, my use of the term 'interpellative performative statement' denotes an utterance that appears as descriptive, but actually works to produce that which it names. Butler uses the example of the moment a newborn infant shifts 'from an "it" to a "she" or a "he", and in that naming, the girl is "girled", brought into the domain of language and kinship through the *interpellation* of gender' (1993: 7, my emphasis). The interpellative statement, 'it's a girl!' does not merely describe the sex/gender of the infant, but produces the infant as a (feminine) gendered subject. As Butler has stated elsewhere, there is 'no doer behind the deed': a 'doer' is constructed in and through the deed (Butler 1999 [1990]: 195). Thus to proclaim your compassion is not merely to describe a pre-existing subjectivity; rather, it is to interpellate and constitute yourself as a compassionate subject. It is then, in the moment of the profession, that a soldier is reconstituted and reiterated as a good and kind subjectivity despite any violences they may have engaged in.

As signalled above, to claim to feel compassion, to engage unthinkingly in its attestations, and to interpellate as a compassionate subject is a highly comforting move. It offers – as use of the word compassion in the religious context during the nineteenth century stressed – 'emotional benefits to the nonsufferer' (Garber 2004: 20). What is uncomfortable, what may be disrupting to who soldiers believe they are, is to confront the possibility that compassion, that good intentions, 'can sometimes be said to be aggressive' (Berlant 2004: 6), or at least have aggressive effects. To do so is not to smooth over the tensions that emerge between a softer and kinder soldier, and the familiar violence s/he (re)enacts, but to confront that tension head-on. Interrogating compassion, or reflecting on its operations, would mean soldiers considering that their experience of the emotion may be more beneficial to themselves than those they are claiming to feel compassion for. It would mean recognising that it is not enough to simply mean to do well, and that good intentions do not always or easily follow through into good effects. It would mean becoming aware of complex intersecting power relations, the legacies of colonialism, and the current workings of the global economy (Duncanson 2013: 103–4) that surround and produce a soldier's encounter with those they then claim to feel compassion for.

## Appropriated and redirected compassion

It is not, however, just that proclamations of compassion can work to obscure and conceal the ongoing physical violence of counterinsurgency. Tracing the etymological roots and history of compassion, its different operations can be revealed. The word itself derives from the Latin *com*, together, and *pati*, to suffer. From the fourteenth to the beginning of the seventeenth century, the word 'was used to describe both *suffering together with one another* … and an emotion felt *on behalf of another who suffers*' (Garber 2004: 20, emphasis in original). The latter description – an emotion felt on behalf of another who suffers – is that which tended to be on display or in operation during the previous section's discussion. In that section, the ways in which soldiers' announcements of compassion worked to both disguise the continuing violence and obscenity of war, and (re)articulate a soldier as a 'good' and innocent actor, was unpacked. As Majorie Garber points to, such a description of compassion is not one that always takes place between equals; rather, it can operate from high to low, hovering somewhere 'between charity and condescension' (ibid.: 20). It is, however, the former description – suffering together with one another – with which this section is primarily concerned. For, despite being an emotion that depends upon an Other for its experience and, at least superficially, places that Other at the centre of its operations, the compassion experienced and declared by soldiers places their selves as the referent subject of and for compassion.

Compassion, as Lawrence Blum (1980) has argued, involves both a difference in the actual situation of the sufferer and compassionate actor, and something of a shared vulnerability to suffering. Summarising his argument, Elizabeth Spelman writes:

> In compassion, I am moved by what *you* are going through, not what *I* am going through, concerned about *your* condition, not about *mine*. At the same time, while I need not have gone through what you have, your

'suffering … is seen as the kind of thing that could happen to anyone, including [my]self insofar as [I] am a human being.

(Spelman 2001: 120, emphasis in original)

So, while compassion is an emotion directed externally, it requires an awareness of the Self and an awareness of a similarity, a connection, between Self and Other. However, one of the hazards of compassion is that a 'compassionate person's attention doesn't necessarily stay fixed on the object of her (sic) compassion and all too easily may roam towards herself as the subject' (ibid.: 161). In effect, the compassion felt for another can easily be redirected *internally*, towards the Self. One way in which this attention may be redirected is toward the compassionate actor's 'interest at excelling at being empathetic or compassionate [and this] dwarfs careful solicitude for the objects of their care' (ibid.: 161). Evidence for such interest in their own internal empathy and compassion is common within the 'TiC-lit' genre, and supports soldiers' attempts at interpellating themselves as compassionate actors. For example, in his memoir, Leo Docherty spends a significant amount of time detailing the 'nation-building' aspect of the British military's involvement in Afghanistan, describing it as sounding 'fascinating and very honourable' (2007: 45). He's visibly excited during an operational briefing, and optimistic about the possibilities of success through a 'comprehensive approach', bringing together not just military capabilities, but governance and development projects. Docherty is 'increasingly thrilled' at his involvement in what he sees as 'an important cutting-edge project' and 'mustard keen on … getting really involved with the Afghans' (ibid.: 48). While Docherty's excitement and unselfconscious desire to 'do good' marks a departure from soldiers who prioritise and valorise combat and the annihilation of the enemy, his attention remains very much internalised and focused on what this means for him and his experience. He takes pleasure in being 'at the epicentre of something so huge, important, maybe even historic' (ibid.: 55), and positions himself, not the Afghan people such nation-building is claiming to assist, as the central figure in his imaginings, picturing himself 'speaking Pashtu and cutting deals with Pashtun tribal elders while drinking tea in the Hindu Kush' (ibid.: 45). It is Docherty's compassion and embodiment as a 'latter-day Great Gamer' (ibid.: 44) that is the focus.

In these extracts we can see both the ways that interpellation operates through time – the ways in which 'interpellation echoes past interpellations' (Butler 1993: 226), and that the 'founding interpellation is reiterated by various authorities and throughout various intervals' (ibid.: 8) – and operates at both individual and group levels. Through this recitational and reiterative process there is a 'setting of the boundary' (ibid.: 8), a subject is performatively (re)produced, even if it is 'always and only provisional' (ibid.: 226). Interpellation thus emerges as a process integral to identity construction more broadly. Who soldiers think they are and what they think they are doing is forged through interpellation: social bonds are formed, subjects become intelligible, and interpellative statements 'bind ... the speakers, as if they spoke in unison across time' (ibid.: 226).

Attention may also roam towards what Spelman has referred to as the 'paradox of appropriation' (2001: 117). The paradox of appropriation refers to the contradiction that exists between what is 'repugnant in so distancing oneself from the experience of others that one cannot see oneself as having anything to do with such an experience', while at the same time, to see 'so much of oneself in another's experience ... one completely obscures the existence of that other subject' (ibid.: 118). Thus, in soldiers' rush to be and to be viewed as compassionate, in their desire to identify with and respond to the local population they encounter, they risk both eliding their own suffering with that of others, and appropriating the experiences of others to such an extent that they erase the fact that these others were indeed the subjects of those experiences. Claire Duncanson has pointed to this tension between soldiers simultaneously empathising with the local population and placing themselves as equal recipients of compassion. Duncanson uses the example of Sergeant Mills reflecting on the devastation caused by the British military in Al Amara in Iraq. Mills recognises the population of Al Amara were 'utterly innocent civilian victims' and the longer the fighting went on 'the more we began to feel for them'. One family in particular are the recipients of Mills' compassion: their house had all but been destroyed by rounds aimed at the British base located nearby, and when Mills went to speak with them, they told him they could not leave as they had 'nowhere else to go'. On hearing this, Mills writes, 'It was no way to live. For them or us' (Mills cited in Duncanson 2013: 151). As Duncanson notes, 'There is care and empathy here; he feels for this family, notes the challenges they face.' However, Duncanson also notes, 'Just when you think that Mills is going to start to question British strategy and even perhaps presence in Iraq, in that "or us" it becomes all about him again' (ibid.: 151). This redirecting of compassion towards the subject who professes to experience it is in evidence in another of the soldier memoirs Duncanson details. Doug Beattie's second memoir charts his return to Afghanistan. As Duncanson states:

> Beattie structures his second book around a little Afghan girl who is wounded and killed by British fire: the story of her death and its effect on him, having just become a grandfather is the prologue to the book and he refers back to her repeatedly.
>
> (ibid.: 116)

In this example, while Beattie is clearly deeply touched by the death of this girl, the focus remains on him – her death is used to structure *his* story about his return to Afghanistan, and her death is framed around its effect on him.

In both these instances, while compassion is felt for the local population, for innocent victims and so-called 'collateral damage', it is all too swiftly repackaged and redirected toward the subject announcing their compassion to an Other. Here it appears that acknowledgement of another's suffering serves primarily to bring attention to the suffering of soldiers. The paradox of appropriation points to the ways that, while this invocation of a shared sense of suffering and hardship is an attempt at common experience and a relation between the compassionate actor and those they encounter, to borrow another's suffering in order to make sense of your own can have other effects. As Spelman asks:

> [W]hat if the borrowers are in fact more like scavengers, interested in the suffering of others not as a way of marking deep and pervasive similarities among suffering humanity and making a case for mutual care, but mainly as a way of trying to garner concern simply for themselves?
> (Spelman 2001: 10)

As a 'scavenger' of suffering, compassion directed externally towards others is useful only insofar as it can be used to highlight a soldier's own experiences of suffering and their own need for compassion. Thus, in today's self-styled compassionate wars, the hardships of Afghan civilians are read through the suffering of our own soldiers – it is a soldier's own death, their own injury, and their own physical and emotional hardships that inform us of Afghans' plight. Despite proclamations of a war fought for those 'less fortunate than ourselves' and enacted against the background of an imperilled local population, it is our own soldiers who remain the referent objects of compassion. Hennessey, in his second memoir –one that focuses explicitly on the Afghan National Army (ANA) rather than exclusively his own experiences – has some self-awareness of this redirected attention. On a return trip to Afghanistan as a 'civvy', Hennessey meets with a number of ANA soldiers he fought alongside during his tour of duty. Excitedly he tells them, 'I wrote a book about you', referring to his first memoir, *The Junior Officers' Reading Club*. However, as Hennessey flicks through the pages of a copy, trying to find some sections to share with them, he realises that he 'hadn't written a book about them at all; like all first-time writers I had just written a book about myself' (2012: 161–2). In returning to his book, his own reflections on his tour of duty, Hennessey becomes all too aware of whom his referent object of attention was.

Not only does this appropriation render all but obsolete the suffering of the local Afghan population, but by presenting a soldier as co-sufferer, whatever role they may play as perpetrator of the misery is obscured (Spelman 2001: 127). That much of the local population's suffering may be as a direct result of the conflict raging in their country, and that soldiers are intimately connected to this, is papered over in soldiers' attestations of compassion and their positioning as equal or comparable victims. And it is here that we can again see the comforting nature of compassion for those who proclaim to experience it. For when compassion operates as 'suffering alongside', and is announced by soldiering subjects, they can again come to understand themselves as innocent and deserving of the comfort compassion brings. Soldiers can understand themselves as not only disconnected from the violence of war, but as the victims, not perpetrators, of it.

## Conclusion

Compassion, an emotion that has at times appeared as antithetical to soldiering and warfare, was at the heart of the conflict in Afghanistan. It was entrenched in counterinsurgency policy that foregrounded the needs of the local population and political rather than military advantage; it was present in our understandings of why the military is fighting a war located thousands of miles away; and it was a central framing device for soldiers engaged in the conflict, helping them make sense of who they thought they were and what they thought they were doing. As has been shown, however, compassion is not a simple or straightforward emotion. While there may be a desire for it to be taken as simple, for it to be understood as a 'positive, world-building social relation', its operations and effects are not so easily understood. For while social relations between subjects are essential for compassion's emergence, its emergence doesn't always or necessarily result in simple and straightforward 'good'. Indeed, when experienced or proclaimed to be experienced in settings marked by highly unequal power relations and violence, compassion may not be concerned with an Other at all. Rather, compassion works as a self-reinforcing, self-rearticulating tool and offers comfort not to those it is claimed to be directed towards, but towards those who profess to experience it.

This chapter has sought not to destroy compassion, but rather to critique its processes. It has detailed two specific operations of compassion in relation to the counterinsurgency war-fighting that took place in Afghanistan and the effects it has. Firstly, when compassion is felt on behalf of another who suffers, when a soldier professes a desire to help others, or when the enemy are humanised and the local population empathised with, it elicits something of a 'writing out' of the continuing violence and obscenity of war. For while compassion may be felt and soldiers may want to do good, in the context of war this is likely to involve the expelling of bullets, the dropping of bombs and a continuation of kinetic operations. Secondly, when compassion operates as suffering alongside another, the emotion can all too easily be redirected away from its initial object of attention. This can take place in two ways: the individual who professes their compassion may become more concerned with excelling at the *feeling* of compassion and empathy, rather than considering those it is supposedly directed toward. Compassion, or rather the suffering in relation to which it is experienced, can also be appropriated through the elision of a soldier's experiences of war with those they claim to feel compassion towards. In these instances, while there is evidence of care and empathy felt towards those Others with whom soldiers come into contact, compassion itself is redirected towards the soldiers while the Afghan population fade from view altogether. It is the physical and emotional hardships of soldiers that signal the plight of local Afghans, and it is soldiers who are deserving of compassion. Compassion directed externally here is useful only insofar as it signals a soldier's own deservingness of it.

What both operations of compassion offer, however, is a degree of comfort. Comfort felt not by those towards whom it is professed to be aimed, but comfort felt by those experiencing the emotion. And while soldiers' announcement of compassion may not be 'genuine', inasmuch as its operations may not reflect its intentions, this interpellative move remains an emotional process at the individual level. For, when soldiers proclaim compassion for another, they not only interpellate themselves as 'good' subjects, but they experience a positive social relation and align themselves with other compassionate (soldiering) actors. Furthermore, the emotional process of claiming to experience compassion allows soldiers to disconnect themselves from the devastation of war, or at least disconnect from their potential complicity in it. Announcing their compassion can even serve to locate them not as perpetrators, but as victims of this devastation. Compassion then is not as simple as caring for others: it can obscure, it can paper over complicity, and it can redirect attention away from those with no choice but to live amongst the horrors of war. When war continues to be waged through strategies and tactics where force and violence remain integral – even when enacted by 'softer' soldiering subjects – we should be wary of claims to compassion and pay careful attention to its operations, effects and exclusions.

## Notes

1 However, in the colonial context, compassion was an essential part of the paternalistic framework that underpinned colonial intervention. Not only was compassion one of the faultlines along which the civilised white European man was distinguished from the barbaric non-white, non-European man, but to be seen to show compassion was integral to constructing the 'image of a lone, dashing Englishman dispensing justice, wisdom and righteous retribution upon his brown subjects' (Rutherford 1997: 13). So while compassion has been considered as disconnected from day-to-day soldiering, its use in the legitimation of violence, occupation and dominance has a long history.

2 Carol Cohn's (1987) writing on the 'war talk' of nuclear defence intellectuals remains seminal to discussions of turning people into targets.

3 For example, the prosecution in 2010 of a number of American soldiers who, as part of a secret 'kill team', murdered unarmed Afghan civilians and collected body parts as 'trophies' (McGreal 2010).

4 Patrick Hennessey, in his memoir of time spent fighting in Afghanistan, recalls that pulling his gun trigger and seeing a Taliban fighter fall back were 'no longer distinct but part of one chain, in which to think about it and will it, is for it to happen'. In the heat of battle – 'completely alone and with no time to think stop or think or wonder' – it dawns on Hennessey 'that we're doing all the things I'd scoffed at in training' (2009: 233, 2012).

5 The UN-mandated international military force created to assist the Afghan government in establishing a secure society. ISAF soldiers were involved with both combat operations and humanitarian missions.

6 Richard Dannatt was Chief of the General Staff, the professional head of the British Army, between 2006 and 2009.

7 While British soldier memoirs tend to construct British military masculinities as 'caring, compassionate and ethical' (Duncanson 2013: 85), the same cannot be said about the portrayal of their Afghan National Army (ANA) counterparts. References abound of ANA soldiers not caring for their fellow men, committing war crimes against captured enemy forces or even the local population, and being less than trustworthy in their relations with the Taliban.

8 The Afghan word for 'consultation': senior ISAF officers will meet with Afghan village elders to keep local populations up-to-date with the security situation in their local region.

## Bibliography


Althusser, L. (2001 [1971]) 'Ideology and ideological state apparatus: Notes towards an investigation', in *Lenin and Philosophy and Other Essays*, Brewster (transl.). New York: Monthly Review Press, 85–126.

Aylwin-Foster, N. (2005) 'Changing the army for counterinsurgency operations', *Military Review*, 85(6): 2–15.

Beattie, D. with P. Gomm (2009) *An Ordinary Soldier*. London: Pocket Books.

Berlant, L. (2004) 'Introduction: Compassion (and witholding)', in *Compassion: The Culture and Politics of an Emotion*, Berlant (ed.). Abingdon: Routledge, 1–13.

Blum, L. (1980) 'Compassion', in *Explaining Emotions*, Oksenberg Rorty (ed.). Berkeley, CA: University of California Press.

Butler, J. (1993) *Bodies That Matter: On the Discursive Limits of 'Sex'*. London: Routledge.

Butler, J. (1999 [1990]) *Gender Trouble: Feminism and the Subversion of Identity*. London: Routledge.

Cohn, C. (1987) 'Sex and death in the rational world of defense intellectuals', *Signs*, 12(4): 687–718.

Dannatt, R. (2011) 'The Battle for Hearts and Minds: Morality and Warfare Today', Theos Annual Lecture. Available online at: www.theosthinktank.co.uk/files/files/FINAL%20ANNUAL%20LECTURE%20PDF%202011.pdf (accessed 23 December 2013).

Docherty, L. (2007) *Desert of Death: A Soldier's Journey From Iraq to Afghanistan*. London: Faber and Faber.

Duncanson, C. (2013) *Forces for Good? Military Masculinities and Peacebuilding in Iraq and Afghanistan*. Basingstoke: Palgrave Macmillan.

Garber, M. (2004) 'Compassion', in *Compassion: The Culture and Politics of an Emotion*, Berlant (ed.). Abingdon: Routledge, 15–27.

Gilligan, C. (1982) *In a Different Voice: Psychological Theory and Women's Development*. London: Harvard University Press.

Gregory, D. (2010) 'War and peace', *Transactions of the Institute of British Geographers*, 35(2): 154–186.

Harding, T. (2008) 'A year in Helmand: 4m bullets fired by the British', *The Telegraph*, 12 January. Available online at: www.telegraph.co.uk/news/worldnews/1575364/A-year-in-Helmand-4m-bullets-fired-by-British.html (accessed 20 April 2012).

Hennessey, P. (2009) *The Junior Officers' Reading Club: Killing Time and Fighting Wars*. London: Penguin.

Hennessey, P. (2012) *Kandak: Fighting with Afghans*. London: Allen Lane.

McGreal, C. (2010) 'US soldiers "killed Afghan civilians for sport and collected fingers for trophies"', *The Guardian*, 9 September. Available online at: www.theguardian.com/world/2010/sep/09/us-soldiers-afghan-civilians-fingers (accessed 6 March 2014).

Rayment, S. (2011) *Bomb Hunters: In Afghanistan with Britain's Elite Bomb Disposal Unit*. London: Harper Collins.

Ruddick, S. (1983) 'Preservative love and military destruction: Some reflections on mothering and peace', in *Mothering: Essays in Feminist Theory*, Treblicot (ed.). Lanham, MD: Rowman & Littlefield, 231–262.

Rutherford, J. (1997) *Forever England: Reflections on Masculinity and Empire*. London: Lawrence & Wishart.

Spelman, E. (2001) *Fruits of Sorrow: Framing Our Attention to Suffering*. Boston, MA: Beacon Press.

Tootal, S. (2009) *Danger Close: The True Story of Helmand from the Leader of 3 PARA*. London: John Murray.

# 10 Waiting for war

## Soldiering, temporality and the gendered politics of boredom and joy in military spaces

*Victoria M. Basham*

International Relations has repeatedly overlooked how 'emotions not only represent a particular feeling or sensibility but also actively shape the world around us and the bodies of those that populate it' (Crawford 2000; Sylvester 2010; Åhäll and Gregory 2013: 117). With notable exceptions (inter alia Hockey 1986; Higate 1998; Eichler 2012; MacKenzie 2012), much research on armed forces similarly fails to concern itself with the emotions and sensory experiences of those whose bodies are trained in inflicting state-sanctioned violence. This is rather curious, as it is soldiers, and their bodies, that enable that very violence. The so-called 'revolution in military affairs' (RMA) – a shorthand for ongoing technological advancements taking effect in many state armed forces – means that for some, state-based warfare is now far more a 'contest, between machines that are served, maintained and operated by men [sic]' than something 'waged by men [sic] employing machines' (Van Creveld 2010: 225). However, soldiers remain integral cogs in the war machine. A continued reliance on their bodies, whether operating technology or not, ensures that it is not technology alone, but also soldiers, that enable war.

Socialising individuals in the possible and actual enactment of military violence is emotional work, therefore. Soldiers quickly learn the value of controlling and displaying their emotions; of when it is and is not appropriate to express emotions of one kind or another. An oft-repeated notion is that 'wars consist of '5% horror and 95% boredom' (or waiting)' (Maeland and Brunstad 2009: 2). Thus, in an institution where boredom is almost a constant, but danger an ever-present possibility, knowing when to take matters seriously and knowing when to take a joke both become integral to soldiering. One means correctly anticipating real and present dangers; the other means being able to 'let off steam' with comrades to cope with those dangers. In both cases, emotional control and display can become a matter of life and death.

Importantly, displays of emotion are also very often reliant on gendered logics of in/appropriateness. The sharing of stories of sexual conquest may be a common way of 'letting off steam' for military men (Barrett 2001; Basham 2013), for example, but women soldiers frequently find themselves characterised as sluts or dykes for the 'inappropriateness' of having more than one sexual partner or none at all (Miller 1997; Basham 2013). Similarly, deriving pleasure from combat is often regarded as 'normal' for military men but suspect for military women. Militaries have traditionally been (and remain) dominated by men, so much so that warfare has historically been 'wherever "women" are not', regardless of their experiences and war's effects on them (Enloe 1983: 15). Although what comes to be understood as 'manly' varies by time and place (Nagel 1998), armed forces globally are still comprised primarily of men and shaped by their practices, beliefs and experiences, as has been the case throughout history (inter alia Morgan 1987; Bibbings 2003). Militaries continue to be valued in societies as key sites for the making of men, regardless of women's increased participation in military roles[1] (Basham 2011). Thus, as a gender-conforming role for men but not for women, the ways in which men and women perform emotion in military settings, and how this comes to be understood, is often highly dependent on wider gendered assumptions about what men and women are and should be.

This chapter examines some of these gendered emotional expressions that so frequently characterise what it means to soldier. In particular, I focus on the gendered politics of lives regulated not only by violence, but by waiting for it and enjoying it. By drawing on insights from research with serving British soldiers, I consider how the mundaneness of everyday life on the base and the exhilaration of the combat mission can shape the lives of soldiers in particular, often divergent ways. I suggest that military boredom and joy are particularly important emotions because war relies on the simultaneous inclusion and rejection of particular bodies to function (Basham 2013), and gender-appropriate and -inappropriate displays of emotion can reveal aspects of how the gendered socialisation and regulation of emotion make military violence and war possible.

## Not your average nine to five

> Suggested techniques for the Marine in the avoidance of boredom and loneliness: masturbation. Rereading of letters from unfaithful wives and girlfriends. Cleaning your rifle. Further masturbation … Discussing in detail every woman the Marine has ever fucked … Left- versus right-handed masturbation.
>
> (Mendes, *Jarhead* 2005)

A few weeks into every autumn semester, I sit down with undergraduate students, all taking my class in 'Gender, Militarization and Resistance', to watch Sam Mendes' *Jarhead* (2005). There are a number of reasons for this, aside from the war it depicts, its upbeat soundtrack, and a fine performance from Jake Gyllenhaal in the central role of US Marine Anthony Swofford, as he 'proceeds' through basic training, to deployment in the 1990–91 Gulf War, to 'homecoming'. One such reason is how well the film depicts the process of becoming and remaining recognisable as a soldier. Through *Jarhead*'s depiction of basic military training, it reveals some of the ways in which soldiers begin to produce, maintain and then embody very particular corporeal, psychological and social capitals. From marching, standing tall and meticulously cleaning uniforms, to exhibiting valued traits to peers like loyalty, courage and a good sense of humour, becoming a soldier is an unending performance (Hockey 1986; Higate 2003). Moreover, that depiction of basic training takes place in an all-male environment and highlights some of the pleasures men have long derived from the transformative process from civilian to soldier that confirms recruits have opted out of the usual 'nine to five' (Woodward 1998). Though Swofford and his comrades find training tough, brutal even, this very brutality affirms that each of them can 'make themselves into the man they want to be' (Dawson 1991: 119).

Although women also now undergo military training, its physical regimes, standards, equipment, machinery and even uniforms have developed with male bodies in mind. An enduring legacy of women being traditionally deemed unsuited to combat, and more suited to being war's sweethearts, wives, mothers, nurses and clerks (Enloe 2000), is that their bodies are suspect in military settings. Though, as popular culture reflects, the desire of men to fulfil fantasies of warfighting is somewhat commonsensical, women's desires to reject the nine to five are still an irregularity. This is reinforced through the habitual denigration of the 'feminine' in military training. Recruits become soldiers precisely by proving they are not women or 'effeminate'. Gendered insults – 'pussies' – hurled at recruits lagging behind serve as frequent reminders (inter alia Hockey 1986; Harrison and Lailberté 1997). Appearing 'unmanly' in the eyes of other men often elicits shame (Kimmel 1994), an especially negative emotion in an institution that reveres pride. Furthermore, for many, biological functions such as menstruation, and more general perceptions of the inferiority of women's bodies and their inability to 'stomach' war, fully justify the marginality of women (Cohn 2000). When women in Western armed forces were deployed in substantial numbers for the first time during the 1990–91 Gulf War, many newspapers reported the tears of 'girl soldiers' whilst their male counterparts stoically comforted their tearful wives and girlfriends (Forde 1995). Though it is not uncommon for *men* under fire to tremble, sweat, piss themselves, vomit or even shit themselves (inter alia Holmes 2003), the salience of the idea that 'the soldier' is a man elides this.

Importantly, some acts of becoming, such as cleanliness, tidiness and domesticity, that are more commonly associated with the feminine, can also be reconstituted as ways of 'being a man' if they become controlled military activities. An orderly bunk and a well ironed shirt, when carried out within the parameters of the masculinised environment of basic training, all symbolise the rejection of the civilian and the primacy of military efficiency. As military efficiency has a male face, these activities reinforce the 'manly'.

*Jarhead* depicts such everyday mundane tasks as integral to the soldier-self. As the above quote suggests, *Jarhead* reveals war to be a waiting game; one of military service's key features is the 'queuing, being "processed" for this or that, [the] waiting' (Morgan 1987: 9). The prevalence of boredom in military settings is both an enduring feature of war and something soldiers must endure (Maeland and Brunstad 2009). Military officials take this seriously; boredom potentially undermines soldiers' abilities to 'switch on'; those ways of 'moving, seeing, hearing, touching and smelling' that enhance a soldier's 'individual and collective capacity to kill the enemy' (Hockey 2009: 481).

Many attempts at mitigating military boredom are also gendered. From military officers providing 'rest and recuperation' for servicemen in brothels (Morgan 1994; Enloe 2000) to 'jokes' about servicewomen's alleged sex lives, mitigating the mundane relies on gendered assumptions about appropriate sexuality (Miller 1997). Preparing for and going to war is still a 'boy's own adventure', not a girl's. As most 'real soldiers' tales', written almost exclusively by men, attest, this is an idea central to both boyhood and military culture (Woodward 1998: 288). Moreover, taking an interest in, and in some cases pleasure or joy in, combat is also gender-conforming for men but not for women (Sasson-Levy 2003). Moments of military boredom and joy thus often reinforce the gender-conformity and non-conformity of men and women's military service, respectively.

A final reason for screening *Jarhead* is that it toys with the stability of time and space. The military is a prime example of the power of particular configurations of time and space in facilitating social identity. Time and space have traditionally been dichotomised as fluid and static, respectively (Massey 1994). Time has come to be thought of as a matter of progression; life is often considered in cradle-to-grave terms, as 'a straight line or number of straight lines' (Deleuze and Guattari 2004: 230). Space, in contrast, has often been conceptualised as timeless, as territorially or structurally bound, as fixed and autonomous (Agnew 1994). However, the characterisation of time and space in such ways, and their compartmentalisation, rely on the production of sets of boundaries and distinctions that remove temporality and spatiality from the historical, social and political struggles that make them intelligible (Walker 1993; Agnew 1994; Lundborg 2012). In everyday life, spaces and times become intertwined and invested with meaning. The notion that there is a 'time and a place for everything' has become so normalised that a failure to utilise time and space appropriately can elicit emotional responses, from guilt over relaxing and not working, to excitement at one's own fashionable lateness (Halberstam 2005).

Space and time are not fixed or stable. To become so normalised, so entrenched in our daily lives requires that they become technologies of thought and action through which individuals 'may give expression to themselves' (Lefebvre 1991: 33). *Jarhead* provides an insight into how these technologies can operate in military settings; how they can ensure that a man is always 'of' the military even if not 'in' it. Though we follow Swofford from basic training to war and to 'homecoming', we are also told his story is one where:

> A man fires a rifle for many years and he goes to war. And afterwards, he turns the rifle in at the armoury and he believes he's finished with the rifle. But no matter what else he might do with his hands, love a woman, build a house, change his son's diaper, his hands remember the rifle.
>
> (Mendes, *Jarhead* 2005)

Reiterated constructions of soldiers' bodies are integral to becoming and being made recognisable as a soldier. It follows that being a soldier can leave marks on the body, marks that therefore 'cannot easily be erased' (Godfrey *et al.* 2012: 551). As already argued, the functionality, meaning and construction of men's and women's bodies in military settings varies. Whereas men's bodies are often imagined as resilient, adaptable and strong, women's are more often problematically sexual, reproductive, weak and leaky. Male and female bodies are appropriate for different and specific military tasks (Basham 2013). Men's bodies are the measure of ability in being distinguishable from women's. In military contexts, interlockings between gender, spatiality and temporality similarly and frequently de/legitimise the expression of emotion and its social meaning. Crying over the death of a fellow soldier is more acceptable than crying over brutal training for servicemen, for example. As I found in my research with British soldiers, the military is therefore an institution with a profoundly gendered ordering of socially in/appropriate behaviour; there is a time and place for each emotional expression of soldiering, the intelligibility of which relies on gendered logics.

## Behind the wire

> Cousin Sally rang tonight – I cannot stress enough how good it was to have some outside contact. I feel claustrophobic and I'm so bored. I guess it's just a bit weird being surrounded by military personnel the whole time. I mean, just the fact that when Chloe and Rachel (the two women soldiers I met on the course yesterday) go off for a run, it's always on the base – it's so enclosed here. Oh well, maybe I'm just a mega civilian! Really looking forward to escaping on Friday though …
>
> (Extract from fieldwork diary, April 2005)

Between the winter months of 2003 and those of 2005, I visited, ate at, and occasionally slept at a wide range of British military bases. I was in these places to carry out fieldwork-based research with members of the British Armed Forces. Through interviews and generally waiting around, I explored the significance of gender, race and sexual orientation to the self-identities and relationships of the military personnel I encountered. I reflected on the implications of their stories for them, for military culture, for societal relations with the military, for war itself, and for preparations made for its inevitability, and built a doctoral thesis, book and a career based on knowledge claims about their lives (Ramazanoglu and Holland 2002). It is perhaps unsurprising therefore that carrying out fieldwork was a profoundly emotional experience. At different times and settings and to varying degrees, I found it challenging, unsettling, humiliating, rewarding, tedious, fun and funny. I experienced dismay, anger, hurt, fear, happiness, laughter, friendship and, as alluded to above, boredom. How I have come to understand this research and those I spoke to has been profoundly shaped in and through emotional encounters. Whilst scholars are disciplined, with both small and large 'd', into making 'distinctions between scholarly activity and "real life", in practice this is not a distinction that holds up to close examination' (Morgan 1998: 657; see also Jauhola, Chapter 7 in this volume).

Two especially resounding emotions for me were sympathy and empathy, from the tale of the chaplain leading his first religious service following the deaths of four of his fellow soldiers, to the homesick St Lucian clerk who had enlisted to send money to her family back home, I felt sympathy. I also empathised with many of those I encountered by virtue of sharing their temporal and spatial frames, albeit in a fleeting way. The boredom and tedium of life behind the wire was one such empathetic encounter. As the above extract suggests, I found life behind the wire difficult, even though I only experienced it a few times and in short bursts. On one particular visit to private soldiers at an Army base in the middle of the countryside, I was especially struck by the greyness of the canteen walls where they ate, of the garages and offices where many worked, and of the barrack blocks where most slept. On talking to these soldiers, most of whom were in their late teens and early- to mid-twenties, I was overwhelmed by just how mundane their lives seemed to be. When I asked them what they did socially, they told me:

ME: What do you do, like socially, where do you go? Whereabouts?
KELLY: Just across the road, only there, to the barracks bar.
WILL: Nothing. I've never got no money.
TONYA: Salisbury's too far to go out, it's like, 25 quid a taxi there and then 25 quid back, so we go over the road most nights.

Life behind the wire for these soldiers meant living out time in particular spaces over and over again (the office/garage, the mess, the barrack block, the barracks bar). This shaped their emotional responses to their lives in the military, as the following exchange suggests:

ME: Are you happy with what you're doing?
KELLY: Sometimes. It's just boring, doing the same things every day.
ME: How do the rest of you feel? Are you happy with your Army career?
MARK: There's always room for improvement I guess. [long pause]
ME: So what about these adventure sports things that you hear about in all the recruitment campaigns?
WILL: I went sailing, that's all I've done.
KELLY: Other people do skiing and things like that.
ANGUS: Yeah.
ME: Have any of you done skiing or anything else?
WILL: Sailing from Gibraltar to here.
ME: Wow, sounds great.
WILL: That was emotional, shall we say?
KELLY: Someone just asked us to join the skiing team, never skied in me life … 3 months away from the regiment, I'll gladly do it! [Laughter]

Many of these soldiers shrugged when I asked them whether they enjoyed being in the Army; others expressed that it was 'ok', 'could be improved'; most suggested, when probed, that life in the Army was quite different from the life of adventure conjured up by recruitment ads. The overwhelming impression these soldiers left me with, though, was that they had a sense of humour well honed for their mundane circumstances. Boredom has long been seen as an integral part of military life but a potential threat to military readiness (Maeland and Brunstad 2009). Humour has long been seen as an integral part of military life *and* the alleviation of boredom. Humour in military settings has been variously conceptualised as a 'compensatory device making the fear and tragedy of the moment seem only temporary' for military personnel (Hockey 1986: 137) and 'a way of practicing positive emotions, which enables building personal resilience and capacity to respond to life challenges, as well as building relationships with others' (Brown and Penttinen 2013: 125). The stories of the soldiers above suggested that whilst life behind the wire could be mundane, humour could help one endure it.

However, many attempts to mitigate military boredom rely on the normalisation of the 'heterosexual potency' of military men and the simultaneous policing of servicewomen's sexuality (Hockey 2003; Basham 2013). Whereas servicewomen are required to wear uniforms that satisfy heterosexual definitions of feminine attractiveness, frequently find their sex lives the subject of gossip, are maligned for falling pregnant, and are advised to carry condoms and birth control because they are outnumbered by men (Basham 2013), expressions of male sexuality are habitually normalised, privileged and reinforced in military settings. From the common refrain that anyone falling behind on a run is a 'tart' and stories of sexual conquest, to the organisation of prostitutes 'to service' servicemen as a form of rest and recuperation (Kane 1993; Morgan 1994; Brighton 2004), sexual joy among servicemen is appropriate in ways that women's sexual joy simply is not. During the 95% of the time that soldiers spend waiting for war, emotional expressions are thus often regulated by gendered norms.

### *War isn't hell. It's entertainment*[2]

Death and injury are still ever-present possibilities for soldiers, despite the revolution in military affairs. In recent large-scale military deployments, more soldiers in support roles, not only those in combat arms, have found themselves endangered, due to their skills being called upon in complex 'restructuring' missions and in light of the increasingly slippery nature of the 'frontline'. However, for some, combat and close proximity to it is the very purpose of enlisting and can be an emotionally uplifting experience. For example, Terry, a male officer in the Royal Air Force, spoke fondly of combat as an intense emotional experience:

> 'You realise how good it was by the number of human emotions that you experienced. When in just one day you can go through utter sadness

> where you cry – you're a grown man crying – to things being the funniest things you've ever seen or laughed about, to [the] sheer terror of 'I think I'm actually going to die', and you can experience all that in one day and you think, blimey! You reflect on that and actually it's a really positive experience.

In some military settings, how soldiers experience and display emotions, and how these displays are made socially intelligible to others, is often highly dependent on whether the soldier is a man or a woman, and also whether the soldier's actions are comprehensible as masculine or feminine (Sasson-Levy 2003; Taber 2005). For example, a serviceman falling behind on a run is more likely to be chided as a weak *individual*, whereas, a servicewoman falling behind on a run is more often 'held up as representative of their gender' because military service is gender conforming for men but not women (Taber 2005: 292).

The private soldiers I encountered above belonged to a support arm of the Army, not a combat one. Both men and women served in the unit, though there were far more men than women on the base, and far more women among the office clerks than men, and many more men among the mechanics than women. Women are still currently excluded from close combat (infantry) roles in the British military, but they can and do serve in combat support arms. They have deployed in increasing numbers in recent years to dangerous war zones, with some casualties. Regardless of their proximity to the core function of the armed forces, the notion still abounds that women are more suited to administrative roles and other traditionally feminine trades such as nursing. As Stuart, an Army officer I encountered, put it: servicewomen have 'a sharper eye for detail' and are 'better on the administrative side than men are'. This institutional logic of time (traditional roles/modern roles) and space (rear party/frontline) normalises and reinforces gendered temporalities and spatialities that mean some servicewomen can come to find themselves regarded as 'out of place'.

This is especially relevant to women who express pleasure at having a role in combat or in close relation to it. Emma, a sailor who worked in a non-traditional role as a weapons trainer in a Navy warfare unit, told me that her male colleagues still made 'jokes' like 'a woman's place is at home making the tea' in spite of her extensive experience in combat training. Similarly, Rachel, who described herself as enjoying serving in a unit where she got to do things associated with the 'more war-ry side of the Army', identified a number of challenges she had to endure – from false allegations of a sexual affair with a soldier after chatting to him in a bar, to having to work harder than male counterparts to prove herself – because of her desire to serve in a less traditionally feminine role. Women, as still largely exceptional, alien and strange to militaries, can often find that they are 'not perceived as individuals, but are instead regarded as strangers of a certain type' (Simmel 1971: 148; Basham 2013). Emma's and Rachel's ability to express joy at being in combat-facing roles and as individuals was thus limited by its gender-nonconforming qualities.

For Terry, unlike for Emma and Rachel, the joy of combat was gender-conforming. Even as a 'grown man crying', as a social being meant to carry out military operations, Terry's sense of enjoyment and fulfilment was simply that. It was not a subject of ridicule, as it was for many of the servicewomen I encountered. Servicewomen's tears are often lauded as further evidence of their unsuitability for military service, whereas an emotional but 'masculine, aggressive, violent reaction', such as banging one's fist into a wall, is more readily normalised in military settings (Taber 2005: 296). Such gendered logics of intelligibility around the display of emotion can thus profoundly affect what men and women do, and what and where they should be.

Other servicemen expressed similar joy to Terry's at being able to 'do what we actually got paid for' and 'getting shot at' (Shaun, RAF sergeant); and at being deployed, at being in engaged in the 'real' deal of there being 'bullets in the gun' (Peter, Army officer). Indeed, for some the 'enticing elixir' (Hedges 2003: 3) of war was so enjoyable that being left behind elicited sadness. Christopher, an Army sergeant, told me that missing out on deployment was a real 'low point', leaving him unable to 'join in' with the war stories and be considered a full member of his unit. However, even in the context of the combat mission, soldiers can find that soldiering's emotional spaces and temporalities are not as straightforward as the 95% boredom and 5% horror/joy tale suggests. As previously discussed, and well illustrated by Swofford's monologue in *Jarhead* on the merits of masturbation, reading letters from unfaithful wives and girlfriends and discussing sexual acts at length, sex can be a source of alleviation of boredom for military men. In Shane Brighton's (2004: 52) reflections on the tour of duty, on the combat experience 'beyond the wire', he observes how sometimes, as in Swofford's frustrating experience in the 1990–91 Gulf War, 'the foreign, dangerous places soldiers visit are not dangerous or foreign enough'. Thus, in Northern Ireland for example, British soldiers would 'spice up patrols' with 'near suicidal leaps between speeding vehicles' and 'divert patrols and stand guard while some lucky individual did a bit of sexual tourism with a friendly local' (2004: 52). Whereas servicewomen's desire for risk and sexuality is treated as suspect, out of place, bounded by the temporality of what women have traditionally done, and thus as gender non-conforming, men's risk-taking and sexual encounters (as long as they are potently heterosexual) are the norm. This entails that the intelligibility of the joy in combat, as an emotional response, becomes appropriate or inappropriate through interlockings of gender, spatiality and temporality.

## Conclusion

The emotional desires of (heterosexual) military men to wage war continue to be normalised and reinforced, whether in the social practices of servicemen themselves through the tacit and more obvious support of military authorities, or in popular culture and wider logics of war and gender that cast war as a manly pursuit. Expressions of combat as a pleasurable experience for servicemen are gender-conforming; they are supported by wider and salient beliefs about men making the best warriors. Similar emotional expressions from women are not.

In Britain and much of the global North, war has become marked as a distinct sphere of life, something beyond the everyday lives of most people that is 'done' by a particular set of embodied actors. War has come to be thought of as a coherent 'event' with a clear before and after (Lundborg 2012), even though seeing war this way entails the erasure of multiple experiences of war as an everyday, lived experience that resurges rather than proceeds. For the soldier viscerally experiencing post-traumatic stress, to the civilians living in 'post-conflict zones', and the grieving families of the war dead, war is a continuum (Sylvester 2010). One of the key ways in which war becomes a distinct space and time, though, is through the legitimacy granted to men's emotional experiences and tales of fighting war, and the proscription of women's legitimate emotional responses to it. Whether as a 'boy's own adventure' or a horrifying ordeal, war entails that it is men who fight as they have 'always' done and that it is women who support men as they have 'always' done. Such boundaries are breachable in modern armed forces, but often not without a cost.

The ongoing prioritisation of men's desires in warfare and the marginalisation of women's are not based on the necessity of gender and sexual uniformity for the military to function. The appropriateness of servicewomen's desires to find joy in combat remains contingent because women's bodies fulfil important symbolic roles for servicemen. The desires of military men for a boys' club can make it easier for military institutions to motivate the predominantly male soldiers they have to coax into combat. Thus, even though their actual contributions to military service could enable the functioning of the military, could contribute to the application and normalisation of state-sanctioned violence, for that pleasure to become socially intelligible as legitimate would entail a reconfiguring of time and space. That reconfiguration could reveal the historical, political, cultural and social contingency of military tradition, gender norms and warfare itself, with destabilising effects. As such, soldiering's emotional spaces and temporalities have long been, and are likely to remain, gendered.

## Notes

1 Women's representation in the vast majority of state armed forces remains liminal, both statistically and in terms of the roles they perform. For example, among the four largest financial contributors to NATO, women account for just 14% of military strength in the United States, 8.8% in Germany, 9.7% in the UK and 15.2% in France (NATO 2012). Servicewomen in a wide range of state armed forces are also still largely concentrated in traditionally feminised or 'pink-collar' roles such as nursing and administration (Shields 1988).

2 I have borrowed this phrase from the title of Schubart *et al.*'s 2009 edited collection on visual media and the representation of conflict.

## Bibliography

Agnew, J. (1994) 'The territorial trap: The geographical assumptions of international relations theory', *Review of International Political Economy*, 1(1): 53–80.

Åhäll, L. and Gregory, T. A. (2013) 'Security, emotions, affect', *Critical Studies on Security*, 1(1): 117–120.

Barrett, F. J. (2001) 'The organizational construction of hegemonic masculinity: The case of the US Navy', in *The Masculinities Reader*, Whitehead and Barrett (eds). Oxford: Polity Press, 77–99.

Basham, V. M. (2011) 'Kids with guns: Militarization, masculinities, moral panic and (dis)organised violence', in *The Militarization of Childhood: Thinking Beyond the Global South*, Marshall Beier (ed.). New York: Palgrave Macmillan, 175–193.

Basham, V. M. (2013) *War, Identity and the Liberal State: Everyday Experiences of the Geopolitical in the Armed Forces*. London: Routledge.

Bibbings, L. S. (2003) 'Images of manliness: The portrayal of soldiers and conscientious objectors in the Great War', *Social and Legal Studies*, 12(3): 335–358.

Brighton, S. (2004) 'The embodiment of war: Reflections on the tour of duty', *Journal for Cultural Research*, 8(1): 51–54.

Brown, K. E. and Penttinen, E. (2013) 'A "sucking chest wound is nature's way of telling you to slow down ....": humour and laughter in war time', *Critical Studies on Security*, 1(1): 124–126.

Cohn, C. (2000) '"How can she claim equal rights when she doesn't have to do as many push-ups as I do?" The framing of men's opposition to women's equality in the military', *Men and Masculinities*, 3(2): 131–151.

Crawford, N. C. (2000) 'The passion of world politics: Propositions on emotion and emotional relationships', *International Security*, 24(4): 116–156.

Dawson, G. (1991) 'The blond Bedouin: Lawrence of Arabia, imperial adventure and the imagining of English-British masculinity', in *Manful Assertions: Masculinities in Britain since 1800*, Roper and Tosh (eds). London: Routledge: 113–144.

Deleuze, G. and Guattari, F. (2004) *A Thousand Plateaus*. London and New York: Continuum.

Eichler, M. (2012) *Militarizing Men: Gender, Conscription, and War in Post-Soviet Russia*. Palo Alto, CA: Stanford University Press.

Enloe, C. (1983) *Does Khaki Become You? The Militarisation of Women's Lives*. London: Pandora.

Enloe, C. (2000) *Manoeuvres: The International Politics of Militarizing Women's Lives*. Berkeley, CA: University of California Press.

Forde, C. (1995) 'Women warriors: Representations of women soldiers in British daily newspaper reports of the Gulf War (January to March 1991)' in *(Hetero)sexual Politics*, Maynard and Purvis (eds). London: Taylor & Francis, 118–122.

Godfrey, R., Lilley, S. and Brewis, J. (2012) 'Biceps, bitches and borgs: Reading *Jarhead*'s representation of the construction of the (masculine) military body', *Organization Studies*, 33: 541–562.

Halberstam, J. (2005) *In a Queer Time and Place: Transgender Bodies, Subcultural Lives*. New York: NYU Press.

Harrison, D. and Laliberté, L. (1997) 'Gender, the military, and military family support', in *Wives and Warriors: Women and the Military in the United States and Canada*, Weinstein and White (eds). Westport, CT and London: Bergin & Garvey, 35–53.

Hedges, C. (2003) *War is a Force that Gives us Meaning*. New York: Anchor.

Higate, P. R. (1998) 'The body resists: Everyday clerking and unmilitary practice', in *The Body in Everyday Life*, Nettleton and Watson (eds). London: Routledge, 180–198.

Higate, P. R. (2003) '"Soft clerks" and "hard civvies": Pluralizing military masculinities', in *Military Masculinities: Identity and the State*, Higate (ed.). Westport, CT and London: Praeger, 27–42.

Hockey, J. (1986) *Squaddies: Portrait of a Subculture*. Exeter: Exeter University Publications.

Hockey, J. (2003) 'No more heroes: Masculinity in the infantry', in *Military Masculinities: Identity and the State*, Higate (ed.). Westport, CT and London: Praeger, 15–25.

Hockey, J. (2009) '"Switch on": Sensory work in the infantry', *Work, Employment and Society*, 23(3): 477–493.

Holmes, R. (2003) *Acts of War: The Behaviour of Men in Battle*, second edition. London: Cassell.

Kane, S. C. (1993) 'Prostitution and the military: Planning AIDS intervention in Belize', *Social Science and Medicine*, 36(7): 965–979.

Kimmel, M. S. (1994) 'Masculinity as homophobia: Fear, shame and silence in the construction of gender identity', in *Theorizing Masculinities*, Brod and Kaufman (eds). Thousand Oaks, CA and London: Sage, 119–141.

Lefebvre, H. (1991) *The Social Production of Space*. Oxford: Blackwell.

Lundborg, T. (2012) *Politics of the Event: Time, Movement, Becoming*. Abingdon: Routledge.

MacKenzie, M. (2012) *Female Soldiers in Sierra Leone: Sex, Security, and Post-Conflict Development*. New York: New York University Press.

Maeland, B. and Brunstad, P. O. (2009) *Enduring Military Boredom: From 1750 to the Present*. Basingstoke: Palgrave Macmillan.

Massey, D. (1994) *Space, Place and Gender*. Cambridge: Polity Press.

Mendes, S. (2005) *Jarhead*, Universal Pictures.

Miller, L. (1997) 'Not just weapons of the weak: Gender harassment as a form of protest by army men', *Social Psychology Quarterly*, 69(1): 32–51.

Morgan, D. H. J. (1987) *"It Will Make a Man of You": Notes on National Service, Masculinity, and Autobiography*. Manchester: Sociology Department, University of Manchester.

Morgan, D. H. J. (1994) 'Theater of war: Combat, the military, and masculinities', in *Theorizing Masculinities*, Brod and Kaufman (eds). Thousand Oaks, CA: Sage, 165–182.

Morgan, D. H. J. (1998) 'Sociological imaginings and imagining sociology: Bodies, auto/biographies and other mysteries', *Sociology*, 32(4): 647–663.

Nagel, J. (1998) 'Masculinity and nationalism: Gender and sexuality in the making of nations', *Ethnic and Racial Studies*, 21(2): 242–269.

NATO (2012) *National Reports 2012*, NATO Committee on Gender Perspectives. Available online at: www.nato.int/cps/en/natohq/topics_101371.htm (accessed 27 February 2015).

Ramazanoglu, C. and Holland, J. (2002) *Feminist Methodology: Challenges and Choices*. London: Sage.

Sasson-Levy, O. (2003) 'Feminism and military gender practices: Israeli women soldiers in "masculine" roles', *Sociological Inquiry*, 73(3): 440–465.

Schubart, R., Virchow, F., White-Stanley, D. and Thomas, T. (eds) (2009) *War Isn't hell. It's Entertainment: Essays on Visual Media and the Representation of Conflict*. Jefferson: MacFarland.
Shields, P. M. (1988) 'Sex roles in the military', in *The Military: More than Just a Job?* Moskos and Wood (eds). Washington, DC: Pergamon-Brassey's, 99–113.
Simmel, G. (1971) *On Individuality and Social Forms*, selected writings, Levine (ed.). Chicago, IL: University of Chicago Press.
Sylvester, C. (2010) 'War, sense and security', in *Gender and International Security: Feminist Perspectives*, Sjoberg (ed). London and New York: Routledge, 24–37.
Taber, N. (2005) 'Learning how to be a woman in the Canadian forces/unlearning it through feminism: An autoethnography of my learning journey', *Studies in Continuing Education*, 27(3): 289–301.
Van Creveld, M. (2010) *Technology and War: From 2000 B.C. to the Present*. New York: Free Press.
Walker, R. B. J. (1993) *Inside/Outside: International Relations as Political Theory*. Cambridge: Cambridge University Press.
Woodward, R. (1998) '"It's a man's life!" Soldiers, masculinity and the countryside', *Gender, Place and Culture*, 5(3): 277–300.

# 11 Making war work

## Resilience, emotional fitness, and affective economies in Western militaries

*Alison Howell*

This chapter examines the affective relations that underpin current military mental health programming in a number of Anglo-American militaries, including the Australian Defence Forces, the British Armed Forces, and in particular the United States Armed Forces and the Canadian Forces. It will show that soldiers themselves are now being made responsible for their own resilience, mental wellbeing and emotional states. This, I argue, has entailed a shift in the disciplining of the emotional lives of soldiers from a model of stoicism to one based on self-governance. The chapter also illustrates how military families are increasingly being enlisted into an affective economy (Ahmed 2004) for returning soldiers: an economy that is highly gendered, given that 'family' is most often euphemistic for wives. The generally unpaid emotional labour involved in caring for returning soldiers is thus very much gendered. The chapter demonstrates how affective labour (Hardt 1999) is intentionally harnessed by military resilience programmes in an attempt to reduce mental health care expenditures, but also to maintain or improve the strength of the forces overall. 'Families' are now considered 'force multipliers', that is, they have come to be seen as integral to the making and maintenance of soldiers. Women's unpaid affective labour, in particular, is relied on for the functioning of militarism, and thus gendered care work is essential to the making of war. Hence the title of this chapter, 'Making war work', is intended to convey both the sense that war makes work for those who surround the military, and that this work, in turn, makes war itself possible because unpaid affective labour is being used as a tool of force multiplication in war efforts.

The chapter proceeds through three sections in order to illustrate this phenomenon across a range of Anglo-American militaries, focusing in particular on the US Army and the Canadian Forces. It begins by setting out some of the major pressures that have come to bear on these militaries in terms of the mental health of their personnel, particularly with the high tempo of deployments to Afghanistan and Iraq. The following section looks at how these militaries are making it the responsibility of armed forces members themselves to maintain their own good mental health through a shift from stoicism to emotional self-governance. The third section considers how the spouses of soldiers are being asked to do unpaid affective labour for soldiers, thereby instrumentalising intimate relationships. The process of off-loading the burden of mental health care, then, requires that both men and women conform to a number of expectations. The chapter concludes by illustrating how militarism and the work involved in making war are very much affective processes.

## Mental health in military contexts: controversies and responses

Most, if not all, Western militaries have been under pressure to address the mental health of their troops. This section outlines some of the empirical specificities of these pressures, as well as responses to them, as they have formed around Anglo-American militaries from the early 2000s onwards. The section traces the contexts in which a turn to 'resilience' occurred in military mental health programming, a context that includes: 1) public controversies over soldier wellbeing; 2) ballooning war costs which gave rise to pressures to cut health care costs for soldiers and veterans; and 3) the shift in military strategy to counterinsurgency (COIN), with which came the apparent need for 'emotionally agile' armed forces.

First, it is significant that public controversies about the mental health of soldiers have been a common feature of the post-9/11 political landscape in Western countries that have committed troops to Afghanistan and/or Iraq. For example, in Canada (which committed forces to Afghanistan, but not Iraq), such controversies began to emerge in the mid- to late-1990s in the context of peacekeeping missions, and have continued in the context of Canadian deployments in Afghanistan. Notably, Senator Romeo Dallaire, the Canadian General who commanded the failed mission in Rwanda, went public with his experiences of post-traumatic stress disorder (PTSD) and alcoholism in the wake of the failure to prevent genocide in Rwanda. Public concerns over the mental health of soldiers, and their treatment, mounted further during the years of their deployments to Afghanistan. Soldier and veteran mental health concerns came to be a common feature of reporting on Canadian military commitments in Afghanistan, especially surrounding the re-deployment of soldiers with mental health troubles (Esau 2007), barriers to service provision such as excessive paperwork (Perreaux 2011), and issues of social isolation and stigma (ibid.).

In both Australia and New Zealand, there has been similarly sustained media attention and public scrutiny concerning the mental health of soldiers. For instance, in Australia there have been public controversies over rates of Australia soldier suicide (Healy 2011), the ability of soldiers and veterans to access mental health care (ABC 2007), the comprehensiveness of post-deployment mental health checks (ABC 2008), amongst other issues. Much of this public debate over the mental health of military personnel has been spurred on by public interest and activist groups, especially those with links to the medical field, such as the Australia-based Medical Association for the Prevention of War, and the Royal Australian and New Zealand College of Psychiatrists.

Public debates over the quality of mental health care for soldiers and veterans in the US are numerous. In early 2007, *The Washington Post* published a series of articles condemning the lack of timely access and conditions of treatment, particularly mental health treatment, at the Walter Reed Army Medical Center (Hull and Priest 2007). There have also been a series of controversies surrounding diagnostic practices. The tendency to deny PTSD diagnosis in order to curb compensation claims became especially controversial with the release of the leaked so-called 'Perez email': a communication sent in March 2008 by a PTSD programme coordinator, stating that 'Given that we are having more and more compensation seeking veterans, I'd like to suggest that you refrain from giving a diagnosis of PTSD straight out.' Until recently, veterans were required to provide documentation showing that a particular event was at the root of their diagnosis before getting treatment (Martin 2010). Additionally, in numerous cases US armed forces members have been diagnosed with pre-existing 'personality disorder' (PD): such diagnoses have been used to discharge thousands of soldiers without paying them disability or medical benefits. Armed forces members have been retroactively diagnosed with a purportedly pre-existing personality disorder, despite the standard psychological screening that soldiers undergo upon enlisting (VVA 2010). Because PD was deemed to be a pre-existing condition, the military abdicated responsibility for medical treatment, while those diagnosed with the disorder were then also denied access to disability pay, and in some cases made responsible for paying back a part of their enlistment bonus, often thousands of dollars. The result is that the diagnosis of PD has saved the US Army a sum in the range of \$12.5 to \$17.2 billion (ibid. and Kors 2012). Veterans' organisations have been particularly active in bringing these issues to light, and such issues were the subject of an exposé in *The Nation* (Kors 2009).

Additionally, much has been made of soldiers' heavy reliance on pharmaceuticals, including not only anti-depressant and anti-anxiety medications, but also the mixing of these with anti-convulsant medication. A 2008 *Time* magazine cover article, titled 'America's medicated army', drew attention to the systematic over-prescription of pharmaceuticals to armed forces personnel, likening the use of such medication to a troubling technological innovation in warfare, supporting the high tempo of deployments. Perhaps most crucial, however, has been the widely reported high rate of soldier suicides: a rate that in the US armed forces began to outstrip the rates of suicide in the civilian population for the first time in history as of 2008 (US Army 2010).

The context for the turn to resilience models of mental health programming also arose out of a second context: the pressures of escalating costs associated with the wars. The post-9/11 wars have been estimated by the Costs of War project to have come at the hefty price of at least \$3.1 *trillion*, just for the US alone (www.costsofwar.org). US medical and disability expenditures related to the wars have totalled at least \$32.6 billion (Bilmes 2011), yet this is just the tip of the iceberg. Costs associated with veteran care tend to peak 30 to 40 years after the end of war, because service members who have been deployed are entitled to receive free or subsidised medical treatment for the rest of their lives, and because costs associated with medical care tend to rise as the population of veterans ages (ibid.). Additionally, a significant percentage of veterans are eligible to receive permanent disability compensation for physical or mental disabilities (or both) if these disabilities stem from their wartime service. Because of this, the costs associated with caring for American veterans of the Iraq and Afghanistan wars are expected to be in the range of $600 billion to $1 trillion over the next 40 years (ibid.). This is an astronomical sum. While other Western militaries will not incur costs of quite this magnitude, these figures give us an idea of the kinds of financial pressures that Western governments are facing in service provision for soldiers and veterans. It is in this context that a preventive logic of emotional management came to be seen as desirable: after all, if mental health issues could be forestalled (or if militaries could claim that soldiers are not responsible for their mental states), then these costs could be curbed.

Third, the move to resilience-based models is a matter of military strategy in the context of a shift to COIN warfare from 2006 onwards. Over a decade of a high tempo of deployments placed pressures on all aspects of the 'human resources' of the militaries involved in Iraq and Afghanistan. The new era of counterinsurgency involved the sustained use of ground troops. These troops are meant to circulate amongst the civilian population in the 'host country' in order not only to root out so-called insurgents, but also to win the 'hearts and minds' of the local population. They must also be cool-headed enough to determine who is an enemy and who is a potential ally, in the context of the decision to wage war against so-called 'insurgents' who are not conventional military forces, and therefore do not wear uniforms. Soldiers can no longer shoot first and ask questions later, rather they must often ask questions first (in order to determine who is an enemy), and shoot second. This requires an emotionally stable fighting force. In many ways, mental health must now be at the centre of military strategy.

Because of the confluence of the pressures of public relations, of cutting costs and of winning wars, questions of mental health become particularly attenuated. Ultimately, this led to the release of a series of reports outlining a need for a shift in policy in many Western military contexts. For instance, the Canadian Forces Ombudsman released a series of reports on PTSD (DND/CF Ombudsman 2002). In Australia, David Dunt's 2009 *Review of Mental Health Care in the ADF and Transition through Discharge* report called for more investment in 'resilience training and mental health literacy' (ibid.: 16). In the US, the Army released a detailed report on Health Promotion, Suicide Prevention and Risk Reduction (HP/SP/RR) (US Army 2010). Each reflected a growing consensus in military circles: that mental health care should be oriented towards prevention and the promotion of health and wellness, leading to the launch of a series of resilience-oriented programmes in these militaries.

Of note here is that, while the controversies surrounding mental health care in the US and other militaries have revolved centrally around the lack of access to adequate treatment, the military responses have increasingly involved a focus on *prevention*. Prevention, as a model for dealing with mental health concerns, is a cost-cutting technique in that it attempts to avert treatment. It is cheap in that it places responsibility on service personnel and their families for maintaining the mental wellbeing of soldiers preventively. In drawing on both the inner resources of soldiers and their spouses, these preventive resilience models are attempting to manage and foster both emotional labour and certain kinds of affective relations – all for military purposes.

## Shifting the burden to soldiers? The affective work of self-governance

This section charts how soldiers are now expected to look inwards and govern their own mental health – to prevent their own potential breakdowns and soldier on. It illustrates how, whereas once soldiers were meant to be stoic through resilience, Western military mental health policies are now attempting to work on soldiers' emotional responses by encouraging self-governance.

Before proceeding, it is necessary to delineate some of the theoretical framing that informs this chapter. Following from Critical Disability Studies (Tremain 2005), and also from Foucault's seminal work (Foucault 1988, 2006) or more recently from the work of Foucauldian political sociologists such as Nikolas Rose (1998), I view psychology and psychiatry as technologies of governance. Such scholarship has offered a new way to approach these disciplines, by looking at how they do not always simply help people, but how they also serve (often dominant) social and political functions. Psychology, and in particular new strains of psychology such as cognitive behavioural therapy and positive psychology, asks subjects to govern themselves and their emotions and actions. In Western military contexts, psychology is increasingly being used to foster certain kinds of soldiers who govern their psyches through therapeutic encounters, rather than repressing traumatic memory. Stoicism and repression are no longer seen as fully effective for managing and retaining soldiers. Western militaries now need a new kind of man: one who looks inwards, who works through their emotions, and governs their interior life in order to be emotionally stable, and therefore mission-ready. This entails the engendering of new kinds of masculinities in Western military settings, and it should be noted that these changes precede the turn to counterinsurgency and the wars in Iraq and Afghanistan; rather, they are also deeply tied to peacekeeping (Duncanson 2009).

In the Canadian context, there has been a vast array of programmes that seek to foster soldiers not in repressing, but in excavating and 'working through' their emotions. For example, the use of peer support is institutionalised in the CF through the Operational Stress Injury Social Support (OSISS) programme, to provide peer-to-peer support. Peer support marks a shift in ideas about what soldiers should do with their emotions. While repressing feelings of pain, guilt or fear may have been a feature intrinsic to stoic masculinity (see Whitworth 2008: 117), self-governance demands that soldiers experiencing difficulties seek out peer support, marking a shift in the kind of men the CF wants as soldiers. That is to say, they now want soldiers to seek help and govern their emotions, rather than just repress them, marking a shift in militarised masculinity.

Indeed, these programmes suggest a shift to therapeutics in Canadian military culture that has much to do with masculinity. Soldiers are meant to manage their psyches and their experiences of deployment such that they may be retained and re-deployed: they are being tasked with self-governing so as to maintain their own good mental health. This involves a shift in regimes of emotional management, wherein soldiers are meant less to 'suck it up' than to 'work it out'. This shift from stoicism to therapeutics in the Canadian context is by no means uncontested, however, and resistance to these changes can be seen at multiple levels of military culture (see Howell 2011).

These shifts are perhaps even more pronounced in the US context, where there has been a great deal of emphasis on preventive mental health promotion. The US 2010 HP/SP/RR report sets the agenda for preventive mental health programming for the Army, wherein prevention is seen as a proactive response to mental health difficulties, and treatment is considered 'reactive'. The trouble with this, however, is that while the prevention approach may at first seem progressive, in that it acknowledges that soldiers often have difficulties coping with their experiences of war (unlike the stoicism model which cast soldiers with PTSD as lesser men, not tough or strong enough), it in fact has very regressive consequences. This is because, like the earlier emphasis on stoicism, the prevention approach places the burden of mental health and wellness squarely on the shoulders of soldiers themselves: they are expected to *govern* their emotions. A soldier's relation to their emotions then is meant to pass from repression (as in the stoicism model) to self-governance (as in the prevention model).

This is perhaps best illustrated through the US Army Comprehensive Soldier Fitness programme, which was recently re-branded as Comprehensive Soldier and *Family* Fitness, or 'CSF2'. The programme is based on a fivefold notion of fitness, wherein soldier fitness comprises not just physical fitness, but also emotional, social, family and spiritual fitness (I discuss the category of 'family fitness' in the following section). Of note here is the idea of 'emotional fitness'. Fitness is a word that carries much baggage with it: fitness is an expectation placed on individual subjects, and particularly those in military contexts, to govern their own bodies in order to be physically fit. CSF2 claims to be able to make a resilient fighting force, with enhanced performance. It works by transposing the expectation that a soldier should be responsible for their physical state, to the idea that soldiers must also be responsible for their emotional or mental state. This is a heavy burden in a context in which soldiers have been and continue to be deployed and re-deployed repeatedly in the post-9/11 wars. The CSF2 programme requires that every single soldier take an online test (or 'Global Assessment Tool') that returns results wherein soldiers are told what area of 'fitness' they are lacking in, in terms of this fivefold notion of emotional fitness. So, for example, if a soldier is an atheist, they may perform poorly on the 'spiritual fitness' portion of the test, and may be told: 'You may lack a sense of meaning and purpose in your life. At times, it is hard for you to make sense of what is happening to you and others around you. You may not feel connected to something larger than yourself.' The test is used, then, to enjoin soldiers to improve areas of their fitness that the Global Assessment Tool finds that they are lacking in, and thus to take responsibility for their own emotional fitness. Soldiers are meant to govern their emotions, rather than just repress them. Yet the end result is the same, whether soldiers are meant to be mentally fit, or stoic, that is: they are made responsible for their own mental states, while those who decide to send such soldiers to war largely escape such responsibility.

These kinds of programme aspire to keep the costs associated with providing psychiatric or psychological treatment to a minimum. They also aspire to something even more ambitious: that is, they aspire to change the kind of man that makes a soldier. As detailed above, the new era of counterinsurgency has relied heavily on the use of ground troops, who are meant to circulate amongst the civilian population in the 'host country' in order not only to root out so-called insurgents, but also to win the hearts and minds of the local population (see also Welland, Chapter 9 in this volume). Soldiers can no longer shoot first and ask questions later; rather, they must often ask questions first and shoot second. This requires an emotionally stable and mentally fit fighting force, placing mental health at the centre of military strategy. Because of these changes, Western militaries now need a new kind of man: one who is resilient and self-governing, rather than merely stoic and self-controlled. Western militaries need a new kind of man, but at the same time they are making parallel demands of women associated with the military, as the following section illustrates.

## Emotional labour and 'family fitness'

Even in the late twentieth century, it was unclear to military leadership whether it was better for their purpose for their soldiers to be single or married. For example, writing at the end of the Cold War, Cynthia Enloe noted:

> For a century both British and American military commanders had been weighing up the advantages and disadvantages of allowing their soldiers to marry. Would marriage raise the moral tenor of the troops and cut down on drunkenness and VD? Or would marriage divide a soldier's loyalty, make him slower to mobilize … The debate remains unsettled today.
>
> (Enloe [1989] 2001: 71)

With the passage of over two-and-a-half decades, and with the high tempo of deployments associated with the post-9/11 wars, it seems this debate is increasingly being settled in favour not only of allowing soldiers to marry, but in fact of harnessing soldiers' families, and especially their spouses, to make Western militaries work better, more efficiently, and cheaply. Families, and especially wives, have come to be viewed as critical to supporting the emotional states of soldiers, such that they can be ready for deployment or, moreover, re-deployment. As Zoe Wool (2014) demonstrates, in the US military this forms part of a model that fosters conjugal couplehood.

Per the US Department of Defense: 'The linkage between family readiness and operational success is evident in today's U.S. armed forces, of which the majority are married personnel' (DoD 2009: 1). The title of the DoD report to the congressional defense committees on family issues is telling: *Plans for the Department of Defense for the Support of Military Family Readiness*. The purpose of DoD policies and programming concerning family issues is designed not exactly for 'the support of the family', but for 'the support of military family *readiness*'. In the Canadian Forces, 'family' is considered integral to the success of military efforts. The Canadian Forces' official stance is that 'the military family is truly "the strength behind the Uniform"' (NATO 2009: 5/7). These militaries harness the unpaid affective labour of 'families' in the maintenance of troop strength, and particularly mental health. In the process, the family is instrumentalised as a means to ensure military and operational readiness more generally: the family is treated as a military instrument.

This is a gendered process. It should be noted that, in most cases, the language of 'families' and 'spouses' is euphemistic in a context where the majority of service personnel are men; additionally, men serving in the military tend to be married more often than their female counterparts. In the US military, as of 2013, men outnumbered women by a ratio of six to one amongst active duty service members. Add to this that military men are married more often than military women, and the result is that women comprise the majority of spouses (DoD 2013). In the Canadian Forces, women comprise 15.1% of the total armed forces (regular and reserve) (NATO 2009: 2/7); in the Australian Defence Forces, rates range from 12% in the Army to 18% in the Navy (ADF undated), while the total number of women serving in the British Armed Forces was 9.1% as of 2006 (MoD undated). Further, the language of 'spouses' tends to conceal that the kinds of affective labour expected of military spouses are highly gendered. In other words, these militaries may not expect the same kinds of care work to be done by the minority of male military spouses as it does female ones. For these reasons, we should be cautious when the language of 'families', 'spouses' or 'partners' is used, because most often it is military wives who are implicitly being referred to.

The previous section of this chapter discussed Comprehensive Soldier and Family Fitness, and the ways in which it is shifting the burden of mental health onto soldiers themselves, making them responsible for their own mental resilience. Yet one of the five types of fitness that the programme encourages is what it calls 'family fitness'. In the CSF2 programme, 'family fitness' is understood as '[b]eing part of a family unit that is safe, supportive and loving, and provides the resources needed for all members to live in a healthy and secure environment' (see http://csf2.army.mil). Family members are also asked to take a test evaluating their fitness, in order to help them provide better support for their soldiering family members. According to the Army, '[t]he CSF program is designed to provide Family members with the thinking skills and coping strategies needed to take care of themselves and their Soldier' (http://csf2.army.mil). Yet CSF2 does not do much to support military families and spouses; rather, based on their test results, they are directed to 'immediate results that link to tailored self-development training' (ibid.). In reality, what this amounts to is a paltry online resilience module.

In the Canadian Forces there are parallel programmes. For example, for the past several years the CF has offered its members and their spouses what it calls 'Basic Relationship Training' (BRT). The programme, first piloted in 2005 and fully launched in 2006, comprises a several-session course taken either over a series of weeks, or through intensive weekend sessions. The course was pitched to CF members not as a counselling programme, but rather as a skill-based programme aimed at giving military couples 'support, information, and tools' (DND 2006). BRT is intended to provide soldiers and their spouses with 'relationship skills', including 'recognizing when you have a problem, understanding each other's expectations, communicating without fighting, and – most importantly – maintaining the friendship between you that originally led to the relationship' (DND 2006). Intimate relationships, then, are being harnessed by the CF: they are being militarised in a number of ways.

First, the title of the programme is notable. The inclusion of the word 'basic' is clearly meant to evoke 'basic training'. Relationship skills, then, become likened to military training. And indeed, they are a form of military training: but this training works to reach beyond the CF's paid employees, to their spouses. All of this begs the question: why does the Canadian military need to train military spouses – most often wives – in how to conduct their intimate relationships? The overt rationale for the BRT programme is for soldiers to be operations-ready: the brochure for the programme urges soldiers to recognise that 'strong supportive relationships are paramount to your ability to remain mission-focused' (DND 2006). As one reporter who covered the launch of the programme put it: 'senior military brass recognize that happily attached soldiers are better fighters' (Beeby 2006: F7).

The programme thus aims to instrumentalise the intimate relationships of its fighters: it makes the successful functioning of these relationships into a matter of military strategy. BRT aspires to reach deeply into the personal lives not only of its paid employees, but also of their spouses. To this end, it contains three components: 'relationship building, health promotion, and spiritual encouragement' (DND 2006). The programme thus seeks to work on not only the relationships of its members, but also their health and even their spirituality. The programme aims specifically at providing 'spiritual encouragement'. Like the US Army's CSF2 programme, even the faith of CF's members and their spouses comes to be rendered a tool of military strategy, when the very same programme is pitched as a way to 'remain mission-focused'. Basic Relationship

Training is a tool, then, of force multiplication – and one that asks as much of the CF's unpaid spouses, who are most often women, as their paid employees. As such, wives are enlisted in maintaining the good mental health of soldiers; in other words, their fitness for re-deployment in a kind of affective economy of militarism.

Wives are not only positioned as support systems for soldiers, they are also directly targeted by mental health policies so that they can maintain this support. One CF document warns spouses to be on the lookout for symptoms of their own 'compassion fatigue':

> Empathetic and understanding, you try to maintain a satisfying conjugal relationship and stable family relations during the time it takes for your partner to recover from the [psychological] injuries … The compassion you first felt becomes clouded by feelings of helplessness, doubt, guilt, and anger … You may be going through compassion fatigue. It is essential to take care of yourself in order to prevent exhaustion. Establish your limits and priorities, let certain tasks go, dare to ask for help, award yourself breaks and little pleasures, change only one habit at a time. All this is crucial to your personal well-being and to that of your family member.
>
> (OSISS 2006)

The tone of this entreaty makes it clear that it is women (as soldiers' wives) who are being spoken to, in an effort to get them into a good state of mind, but mainly so as to help the soldier.

A British Army Families Federation (AFF) pamphlet titled *Carers – Prevent Problems after Deployment by Preparing Before!* also makes a similar plea to military spouses. It addresses family members who are carers (again, most often wives) as follows:

> We are all aware of the difficulties families face at the time of deployment … However, we cannot hide the fact that those of us who care for others have differing needs. At a time such as this it is vital to acknowledge this, and make every effort to prevent problems occurring by preparing as much as possible … Remember – after you have made sure the children are okay, walked the dog, done the shopping etc., who is making sure that you are okay?
>
> (AFF undated)

Yet the rationale for intervening in families is not only that it will improve their quality of life; rather, it is that asking them to 'seek help' (and, especially, to 'self-help') will ultimately improve the emotional state of the soldier, making them mission-ready.

A Canadian DND report on family needs suggests that 'it is also considered helpful to involve [family members] in order to avoid having them unconsciously sabotage the victim's treatment' (DND 2004). So, wives are sometimes figured as potential emotional saboteurs, and as a source of potential danger in the recovery of their warrior spouses. For this reason, they too must be intervened upon, and trained to provide support such that their unpaid affective labour can be instrumentalised and used to help make their soldiering husbands able to re-deploy. This has been heightened in the context of the high tempo of deployments during the course of military commitments in the conflicts associated with the post-9/11 wars. When Western militaries expound on the importance of 'family support' for returning soldiers, it is primarily asking for support from women. In effect, these women form an affective workforce for the military.

## Conclusion

It is worth noting that war is often pitched as a dispassionate affair – one of cold and calculated rationalities and strategies. But what these activities demonstrate is that this is far from the case. Rather, militarism entails complex affective systems for the management and governance of the emotional lives of those who labour in war, and those who surround them. The turn to resilience entails something novel in this complex system, as it asks of soldiers, and their families, that they govern their emotions and maintain a high level of mental fitness in order to prevent the need for mental health care. I will leave the reader with a provocation: what does it mean that these preventive systems were largely instituted just as preparations for the withdrawal from the wars in Iraq and Afghanistan were taking place? Why make affective preparations for war, just as war is being wound down? What this suggests is that the turn to resilience is occurring in a context wherein preparations for unending war are replacing demobilisation. New militarised affective economies centered on self-governance and gendered affective labour are taking root precisely in this context of unending war, and of making such war 'work'. This is very troubling indeed.

## Bibliography


ABC (2007) 'Doctors' group slams govt on soldiers' mental health support', Australian Broadcasting Corporation, 11 May. Available online at: www.abc.net.au/news/2007-04-29/doctors-group-slams-govt-on-soldiers-mental-health/2535372 (accessed 18 July 2011).

ABC (2008) 'ADA concerned soldiers skipping mental health checks', Australian Broadcasting Corporation, 26 May. Available online at: www.abc.net.au/news/2008-05-26/ada-concerned-soldiers-skipping-mental-health/2448878 (accessed 18 July 2011).

ADF (n.d.) 'Women in the ADF: FAQs', Australian Defence Forces. Available online at: www.defencejobs.gov.au/womenintheadf/faq.aspx#HowmanyfemalesarethereintheADFandwhatistheratiotomen (accessed 29 July 2011).

AFF (n.d.) *Carers – Prevent Problems after Deployment by Preparing Before!*, Army Families Federation (UK). Available online at: www.aff.org.uk/linkedfiles/aff/health_additional/add_carers.pdf (accessed 5 August 2011).

Ahmed, S. (2004) 'Affective economies', *Social Text*, 22(2): 117–139.

Beeby, D. (2006) 'Serve your country, save your relationship: Military course focuses on soldiers' home front', *Vancouver Sun*, 20 November, F7.

Bilmes, L. (2011) 'Current and projected future costs of caring for veterans of the Iraq and Afghanistan wars', *The Costs of War Report*. Providence: Watson Institute, Brown University. Available online at: www.costsofwar.org.

DND (2004) 'Operational Stress Social Support: Family Support Needs Analysis'. Available online at: www.osiss.ca/pdfs/english/NeedsAnalysisEng.pdf (accessed 11 May 2007).

DND (2006) 'Basic relationship training', *Canadian Forces Personnel Newsletter*, 7(6).

DND/CF Ombudsman (2002) *Special Report: Systemic Treatment of CF Members with PTSD*. Ottawa: Department of National Defence/Canadian Forces, Office of the Ombudsman.

DoD (2009) *Plans for the Department of Defense for the Support of Military Family Readiness, Report to the Congressional Defense Committees*. Washington, DC: US Department of Defense.

DoD (2013) *Demographics 2013: A Profile of the Military Community*. Washington, DC: US Department of Defense.

Duncanson, C. (2009a) 'Forces for good? Narratives of military masculinity in peacekeeping operations', *International Feminist Journal of Politics*, 11(1): 63–80.

Dunt, D. (2009b) *Review of Mental Health Care in the ADF and Transition through Discharge*. Canberra: Australian Government, Department of Veterans' Affairs. Available online at: www.dva.gov.au/sites/default/files/files/consultation%20and%20grants/healthstudies/ReviewofMentalHealth1May2009.pdf

Enloe, C. ([1989] 2001) *Bananas, Beaches and Bases: Making Feminist Sense of International Politics*. Berkeley, CA: University of California Press.

Esau, J. (2007) 'Stressed-out soldiers sent back to Kandahar: Military's chief psychiatrist monitoring mental illness in Afghanistan', *The Globe and Mail*, 5 March, A1.

Foucault, M. (1988) *Madness and Civilization: A History of Insanity in the Age of Reason*, Howard (transl.). New York: Vintage Books.

Foucault, M. (2006) *Psychiatric Power: Lectures at the Collège de France, 1973–74*, Lagrange (ed.), Burchell (transl.). Basingstoke: Palgrave Macmillan.

Hardt, M. (1999) 'Affective labor', *Boundary*, 26(2).

Healy, S. (2011) 'Mental health fears amid suicide surge', *The Courier Mail*, 27 February. Available online at: www.couriermail.com.au/ipad/mental-health-fears-amid-suicide-surge/story-fn6ck51p-1226012609873 (accessed 10 May 2011).

Howell, A. (2011) *Madness in International Relations: Psychology, Security and the Global Governance of Mental Health*. London: Routledge.

Hull, A. and Priest, D. (2007) 'Little relief on Ward 53: At Walter Reed, care for soldiers struggling with war's mental trauma is undermined by doctor shortages and unfocused methods', *Washington Post*, 18 June, A1.

Kors, J. (2009) 'How Specialist Town lost his benefits', *The Nation*, 9 April.

Kors, J. (2012) 'Calling for an end to phony military discharges', *New York Times*, 3 March, A18.

Martin, R. (2010) 'VA eases claims process for PTSD treatment', *NPR News*, 12 January. Available online at: www.npr.org/templates/story/story.php?storyId=128467680.

MoD (n.d.) *Defence Factsheet: Women in the Armed Forces.* London: Ministry of Defence, British Armed Forces. Available online at: www.mod.uk/DefenceInternet/FactSheets/WomenInTheArmedForces.htm (accessed 29 July 2011).

Moniz, D. (2005) 'Army plans to test another increase in recruit bonuses', *USA Today,* 4 May. Available online at: www.usatoday.com/news/washington/2005-05-04-army-recruits-bonus_x.htm (accessed 21 June 2008).

NATO (2009) *Canadian Forces 2009 National Report to the Committee for Women in NATO Forces (CWINF).* North Atlantic Treaty Organization. Available online at: www.nato.int/issues/women_nato/meeting-records/2009/national-reports/canada-national-report-2009.pdf (accessed 29 July 2011).

OSISS (2006) *Life for the Loved Ones: Compassion Fatigue.* Operational Stress Injury Social Support. Available online at: www.osiss.ca/engraph/life_e.asp?topic=compassion&sidecat=2 (accessed 21 May 2007).

Perreaux, L. (2011) 'The Canadian war vet is no longer an old guy', *The Globe and Mail,* July 15. Available online at: www.theglobeandmail.com/news/national/the-canadian-war-vet-is-no-longer-an-old-guy/article592852/?page=all (accessed 27 February 2015).

Rose, N. (1998) *Inventing Our Selves: Psychology, Power, and Personhood.* Cambridge: Cambridge University Press.

Tremain, S. (2005) *Foucault and the Government of Disability.* Ann Arbor, MI: University of Michigan Press.

US Army (2010) *Health Promotion, Risk Reduction, Suicide Prevention Report (HP/RR/SP).* Washington, DC: US Army.

VVA (2010) 'Defense Department wrongfully discharges nearly 26,000 veterans, refuses to release records', Vietnam Veterans of America, 15 December. Available online at: www.vva.org/PressReleases/2010/pr10-024.html.

Whitworth, S. (2008) 'Militarized masculinity and post-traumatic stress disorder', in *Rethinking the Man Question: Sex, Gender and Violence in International Relations,* Parpart and Zalewski (eds). London: Zed Books, 109–126.

Wool, Z. (2014) 'Attachments of life: Intimacy, genital injury, and the flesh of US soldier bodies', in *The Anthropology of Living and Dying in the Contemporary World,* Das and Han (eds). Berkeley, CA: University of California Press.

# 12 Representations of grief and the Falklands War

*Helen Parr*

This chapter takes the example of a small war fought by a British Task Force in 1982 to show that the representation in the public sphere of the emotion of grief had the effect of normalising the practice of warfare as something that was a natural part of the British national experience.[1] Grief was a vital emotion, because it was experienced by civilians as well as by servicemen, and therefore the representation of grief brought this war, fought in a very distant theatre, home. The process of normalising this conflict was achieved by erasing the wild jubilations expressed when the Task Force set sail, in effect, by crushing the excess of a working class crowd and reproducing a vision of middle England, of restrained, masculinised and patriotic grief. This chapter examines grief as it was represented in the tabloid press, and here, representations depended upon the performance of loyal femininity, on a hetero-normative coming together of ideas of family, on the respectable youthfulness of the surviving men of the Task Force and the widows of the dead. It also depended upon whiteness, reinforced particularly through the connection between rituals of burial and elegiac portrayals of deep English countryside.

For the British, the Falklands war was symbolically important and this is why it presents a useful case study of the things that grief can do. World War II was an enormously significant marker of British national identity. The Falklands conflict, a short war fought between Britain and Argentina over the sovereignty of the Falkland Islands, was nothing at all like World War II, but it enabled a reinvention of Britain's past role. The spring of 1982 became 1940 in miniature, when Britain had stood alone against the Nazi take-over of Europe (Smith 2000: 111–129).

This evocation was possible in part because of the particular time of the conflict. The Argentine invasion of East Falkland followed a decade of concern about British drift, decline and crisis, and this meant Thatcher's government, and much of the press, could present Britain's victory as a resumption of national purpose and pride (Dawson and West 1984: 11–13; Monaghan 1998; Eley 2001: 818–20; Boyce 2005). In addition, the nature of the conflict lent itself to simplified discussion of Britain's role in world politics. Although the British military had since 1945 been engaged in wars of the Cold War, the end of Empire and counter-insurgency operations, not least in Northern Ireland, this was the first frontline infantry war since the Korean War in 1950. Britain appeared to be fighting alone, and Britain faced a state enemy headed by a dictator who could be likened to Hitler. When Argentina used force to occupy East Falkland, parliamentarians spoke about British mettle in resisting appeasement, about the right of self-determination of a people, an 'island race' (Barnett 1982: 63–86). The conflict was fought only by a professional military, 28,000 men who had opted to join the services, yet, as Lucy Noakes has shown, the language in which it was discussed created ideas of a past British greatness, a common British experience and a sense of destiny imparted through heritage (Noakes 1998: 103–33).

What has this got to do with grief? As the fleet set sail, crowds on the dockside poured out apparently patriotic emotions, described by Zoe Anderson as 'sexualised nationalism' (Anderson 2011: 189–204). For example, young women bared their breasts at the departing troops, accompanied by the tabloid headline; 'a big lift for our boys' (*Daily Mirror*, 13 May). This eruption of sexualised nationalism was possible precisely because this was a professional military going to war. In Britain, memories of World Wars I and II stressed the significance of the officer class, but the Falklands was a war fought mainly by young working-class men, most visibly paratroopers and marines, memorialised in the statue of *The Yomper* outside the Royal Marines museum (Noakes 1998: 103–4). The emotions associated with the officer corps were emotions of restraint and respectability. As Sonya Rose has demonstrated, during World War II, hegemonic middle-class ideas of men as courageous and heroic, but also as expressing their emotions in a temperate manner, mapped onto notions of Britishness (Rose 2004: 177; see also Rose 2003: 151–96). Martin Francis noted of the 1948 Ealing Studios film *Scott of the Antarctic* that the men of Scott's mission displayed 'quiet gallantry, stoicism and verbal understatement, even in the face of appalling disappointment' (Francis 2007: 173). These were regarded as middle-class qualities, and they represented a dominant view of how men should convey their feelings.

The warriors of 1982 were different. The initial jubilation and sense that this was a fantasy war lent itself to crude and direct expressions of feeling about the enemy, and the injury that the British nation had done. They knew the 'Argies' did not like it up 'em and they were prepared to stick it where it hurt. 'Are you feeling shirty with the enemy?' the tabloid newspaper *The Sun* asked, 'Want to give those damn Argies a whole lot of bargie? Of course you do!' (*The Sun*, 30 April, cited in Harris 1983: 46). The military were supported by young working-class women, for whom exposing themselves on the dockside or sending their underwear to the troop ships, as they were encouraged to do by *The Sun* – 'The Sun says knickers to Argentina' (*The Sun*, 16 April 1982) – was unusual, but also reflective of a more licentious working class and youth culture of exuberance, permissive sexuality and lack of concern about respectability. The sight of a patriotic working class cheering a British nation going to war served to allay some of the class anxieties of the 1970s and early 1980s when, for example, there had been moral panic at black youth rioting in inner cities, fear of football hooliganism and of crime, anxiety at the potential strength of a unionised workforce, and concerns about large numbers of unemployed young men (Hall *et al.* 1978; Vinen 2009: 125–33; Hay 2010: 446).

Once there was loss of British life, the excess of the send-off was erased in favour of a comportment of respectable, moderate, patriotic grief. In some ways, this was surprising. The dominant expectation of the public expression of grief remained restrained in the latter part of the twentieth century, but nevertheless grief was understood to be a sincere and human emotion that individuals should feel and needed to express. The formalities and rituals of mourning, such as the Victorian fashions for black dress and isolation, had been lifted, and individuals had the freedom to live with their feelings in the ways that they could (Cannadine 1981: 240). Individual grief, particularly following the loss of a child, was generally understood to be a terrible rupture to the normal course of life. During World War II, grief had been commonly experienced, but the fact that the numbers of dead during the Falklands were, as a proportion of the population, very small (255 British servicemen died in the war, and there were 777 British casualties) meant that the experience of bereavement through warfare stood out as exceptional, and this also had a bearing on the way in which it appeared.

Patriotism, on the other hand, was generally understood not as an emotion that sprang naturally from human beings, but as something manufactured (Anderson 1983). Even soldiers claimed they did not die for 'Queen and Country', but for each other (Woodward 2008: 363–6). However, the outward expression of grief was moderated through the language, and also the public spectacles, of patriotism. The British mourned gracefully. In public, they could weep but not howl; they could express regret but not bitterness or anger; they were sad, even devastated, but not insane. The emotions of grief reflected a settled country, a country that bore the inevitability of sacrifice just as it bore its history. It was the appropriate aftermath of the war that served to make the Falklands war into an ordinary British experience. To use Jon Lawrence's term, ideas of British national character were not formed from the brutality of military violence, but from the idea of a 'peaceable kingdom' (Lawrence 2003), and for the Falklands war this depended very much on the representation of grief.

## Patriotism and pride

When British men began to die, the press poured out patriotic feeling. This illustrated the intensely political way in which death and grief were talked about. Grief was not represented as an emotion, was not given a separate life as a feeling experienced by individual people, but was talked about in terms of duty and sacrifice, and therefore of inevitability. It was a regrettable, but unavoidable, part of the country at war. Grief meant that the community of British people had to pull together, as a family. Following reports of the loss of a helicopter carrying SAS men, Thatcher said, 'their courage and their skill has brought a new pride to our country and made us realise, once again, that we are all really one family' (*The Sun*, 22 May 1982).

Stories of the national family were enhanced by the involvement of the Royal Family in the war. Britain was headed by the Queen, who was pictured, 'her face lined with a mother's anxiety' about her own son, Prince Andrew, who was piloting a helicopter (*The Sun*, 27 May 1982). The family, without question a family headed by a man married to a woman, felt the same emotions, mourned the loss of all its sons together, thereby blunting acute individual pain. After the sinking of the British ship the *HMS Sheffield,* the tabloids accused the BBC of 'treason': 'there are traitors in our midst'. The BBC had treated Britain and Argentina 'as if they had an equal claim to justice, consideration and loyalty' (*The Sun*, 7 May 1982). In the face of death, the opposite of patriotic emotion was treachery.

The emotions associated with loss were therefore sadness, regret and pride. Families were reported as deeply sad that their husbands and sons were dead, but enormously proud of the way in which they had died. For some, patriotism was the traditional notion of duty, Queen and country; for others, it was a shifting patriotic expression that he died 'doing the job he loved'. *The Sun* reported the father of Lt Nicholas Taylor: 'I'm proud to have a son who died doing a job he loved for the country he loved' (6 May 1982). The father of an SAS soldier said: 'to Stephen the SAS was his life and his home. I'm proud he died serving his country and doing the job he loved' (*Daily Mail*, 24 May 1982). The feeling of pride was of course also loyalty to the cause for which he had given his life and admiration of his qualities: courage, lack of selfish will, dedication to his role and his rank, uncomplaining sacrifice.

## Women

Central to the representation of grief was the performance of loyal femininity (see also Damousi 2001: 193). The press preferred to concentrate on widows rather than on mothers, believing that young women, sometimes with babies or young children, were more newsworthy than older people. The tabloids revealed a seventeen-year-old, only three weeks wed; a widow described as an 'eight-hour bride'; another just-married teenager whose husband and best man were killed (Taylor 1992: 21). Focus on the bereaved young might have been thought to emphasise the futility of their loss, but it actually served to demonstrate the nation's vigour and resilience in the face of death. Interviewed in the *Daily Mirror*, the widow of Bob Fagan, killed on the *HMS Sheffield*, said that he had wanted to leave the Navy. She was proud of him but never got used to the separations. He would have wanted her to cope, she had to 'be brave, like he was' (7 May 1982). A kind of transferred pride amongst children too young really to know that their fathers were never coming back could also be seen as carrying the best British qualities into a new generation.

As with other conflicts, mothers were the group amongst whom there was the greatest potential anger about what had happened (Acton 2007: 2). Terry Burt, mother of seventeen-year-old Jason, argued that her son, too young to vote or to buy a drink in a pub, should never have been sent to the Falklands (Carr 1984: 67–70). Freda McKay, whose son Ian was to win the Victoria Cross, maintained that all families should be recompensed equally for their loss. She believed that she had a right for her son not to die (Carr 1984: 107–9). However, while there was a campaign in the tabloid press for better treatment for bereaved families, maternal bitterness was not given priority.

Rather, maternal grief was represented as the highest form of grief, and hence in a sense naturalised any animosity mothers might feel towards the conflict. The death of a child was, for the woman who had carried, birthed and nurtured that child, acknowledged to be a singularly dreadful event. Pauline Hatfield, mother of severely burnt Welsh Guard Simon Weston, wrote later of an 'extraordinary bond' between mothers and their children. Referring to the 2003 Gulf deployment, she said: 'I know that mothers will be finding the waiting and the not knowing excruciatingly painful' (MercoPress, 31 March 2003).[2] The singularity of maternal grief positioned the mother as almost untouchable in the hierarchy of grief, having made the ultimate sacrifice for the nation. If they were angry, this became understandable, as motherhood was the most significant role women could perform, and that function had been brutally taken away.

The focus on widows and their offspring also illustrated the odd relationship between grief and sexuality. In one sense, mothers whose child-bearing years were over were simply airbrushed from public view, aping a more widespread eclipse of female public appearance once fertility had declined. In another sense, while the widows were still young enough to reproduce, it was important that they were also seen to be chaste. When, for example, on a trip to the Falkland Islands early in 1983, some young widows, women probably in their late teens or early twenties, sunbathed on the deck of the ship in their bikinis, some parents complained at their unseemly behaviour (Carr 1984: 144).

Sara Jones, the widow of Colonel H. Jones, the highest-ranked soldier to be killed, represented the public face of respectable grief. At forty, she was a similar age to some of the bereaved parents, but she was older than most of the widows, she had teenage sons, and she was upper middle class. She spoke to the press hours after her husband's death, and said that if he had to die, he would have wanted to die in the service of a job and country he loved (*The Sun*, 31 May 1982). She has never remarried: 'I never met the right person. One would be tempted if one had. It would be stupid to say otherwise' (Sara Jones interviewed in *The Daily Telegraph*, 2 April 2012). Despite Jones' sensible words, in the public eye female reproductive potential was less important than loyalty to the man who had died in service. A demure covering of the female body, and suppression of joy, exuberance or female sexual desire, was a necessary part of mourning. The link between grief and repression of sexuality also suggests that other men would regard a woman whose husband had died in the service of the nation as off-limits. Men, too, would display sexual fidelity to the memory of the dead.

## Men

Men's feelings were very rarely described in terms of grief, with the exception of the few fathers who had lost sons, interviewed about their pride. When the survivors of the *HMS Sheffield* returned to the UK, their homecoming and reunion with their relatives was described in moving terms of 'cheers and tears'. The returning naval personnel had emotions. They were not unfeeling. It was just that they were able – just about – to control those feelings. In old-fashioned language that suggested the effort, successful through force of will, to overcome weakness or unacceptable torrents of feeling, the *Daily Mirror* wrote 'every man jack of them tried their damndest to control their emotions'. The tabloid continued, 'some who sailed with the Task Force as boys have returned as men. The men are now legend'. The experience of war, and the ability emotionally to deal with it, quite explicitly had turned these boys into men (*Daily Mirror*, 28 May 1982).

The equation of manhood not just with experience of combat, but with the ability to express an appropriate emotional reaction to that experience, illustrated deeply held assumptions about what it meant to be a man, about the exclusive position of military service in determining attributes of masculinity, and in proscribing values associated to citizenship. Men were supposed not only to conduct military service, but to be able to reintegrate into civilian life without showing any scars of that service. This attitude helped to reinforce an idea that a display of emotion was weakness, that weakness was a feminine virtue, and therefore that what made a man masculine was his ability to bear the pain of death or injury of his friends, and by corollary, the bloody responsibility that went with the duty of serving your country. Perhaps this was the heart of the restraint of the officer corps. It was a reflection that only men should and could witness the horror of state-sanctioned violence, and steadfastly, stoically, bear the consequences of violence. They did so to secure women from that violence and to further the idea of a nation in which women were responsible for the innocent beauty of home (see e.g. Elshtain 1987: 3–13).

When the young soldiers themselves began to write about their own experiences in memoirs published from the late 1980s, what they wrote was quite different. They wrote about the fear they had felt, the awful difficulties they had faced on the battlefield as they slipped between their roles as soldiers and their human disgust and despair at the killing, the death and the carnage. They wrote of crying as their friends died, of breaking down but having to hold themselves together, in order to attain the objective and win the battle. Some of them wrote about the desperation and loneliness of the aftermath of the war, and about trauma, violence and isolation (see e.g. Bramley 1992; Lukowiak 1999; Eyles-Thomas 2007; McNally 2007).

However, these men did not write openly about grief. The aftermath of the war for soldiers was discussed instead in terms of trauma. Post-traumatic stress disorder (PTSD) is of course a separate condition from grief, but it can also be seen as a more alluring topic than grief. In contemporary military memoirs, PTSD was about extremes of experience. The path of trauma was repression of its existence, uncontrollable violence, often alcohol or drug abuse, before an event that triggered a realisation of the condition. The equation of male feelings with trauma rather than grief served to exceptionalise the emotions associated with the aftermath of military violence. Trauma was the preserve of a few, and a few who had been through the privileged initiation rites both of joining the professional military, and then of combat. In one sense, the exceptionalisation placed the experiences of trauma outside the normal canon of respectable experiences. In another, the exceptionalisation, accompanied with the general sense, since the 2003 Iraq War, of the public's compassion towards the plight of soldiers, highlighted the privilege associated with military service to a delineation of citizenship. Ex-soldiers had the strongest claim, in comparison with other groups, to any benefits provided by the state.

These memoirs could also be used to normalise trauma as an experience that could be expected after war. While the young men who wrote about their pain were challenging very traditional writings of military history, and challenging military and political hierarchies, they were also writing in order to memorialise their comrades, and to draw attention to the struggle veterans might face in the aftermath (Robinson 2011: 569–89, 2013: 91–104). The men who wrote these books generally had a great deal invested in the military, and had sometimes learnt their literacy in the services. Their patterns of writing reflected this (Jenkings and Woodward 2014: 1–14). The memoirists never used their own trauma to renounce the experience of war, and in that sense trauma, like death, became part of the sacrifice of war, part of the burden of responsibility shouldered by military men.

The delineation of male emotions following combat as trauma rather than grief had important implications. First, as suggested above, it entrenched the privilege accorded to military service in notions of citizenship. Second, it served further to split the male from the female. The exclusive preserve of men was to experience trauma, whereas women experienced grief. As Noakes observed, men could act, women could weep (Noakes 1998: 103). This helped to circumscribe what grief was thought to be. Grief was regarded as a peaceful, passive, not a violent emotion. It was peaceful in the sense that it inhabited certain individual bodies, but it was not enacted. Whereas the traumatised veteran would behave in certain, expected ways – excessive drinking, sudden violence – grief did not have a code of behaviour associated with it, beyond participation in state-sponsored rituals of mourning.

The absence of a public face of grief, except the loyal widow, the sad-but-proud father, the devastated mother, served to make grief a private emotion, the lived experience of which was contained in private homes, the public face of which was sad and therefore moving for other people, but never unbearable.

The public face of grief obscured so much (Acton 2007: 2–3). It obscured the raw anger in the short term; it obscured the hauntings as mothers felt the spirits of their sons in their homes, widows dreamt vividly of their dead lovers; and as catastrophic rupture shifted into loss, it obscured the corrosive effect that death had on many survivors' sense of self, the ways it could induce shame, and guilt, and a crushing sense of incompleteness. Death was not just about the end of a body, but it was about the termination of hopes, the wrenching of expectations, the burning out of the normal course of life.

## Commemoration

The formal acts of commemoration that followed the Falklands illustrated the expectation that grief, by itself, did not do anything. It could be managed. The Defence Secretary, John Nott, wrote of the memorial service at St Paul's Cathedral, held in July 1982, that it was primarily to 'comfort the families of the dead' (cited in Freedman 2005: loc. 14739). By comfort, Nott believed that families wanted recognition for the loss of their relatives. Families would be comforted by the formal acknowledgement that they had made a deep sacrifice for the state and the nation. The memorial service in 1982 did invoke some contestation with the Church of England, which perceived that Thatcher was too triumphalist in the wake of the conflict; nevertheless, the service followed an established pattern. Church (the service was performed in the Anglican cathedral at St Paul's but was interdenominational), government and armed services came together to memorialise (Freedman 2005: loc. 14728–67). The service did include readings from members of the military, but it was civilian. It acknowledged loss, not the violence of death.

In part as a challenge to the established methods of commemoration, in part as acknowledgement of their anger at the deaths of their sons, and in part because of the fear that if Argentina later claimed the islands, their sons' bodies would be in foreign soil, some families campaigned for the bodies to be repatriated. In a way, the campaign for repatriation insisted on a recognition of death, rather than just loss. Some families were not content with absence, but wanted to see a body, to have evidence of the fact of a death in service, or to reclaim the body from the military. It was a break with military tradition when this wish was granted, but the change in stance of the government reflected primarily the acknowledgement that grieving families should be privileged in order to quell criticism of the war. The 64 bodies arrived in the UK without ceremony, and most were sent home to families and buried privately, albeit with military honours (*East Anglian Daily Times*, 17 November 1982). Some were buried in the military cemetery at Aldershot, and this ritual of burial illustrated much about the public face of grief.

While the ritual of the funeral was to recognise sacrifice, it was also, simply through the reiteration of established practices, a way of containing emotion into a specific shape. The shape of the ceremony was given specific boundaries via the physical space within which it took place – a military cemetery – and by the rituals that accompanied a military burial, such as coffins draped in the Union Flag, the Last Post, a gun salute and sentries standing to attention along the route. Its shape was also formed by the recognised behaviours that accompanied burial. The military presence, the formalities of the well pressed uniform, the stiffness of bodily comportment and the power of the gun salute denoted respect for civilians who had given up their relatives. It emphasised that the military serves the nation.

The military presence also illustrated discipline and composure over the interior world. The cemetery, with its well spaced trees, chosen to bear different coloured leaves, its gravelled paths, its rows of graves, displayed order. The neat distance between the graves mirrored the ways in which people walked, in lines, with space between them. Comfort came in bearing the loss, in maintaining the shape. Comfort was not conveyed in touch, in love between human beings, men and women, rather than love with God, or between military men. Comfort was not conveyed in uncontrollable emotion, not in anything that might smear the shape away.

These practices – distance, respect, sombreness, holding in of engulfment – were embedded into civilian rituals of burial, they were not just military (Jalland 2010: 9–10). The presence of the military added dignity and recognition, reiterated the exceptional nature of bereavement in war. The ritual of burial, as the coffins were lowered into the ground, as soil was scattered onto the coffins, emphasised the inevitability of the sacrifice. Bodies were returned to nature, and the cycle of life continued. The public illustration of this process emphasised visions of a peaceful English farmland of fields and hedgerows – 'inarticulate, reticent England' – the country of John Constable that had taken shape in the 1920s following the militarisation of large parts of Northern Europe in World War I (Potts 1989: 160–86, 175).

Even depictions of the Falkland Islands themselves, in reality barren, rocky tundra more similar to northern Norway or the Scottish Islands than to the fertile agrarian Constable terrain, have appeared as rural England: mountainous, but painted in water colours, romanticised as an English heartland (Asprey 1988). The ritual of burial, and the depiction of the landscape both of the war and of the resting places of the soldiers, iterates the Falklands as a white war (also, Foster 1999: 27–30; Zehfuss 2009: 420–3). It was a war fought by white men on behalf of a white population, mourned respectfully by white civilians in traditional Christian, English settings. The middle-class hegemonic masculinity of World War II was also a white masculinity, the behaviour of white men in extremis, more desirable, more to be emulated and reproduced, than those of unwhite race, whatever the actual colour of their skin.

## Conclusion

Formal commemoration did not succeed in controlling the emotions of those who attended the services and the burials. Rather, it punctuated the everyday life of grief, and the contours of grief as an emotion experienced by the people it affected were more boundless, and usually more awful, than as witnessed in public. But formal commemoration did contain emotion. Militarised commemoration worked because it moved with the grain of social and civilian sentiment of what was appropriate (see also Jenkings *et al.* 2012: 5). Hence the displays of restrained mourning built on ideas that were already embedded in an Anglican, undemonstrative, dominant middle-class culture of respectability.

The context of the Falklands war facilitated the reproduction of certain ideas about Britain's role in World War II. This was true in the political sphere, whereby notions of Britain standing alone against the fascist onslaught in 1940 were re-evoked by the Argentine invasion of a small island in the South Atlantic. It was also true in the reproduction of ideas about military masculinity. The jubilant scenes of the send-off of the Task Force were replaced, once men began to die, by a reassertion of hegemonic sentiments about stoic middle-class masculinity, and this cemented the Falklands as just another British war. It made the extraordinary experiences of a small number of military men and their families into an ordinary, expected part of British life.

Restrained comportment in the witness of state-sponsored violence was an utterly integral part of the British ability to wage war. Control over the emotions was vital to the fighting of the battles, and also to making acceptable what had happened in the aftermath. The understanding of war fighting as a masculine activity, the responsibility for which should be borne by men on behalf of the nation, also reproduced distinct cleavages between ideas of masculine and feminine, between masculine war-fighting and the feminine home-making that made the nation a pleasant place for which to fight. Ideas of femininity were therefore essential to the continuation of the military masculine ideal, and ideas about grief were central to the perpetuation of these notions of femininity. Grief was an indelible part of war, but it was seen as an emotion that afflicted civilians, particularly women (Gregory 1994: 8–9). Grief was thus othered from the war fighting experience, and consequently was dealt with as something that moved and touched the nation, and for which the military, the government and the Church had a responsibility, and for which recognition on behalf of the sacrifice of families should be sought; but it was not dealt with as a lived experience, a daily reality that transformed the lives of those it hit with sometimes devastating and usually long-lasting force.

This also suggests something important about the dominance of public narratives about grief, and the daily living with grief. The aftermath of war for military men was discussed in public not as grief, but as trauma. The point is that there exists a dominant public narrative about fighting war, and also about living with the aftermath for veterans. There is no such narrative for the mothers of teenage sons who died in the Falklands, nor the teenage widows who lost the fathers of their children, nor the brothers of young men who died. The absence of alternative public narratives can perhaps partly be explained because the numbers of people concerned are very small, and organisations that represent them tend to be linked to the military, run by former military personnel, and the people concerned often accept and support military frameworks. The public narratives that do exist, such as in the tabloid press, also tread well worn themes, articulating individuals' pain and inequitable treatment by the state: 'agony of grieving Falklands hero's mum …' (*Daily Mirror*, 11 June 2012).

The narrative of the commemorative ceremonies becomes the dominant memory, and is generally the narrative to which individuals harness their own stories. Many people believe that if he had to die, it is better that he died in the cause of something meaningful, than pointlessly, riding too fast on a motorbike, for example. There is also an obvious comfort in the idea that he died for a good cause doing a job he loved, rather than the possibility that he was cold and frightened and wanted his mother.

In these expressions of support, there is a kind of self-generated optimism. People have a natural desire to find ways to express grief that provides the individual with hope and with a way of belonging to something bigger than themselves (Winter 1998: 5). That something, however, is in this example an expression of a conservative nationalism, problematic both because of its specific position in the Thatcher decade and thus in British post-war history, and also because of its suggestion of universal truths about Britain. It is a narrative that prioritises military service and justifies the use of British military force not only in the absence of alternatives, but by virtue of the stance of the British state and nation in history, and in world politics.

That conservative nationalism does provide comfort to some, but it privileges emotion that is performed through the expectations of the military and the government that deploys it, and eclipses the lived and experienced emotions of the everyday. This process perpetuates the broader social conditions necessary for the practice of Britain at war, delineates and reproduces ideas of masculine and feminine behaviour, and circumscribes the ways in which individuals talk publicly about the aftermath of combat.

## Notes

1 The analysis focuses on representations of grief in the British tabloid press during the conflict, and also in military memoirs published after the war.
2 Hatfield wrote her original article in the *Daily Mail*.

## Bibliography

Acton, C. (2007) *Grief in Wartime: Private Pain, Public Discourse*. Basingstoke: Palgrave Macmillan.

Anderson, B. (1983) *Imagined Communities: Reflections on the Origins and Spread of Nationalism*. London: Verso.

Anderson, Z. (2011) 'Empire's fetish: Sexualised nationalism and gendering of the Falklands War', *National Identities*, 13(2): 189–204.

Asprey, A. (1988) *Unspoilt Beauty of the Falkland Islands: Watercolours of Algernon Asprey*. London: Anthony Nelson.

Barnett, A. (1982) *Iron Britannia: Why Parliament Waged its Falklands War*. London: Allison & Busby.

Boyce, D. G. (2005) *The Falklands War*. Basingstoke: Palgrave Macmillan.

Bramley, V. (1992) *Excursion into Hell*. London: Pan Books.

Cannadine, D. (1981) 'War and death, grief and mourning in modern Britain', in *Mirrors of Mortality: Studies in the Social History of Death*, Whaley (ed.). London: Europa Publications, 187–242.

Carr, J. (1984) *Another Story: Women and the Falklands War*. London: Hamish Hamilton.

Dawson, G. and West, B. (1984) 'Our finest hour? The popular memory of World War Two and the struggle over national identity', in *National Fictions: World War Two in British Films and Television*, Hurd (ed.). London: British Film Institute Publishing, 8–13.

Damousi, J. (2001), *Living With the Aftermath: Trauma, Nostalgia and Grief in Post-war Australia*. Cambridge: Cambridge University Press.

Eley, G. (2001) 'Finding the people's war: Film, British collective memory, and World War II', *American Historical Review*, 106(3): 818–838.

Elshtain, J. (1987) *Women and War*. New York: Basic Books.

Eyles-Thomas, M. (2007) *Sod that for a Game of Soldiers*. London: Kenton Publishing.

Foster, K. (1999) *Fighting Fictions: War, Narrative and National Identity*. London: Pluto.

Francis, M.(2007) 'A Flight from commitment: Domesticity, adventure and the masculine imaginary in Britain after the Second World War', *Gender and History*, 19(1): 163–185.

Freedman, L. (2005) *The Official History of the Falklands War: Volume 2, War and Diplomacy*. London: Routledge, Kindle edition.

Gregory, A. (1994) *The Silence of Memory: Armistice Day, 1919–1946*. Oxford: Oxford University Press.

Hall, S., Critcher, C., Jefferson, T., Clarke, J. and Roberts, B. (1978) *Policing the Crisis: Mugging, the State and Law and Order*. London: Macmillan.

Harris, R. (1983) *Gotcha! The Media, the Government and the Falklands Crisis*. London: Faber and Faber.

Hay, C. (2010) 'Chronicles of a death foretold: The winter of discontent and construction of the crisis of British Keynesianism', *Parliamentary Affairs*, 63(3): 446–470.

Jalland, P. (2010) *Death in War and Peace: Loss and Grief in England, 1914–70*. Oxford: Oxford University Press.

Jenkings, K. N. and Woodward, R. (2014) 'Practices of authorial collaboration: the collaborative production of the contemporary military memoir', *Cultural Studies <=> Critical Methodologies*, 1–13. Available online at: http://csc.sagepub.com/content/early/2014/04/21/1532708614530305 (accessed 7 May 2014).

Jenkings, K. N., Megoran, N., Woodward, R. and Bos, D. (2012) 'Wootton Bassett and the political spaces of remembrance and commemoration', *Area*, 44(3): 356–363.

Lawrence, J. (2003) 'Forging a peaceable kingdom: War, violence and fear of brutalisation in post-First World War Britain', *Journal of Modern History*, 75(3): 557–589.

Lukowiak, K. (1999) *A Soldier's Song: True Stories from the Falklands*. London: Phoenix Books.

Monaghan, D. (1998) *The Falklands War: Myth and Counter Myth*. London: Macmillan.

McNally, T. (2007), *Watching Men Burn: A Soldier's Story.* London: Monday Books.
Noakes, L. (1998) *War and the British: Gender, Memory and National Identity.* London: I.B. Tauris.
Potts, A. (1989) 'Constable country between the wars', in *Patriotism: The Making and Unmaking of British National Identity: Volume 1, History and Politics*, Samuel (ed.). London: Verso, 160–186.
Robinson, L. (2011) 'Soldiers' stories of the Falklands War: Recomposing trauma in memoir', *Contemporary British History*, 25(4): 569–589.
Robinson, L. (2013) 'Explanations of post-traumatic stress disorder in Falklands memoirs: The fragmented self and the collective body', *Journal of War and Culture Studies*, 5(1): 91–104.
Rose, S. O. (2003) *Which People's War: National Identity and Citizenship in Wartime Britain, 1939–45*. Oxford: Oxford University Press.
Rose, S. O. (2004) 'Temperate heroes: Concepts of masculinity in Second World War Britain', in *Masculinities in Politics and War: Gendering Modern History*, Dudink, Hagemann and Tosh (eds). Manchester: Manchester University Press.
Smith, M. (2000) *Britain and 1940: History, Myth and Popular Memory.* London: Routledge.
Taylor, J. (1992) 'Touched with glory: Heroes and human interest stories in the news', in *Framing the Falklands War: Nationhood, Culture, and Identity*, Aulich (ed.). Milton Keynes: Open University Press.
Vinen, R. (2009) *Thatcher's Britain: The Politics and Social Upheaval of the 1980s.* London: Simon & Schuster.
Winter, J. (1998) *Sites of Memory, Sites of Mourning: The Great War in European Cultural History.* Cambridge: Cambridge University Press.
Woodward, R. (2008) 'Not for Queen and country or any of that shit … Reflections on citizenship and military participation in contemporary British soldier narratives', in *War, Citizenship, Territory*, Cowan and Gilbert (eds). London: Routledge, 363–384.
Zehfuss, M. (2009) 'Hierarchies of grief and the possibility of war: Remembering UK fatalities in Iraq', *Millennium*, 38(2): 419–440.

# 13 Constructing crises and articulating affect after 9/11

*Jack Holland*

The events of September 11, 2001, are some of the most recorded, reported and revisited moments in world history. And, yet, it is possible to recall the utter confusion experienced by many viewers across the world, and especially in the United States, as they watched the Twin Towers of the World Trade Center collapse and the Pentagon smoulder. It is this temporary moment of *confusion* that this chapter revisits, contrasting it with the *certainty* that subsequently characterised the speeches of foreign policy elites. This contrast is explored by bringing together two literatures.

The first literature explores the discursive construction of crises. Here, I argue that crises are not objective phenomena, but rather result from decisive (discursive) interventions, most frequently on the part of elected state representatives. This intervention constructs crises, in part, through the writing of temporal rupture, as politicians both identify the underlying morbid conditions in place and present the necessary solution to remedy them. Taking this insight on the constructed-ness of crises, the chapter considers how affect fits into this process. The second literature therefore explores the relationship of affect, discourse and resonance. Here, again, the role of discourse and its (re) production by strategic agents is crucial. Two arguments are drawn out of these literatures. First, that affect is articulated within discourse, often as emotion (Holland and Solomon 2014). And, second, in moments of crisis, this articulation is usually conducted by representatives of the state. Bringing these two arguments together helps us to begin to think about the powerful role played by the state in efforts to articulate and incorporate nebulous affective experiences of events into resonant crisis narratives.

To make this argument, the chapter is structured in four sections. First, the work of Colin Hay, Stuart Croft and Jenny Edkins is introduced to establish a conceptualisation of crises as socially constructed. Second, studies of affect are introduced. Here, in particular, the chapter develops Solomon's Lacanian claim that affect is articulated within discourse as emotion (Solomon 2012; also Holland and Solomon 2014). Like crises, therefore, the chapter outlines the importance of discursive construction in the articulation of affect. Third, the chapter outlines the conditioning role played by culture. And, fourth, the chapter considers the case study of 9/11,[1] analysing the experience of the events of September 11, 2001, for ordinary Americans;[2] the framing of 9/11 pursued by the George W. Bush Administration; and the relationship between the initial (popular) experience and subsequent (elite) construction of the day. Constructivist work in International Relations analysing 9/11 has tended to focus primarily on elite-level constructions of events, rather than the experience of ordinary American citizens.[3] The chapter therefore makes a theoretical and empirical contribution; using insights on affect, discourse and resonance to make sense of the substantive case study of 9/11.

The chapter concludes by reflecting on three overarching arguments. First, September 11 was experienced in particular ways, which can usefully be thought of as affective responses – biological in nature but conditioned by culture. Second, the Bush Administration tapped into, articulated and incorporated these affective responses. Third, this interweaving of affect and strategic framing can help us to understand the resonance of dominant official discourses after 9/11. The broader implications of this argument include that, while individual citizens' experiences matter, during moments of perceived national crisis the state retains an ability to articulate affect in ways that serve particular political and policy agendas.

## Constructing crises

Crises are not objective accumulations of contradictions, nor the sudden and unforeseen eruption of destabilising events. Crises are socially constructed. They are usually constituted through the language of elected officials (e.g. Jackson 2005; Holland 2009, 2013a). They may well incorporate and rework traumatic events and political contexts, but they rely upon the decisive agency of state representatives to articulate a shift of political eras. Usually, the state is portrayed as residing at the very heart of this transition. In this sense, crises reflect what Jenny Edkins (1999, see also 2002, 2004) has termed the shift from 'the political' to 'Politics'-as-normal. 'The political', for Edkins, 'has to do with the establishment of that very social order which sets out a particular, historically specific account of what counts as politics, and defines other areas of social life as *not* politics' (Edkins 1999: 2). And 'Politics' marks the arena of 'elections, political parties, the doings of governments and parliaments, the state apparatus, and in the case of international politics, treaties, international agreements, diplomacy, wars, institutions of which states are members and the actions of statesmen and women' (ibid.). Within this understanding, crises are those 'situations of *the political* that suspended, though temporarily, the stable arena of *politics*' (Peker 2006: 4). Using Edkins' terminology, then, crises such as 9/11 are 'political moments'; they have a founding, open and contingent quality to them, in which the political order and community are (re-)constituted (Holland 2013a: 87; see also Lundborg 2012). It is in the construction of crisis that this (re-)constitution takes place, and which the construction of crisis is itself reliant upon.

So what, then, *is* a 'crisis'? Or, rather, perhaps the question can be rethought as: how does a crisis come to be? The term 'crisis' suffers from the distinct lack of clarity that relative ubiquity brings. Its rhetorical richness and attention-grabbing qualities mean that it has considerable reach in academic, policy and public realms, despite (or perhaps precisely because of) its imprecision (Hay 1999: 318). For Colin Hay (e.g. 1996a: 2–3), it is necessary to trace the etymology of the term to understand the role of diagnosis, prescription and promised healing at its heart. A crisis relies upon the act of diagnosis – the articulation of the causes of malady – *and* the prescription of a remedy – the formulation of policy solutions to be enacted – which, it is promised, will lead to the revived health of the body politic. There is, then, a crucial *double* articulation in the construction of crises: the identification of both problem *and* solution. As Hay suggests, crises are moments of both dusk and dawn (Hay 1996b: 255); they are constructed to mark a change of political eras. 9/11, for example, was constructed as 'the day that night fell on a different world' (e.g. Holland and Jarvis 2014). The notion that 9/11 was a moment of crisis required more than 'just' the events of September 11 2001 themselves. This is because, like facts, events never speak for themselves. Rather, articulating transition to a new era – from post-Cold War peace to post-9/11 War on Terror – required a decisive intervention on the part of the Bush Administration (Holland 2013a: 88; see also Jackson 2005; Croft 2006). As Croft succinctly notes:

> A crisis is … itself constructed in and through social interaction. It is given meaning through social processes, through a decisive intervention which gives meaning to the situation and which also provides a route for future policy. That is, there are no objective ontological criteria that a crisis must fulfil to be a crisis: a crisis is one when it permeates discourse, and creates new understandings and, thereby, new policy programmes.
> (Croft 2006: 5)

A crisis such as 9/11, therefore, is 'brought into existence through narrative and discourse' (Hay 1996a: 225). The success of a crisis discourse, such as that centred on 9/11, relies, in part, upon its 'ability to provide a simplified account sufficiently flexible to "narrate" a great variety of morbid symptoms whilst unambiguously attributing causality and responsibility' (Hay 1996b: 335). Following 9/11, various 'morbid symptoms' were accounted for within the crisis discourse, including previous and ongoing 'terror attacks', white powder scares and anthrax incidents. However, crisis narratives must do more than account for a variety of morbid symptoms; they must do so plausibly and persuasively. Crucially, crisis narratives must resonate with a significant proportion (and ideally a majority) of the electorate (Holland 2013b; see also Holland 2010, 2012). It is this key requirement – the need to craft a *resonant* crisis discourse – to which this chapter adds a crucial insight: one particularly effective way of achieving resonance is to pursue the affective investment of an audience within a crisis discourse.[4] And it is this insight that brings together literature on the social construction of crises, with a useful counterpart on the relation of affect and discourse.

## Articulating affect

Affect has received considerable attention in IR, with some going so far as to suggest that there has been a recent 'affective turn' afoot (see e.g. Crawford 2000; Ross 2006; Bleiker and Hutchison 2008). Less 'coherent' than 'feelings' such as vengeance or anger, 'affective energies' (Ross 2006: 212) can be thought of as 'inner disposition[s]' more akin to a 'mood' than a 'state of mind' (Hutchison 2010: 84). For Shouse (2005), for example (and see also Massumi 2007), affect is a pre-personal phenomenon that lacks a (sense of) biographical understanding. While later reflection upon these energies and inner dispositions, as an individual considers their feelings, might help to achieve a greater coherency of (self-)understanding, affect is notable for being pre-contemplative; affect occurs before and outside of conscious attempts to rationalise, categorise and account for it.

One useful way of thinking about 'affect' is to contrast it with 'emotion'. Although affect is a constitutive component of emotion, the latter is socially produced (Shouse 2005).[5] Political discourse is central within this relationship: emotions 'result when … affect is translated into recognizable emotional signifiers within discourse' (Solomon 2012: 908).

> Affect is understood here as amorphous potential … which is difficult to articulate but nevertheless has effects within discourse. Emotion, on the other hand, can be viewed as the 'feeling' that signifiers 'represent' once names are attached to affect, thereby conferring on them discursive reality.
>
> (Solomon 2012: 908)[6]

Affect, then, is a number of things, and distinct from, although constitutive of, emotion. First, it occurs outside of and prior to language. Second, it is bodily, in the sense that it occurs prior to its consideration, reflection and re-constituting on the basis of intentional contemplation. In this sense, although we must not underplay the interaction of 'thinking' and affect (Connolly 2002),[7] here we can think of affect as occurring just prior to cognitive awareness; it is pre-contemplative. Third, affect is a necessary human response to a stimulus; it is the first building block of experience.

It is usually through discourse that nebulous, dispersed, and often contradictory affective energies and dispositions are comprehended, communicated and brought into line with those of others. Emotions such as 'anger' and 'sorrow', for example, were recurrent and persistent features of post-9/11 US foreign policy discourse (e.g. Jackson 2005; Holland 2013a). They represent named, socially agreed upon signifiers used to label and order particular affective experiences of the events, which were frequently far more elusive at the time of their experiencing. Many Americans can now, for instance, look back and recall a sense of shock, confusion and even horror, but, at the time, silence and a sense of disbelief, or even an emptiness and lack, tended to characterise the affective experience of 9/11. Affect, then, can be incorporated within discourse, to serve as a building block and site of audience investment, through processes of accounting for nebulous experiences or the explicit naming of affect as emotion.

## Conditioning culture

Affect then is, in part, a biological response, which can be articulated or incorporated within discourse for political effect. Affect, however, is not purely biological; rather, as I have noted, affective dispositions are culturally conditioned. Culture, as 'the context within which people give meanings to their actions and experiences and make sense of their lives' (Weldes *et al.* 1999: 1), becomes interwoven with the biological in the production of affective dispositions. For example, we can think of American 'security culture' as a particular pattern of thought and argumentation that establishes 'pervasive and durable security preferences by formulating concepts of the role, legitimacy and efficacy of particular approaches to protecting values' (Williams 2007: 279; see also Katzenstein 1996). These concepts help to shape broadly accepted understandings through a process of socialisation. American security culture therefore helps to shape popular (and elite) expectations of what is likely to become a security issue (as well as how it should be dealt with). This expectation is cultural and biological. Culture seeps into the biological, helping to shape expectations of the everyday and to condition affective responses to events. To borrow Connolly's (2002: 16–17) metaphor, the two – biology and culture – are layered. This layering means that, for example, whether or not (biological) shock will follow exposure to on-screen violence will depend upon a person's cultural background as much as their biological make-up.

In the context of the post-Cold War United States, we can see that a particular security culture, proffered by political elites, media commentary and Hollywood storylines, helped to condition Americans in specific ways that ultimately helped to inspire a particular and relatively prevalent affective response to the events of 9/11. American security culture, during the 1990s, located the dangers of the world far beyond the shores of the United States (e.g. Campbell 1998). Conditioned to expect to witness violence abroad only, the events of September 11 fell correspondingly beyond the comprehension of many watching Americans.

Three pillars comprised American security culture in the 1990s. First, the enduring myth of American exceptionalism continued to shape expectations of the everyday. This myth suggests that the United States is unique and superior (e.g. McCrisken 2003). It serves as the foundation of a particular cultural identity (Katzenstein 1996) and affective predisposition (Holland and Solomon 2014). Second, building upon notions of uniqueness and superiority, the geographical isolation afforded by two vast oceans enabled Americans to perceive the end of the Cold War as a return to isolated invulnerability (Gaddis 2004). And, third, most US citizens had never witnessed external violence manifest on American soil. Since at least Pearl Harbor, or perhaps even the War of 1812, the Homeland was perceived to be free from foreign threat.

This was the cultural context that helped to condition the prevalent American experience of the events of September 11 2001. Piecing together evidence from the Library of Congress's Witness and Response collection enables us to reconstruct these initial affective responses, prior to their realignment with the increasingly hegemonic official discourses that followed in the days and weeks after the events.

## Affect, articulation and September 11 2001

### *Affect*

The Witness and Response collection contains an excellent set of interviews conducted with the general public after 9/11. Here I focus on the first five weeks after the events of September 11. Amateur folklorists, social scientists and anthropologists conducted the interviews across the United States, occasionally with interviewees who had been in Manhattan on September 11, 2001, but usually with people who had simply witnessed events on television. The model for the project was the 'Man on the Street' interviews conducted after Pearl Harbor, which were designed to gather a cross-section of popular views on the events and the US response to them. A good cross-section of ages, cultures and ethnicities is represented in the collection, with the vast majority of interviewees chosen at random. Interviewers wrote and asked their own questions. However, a broadly comparable pattern of topics was replicated across interviews. For our purposes, it is interesting to note two things in particular. First, the comparable evolution of popular 'feeling' that emerges as time since September 11 2001 elapses. And, second, the relative lack of homogeneity in expressed 'feelings' during the event's initial aftermath, in comparison with the following weeks and months.

As Holland (2009) and Nabers (2009) have shown, in the days after 9/11 the popular response to events was fragmented due, in large part, to the failure of language to regulate meaning production, as events seemed to fall beyond existing (cultural and linguistic) templates for understanding. Interviewees were initially far more likely to invoke comparisons and analogies from popular culture, such as film, television, music and the Bible. As time went by, interviewees were increasingly likely to speak about 9/11 in the 'official' terms used by the Bush Administration. In the analysis below, the initial response to the events of September 11 is revisited, in order to consider the role of affect for Americans. Despite some diverse attempts to explain their experiences of 9/11 (e.g. claims that 9/11 'was like War of the Worlds' in contrast to quotations of Psalm 23), interviewees frequently begin from a number of similar (shared) experiences of September 11, due to the prevalence of a conditioning American security culture. Three themes in particular – important to US security culture and understandings of American national identity – continually resurface as interviewees report their experiences of the day. These three themes centre on space, time and normality. In each instance, these prevalent affective themes were articulated and incorporated within the official response of the Bush Administration, helping to craft a resonant crisis narrative.

First, one prevalent theme of affective responses to 9/11, which would later be accounted for in official discourse, was spatial distanciation: the perception that the events of the day did not belong; they were somehow foreign. The 'foreign-ness' of the events was affectively experienced and 'felt' before it was accounted for in the emerging official discourse of the US response. This 'foreign-ness' – the sense that the events did not belong, and that they sat uneasily with the familiarity of the Manhattan skyline – tied in with a more general sense of disbelief, incomprehension and denial. Conditioned to expect to witness violence such as this *elsewhere*, outside of the United States, Americans frequently reported dismissing coverage as likely 'news from some other country' (Castello 2001). The fact that events were unfolding *in America* was what citizens noted was making comprehension so difficult. One interviewee noted, 'I can't believe it … it's happening *here, in the US*. You see these things out there, but *not here* in your own country' (Senor 2001, emphasis added). Elaborating, one interviewee explained their shock as being a direct result of the fact they did not 'believe this could happen *on American soil*' (Farley 2001). While claims that 9/11 was shocking because the events occurred in the United States may seem obvious, the point to be made here is that the events were affectively experienced as shocking precisely because of particular and widely understood cultural norms, which located 'foreign dangers' well beyond the United States border.

Second, and related to the above, 9/11 was also affectively experienced as a moment of temporal rupture, prior to its articulation in such terms. Set off against the prevalent American security culture of the 1990s, the events of September 11 were affectively experienced as ending an era of peace within the American Homeland, before the Bush Administration set about assembling this narrative (Holland and Jarvis 2014). Consider, for example, the words of one interviewee, who expresses a new sense of vulnerability and speaks of a previous sense of security in the past tense and as naive:

> I did not really believe it because we live in the United States and basically the whole concept of living in the United States is freedom, living in a very sheltered world where you just never would think of a war, or attack … I have always felt safe in America … [now] I don't know if I could necessarily say if I am safe … a lot of people in America were feeling so secure, they were feeling like the US is invincible … we are not

> invincible … we need to get out of our bubble and realize that we are just in the same ballpark as everyone else.
>
> (Bauch 2001)

This theme of innocence lost, and the use of the past tense to indicate a change of eras, was replicated by numerous interviewees who, for example, noted: 'I feel … that *I've been* a spoilt American … [living in] an untouched, unspoiled culture' (Grayson 2001, emphasis added). Building upon this, interviewees spoke directly to the theme of American Exceptionalism: 'We no longer appear to be chosen people. We are just as susceptible to mass devastation as any other part of the world' (Anderson, 2001). And several pointed out the perceived return of history to America (see also Croft 2006): '[I] thought it was something in history' (Waters 2001); 'This has made everyone open their eyes … we are not invincible' (Moe 2001). If the 1990s were a 'holiday from history', Americans experienced its end, even before they had been told what would come next. Spatial distanciation was accompanied by an affective experience of temporal distanciation; the events of September 11 were perceived as not belonging in the here *and* now. Again, this experience pre-dated its articulation in the official discourse of the United States government.

Third, interviewees repeatedly expressed an affective experience of the events as beyond understanding (which related to their spatial and temporal distanciation), because the events fell so far beyond expectations of normality. One interviewee, for instance, noted that they 'felt nothing' *because* they 'couldn't understand' (Sato 2001). Repeated themes expressed by interviewees centred on notions of shock and disbelief, as well as denial. Interviewees frequently noted that they could not believe and could not understand what they were witnessing; the events, at the time of their first witnessing, were impossible to make sense of. Others went further still in denying the reality of what they were seeing, insisting that it simply could not be happening. And a large number of interviewees noted that they were waiting for reality to be re-established and the whole thing to be revealed as fiction, for instance through a director shouting 'Cut!'. Here, in particular, we see the unusually explicit invocation of popular cultural sources of meaning-making, as interviewees could often only find parallels and analogies in books and films prior to the emergence of an official 'War on Terror' discourse.

The affective landscape that the events of September 11 carved out comprised (in part) three 'senses': of foreign-ness, or the events not belonging; of rupture, focused upon the ending of an era of peace; and of incomprehension and associated disbelief. Many Americans shared these three important features in their affective experience of 9/11. This prevalence is evidenced in the Witness and Response collection. First, it is possible to account for this prevalence by re-stating that affect is biocultural, that is, whilst biological, affect is also cultural. In this instance a particular American security culture, which was widely accepted as it reached its zenith during the 1990s, conditioned citizens to expect the everyday. Questions of normality and exceptionality found answers through American security culture. 9/11, set against the conditioning context of US security culture, was affectively experienced as clearly exceptional by a majority of Americans. Second, these features comprised some of the building blocks for the formulation of an American response and construction of a resonant crisis narrative, within which citizens would be affectively invested.

### *Articulation*

To ensure the affective investment of Americans within emergent narratives of a War on Terror, the Bush Administration articulated and incorporated the prevalent American experience of 9/11, including the three central themes laid out above. Accounting for the affective experience of 9/11 as 'foreign', the Bush Administration confirmed that the perpetrators and their motivations were wholly external to the United States. Naming Osama bin Laden, Al Qaeda, their Taliban hosts, and the state of Afghanistan, the Bush Administration played down domestic links in the construction of a wholly external and foreign enemy. This is an argument that Dan Bulley (2008) has made persuasively following 7/7 and the construction of 'foreign' terrorism in the United Kingdom. In the US, after 9/11, it is a construction that built upon and accounted for 'feelings' of foreign-ness. It was reinforced by the search for motivations and the asking of questions such as 'why do they *hate* us'? Such questions contained their own answer: they hated Americans because they were, by their very nature, so hateful and so filled with hate. They hated 'us' simply because of who 'we' were, certainly not what 'we' had done. As Bush repeatedly urged Americans to unite in *love* for family, friends and country – think, for instance, of calls to 'hug your children' – he juxtaposed American love and compassion with an external and entirely foreign hatred, which helped to account for American affect, as well as affectively to invest Americans within a War on Terror discourse (see also Diken and Laustsen 2005; 2008). Americans were told that the events felt foreign because in two senses they were: foreigners perpetrated them; and they were motivated by intense emotions that were foreign to Americans. 'Binaries of love and hate, inside and outside, America and Afghanistan, good and evil, us and them, were central to the official construction of "9/11" and built upon the affective experience of September 11 as a foreign, external and wholly "Other" event' (Holland and Solomon 2014). The tensions and unease of spatial distanciation were explained and resolved through the language of the Bush Administration, which enabled the affective experience of 9/11 as foreign to be folded into the emerging discourse of the War on Terror. A resonant crisis narrative was achieved, in part, through the affective investment of the American audience.

Likewise, after 9/11, the Bush Administration set about constructing September 11 2001 as a moment and marker of historical discontinuity and crisis. September 11 became the day 'night fell on a different world' (Bush 2001). Temporal rupture was constructed in abrupt and dramatic terms:

'September 11 marked a dividing line in the life of our nation' and a new time of war (Bush 2002a). Bush argued that 9/11 'cut a deep dividing line in our history – a change of eras as sharp and deep as Pearl Harbor' (Bush 2002b; see also Silberstein 2002; Weber 2002; Jackson 2005; Jarvis 2009; Holland and Jarvis 2014). For those who wondered if the now-ended era of peace might ever fully return, Bush insisted that 'it never will' (Bush 2002b). Speaking directly to the security culture that conditioned Americans' affective experiences of temporal rupture, Bush argued, 'After September the 11, the world changed … we're no longer protected by two big oceans … It used to be oceans could protect us from conflict and from threats.' As Silberstein (2002), Jackson (2005) and others have shown, the Bush Administration constructed a vision of the new era as replete with omnipresent and existential threats; the dividing line of 9/11 symbolised the shift from peace to war. And within this war, America was now a battlefield. In constructing 9/11 as a moment of crisis, the Bush Administration was clear in outlining the morbid underlying conditions that were said to manifest that day. It was also clear in outlining the solution to those morbid underlying conditions: fight and kill terrorists. Americans were affectively invested in this discourse and its associated policies, by virtue of the crisis narrative accounting for and confirming the prevalent experience rupture. Now, however, 9/11 was both dusk and dawn: the ending of an era of peace and the start of an era of war.

Emotional signifiers were, of course, important within these articulations. Just as a sense of the events as 'foreign' was confirmed and accounted for through the naming of 'love' and 'hate', so too temporal rupture was explained with recourse to the emotion 'fear'. Freedom and fear, Americans were told, were at war. It was necessary to remain vigilant but not afraid, despite the attack from the 'evil-doers'. And despite repeated reminders of omnipresent threat. The American response to the spread of fear, the Bush Administration suggested, was the heroism of individual acts of bravery (such as those on US Flight 93) and collective resolve. Significant investment in narratives of American Exceptionalism followed. Consider the emotive eulogy to first-responders, police officers and fire-fighters, as well as 'ordinary citizens' who embodied American spirit when displaying feats of heroism. Todd Beamer and the passengers of Flight 93 were amongst those spoken of as the embodiment of bravery and American resolve (e.g. Jackson 2005; see also Weber 2008). Such discourses were designed to encourage Americans to feel brave in the face of an attack designed to spread fear, just as they were told to love each other in the face of an attack motivated by pure hatred. In each instance, the Bush Administration, first, accounted for affect by rendering difficult and nebulous 'feelings' as appropriate and logical. And, second, the Bush Administration, at times, named the emotions that Americans should be feeling in order to incorporate affective experiences of the day and affectively invest citizens within the discourse of the response.

A third and final example of the relationship between affect, discourse and resonance in the American response to 9/11 is the incorporation of affective *incomprehensibility* into a constructed *inexplicability*. Shock, disbelief and incomprehension were some of the most frequently expressed affective experiences of 9/11 for American citizens. The Bush Administration reworked these expressions of confusion and accounted for them within the emerging War on Terror discourse. 'Culturally informed incomprehension was replaced with a politically efficacious inexplicability, which transformed September 11 from a series of events beyond understanding into "9/11": a series of events that cannot be justified or explained' (Holland and Solomon 2014; see also Lundborg 2012). The story that Americans were told was that they could not make sense of the events precisely because it was not possible to find logic in them. The events were constructed as so abhorrent that they were beyond moral reasoning, and motivated by a degree of hatred that was entirely antithetical to American thinking and emotions. In this framing, 9/11 was a pure form of evil, entirely incompatible with the American way of life. Of course, such a construction had important policy ramifications, helping to render particular policy responses (such as diplomacy) off limits, whilst naturalising others (such as military intervention). But, for our purposes, it is most important to note that, by accounting for affect, the Bush Administration was able to affectively invest Americans within the emerging War on Terror discourse. This investment was central to the crafting of a resonant and ultimately hegemonic discourse, which would help to shape the contours of political possibility during the coming decade and beyond.

## Conclusion

As a growing body of literature has identified, affect plays an important role in (international) politics and (international) security. Here, however, I have set out an important rejoinder, highlighting the continued importance of the state, its elected representatives and their strategic narratives of security. Far from affect potentially wresting power away from practitioners of security, as a potential locus of resistance, in times of crisis at least, the state retains an ability to articulate 'affect' in the service of a particular political agenda. To make this argument, the chapter has briefly revisited and reconnected the (popular) experience and official (elite) framing of 9/11. Three principal arguments have been put forward.

First, September 11 was experienced in particular ways, which can usefully be thought of as affective responses – biological in nature but conditioned by culture. In the case of 9/11, the layering of a particular American security culture, which had reached its apogee just previously, within biological predispositions, helped to generate the conditions for an affective experience of the events that was broadly and widely shared by many watching US citizens. Second, the Bush Administration tapped into, articulated and incorporated these affective responses within the emerging discourse of the War on Terror. Three themes in particular – space, time and normality – organised the prevalent American affective experience of 9/11 and (later) came to be central components of the War on Terror discourse. Third, this interweaving of affect and strategic framing can help us to understand the resonance of dominant official discourses after 9/11. By accounting for, explaining and legitimising affective experiences of September 11, the Bush Administration invested its audience in the emerging crisis narrative and its associated policies of the War on Terror. The broader implications of this argument include that, while individual citizens' experiences matter, during moments of crisis the state retains an ability to articulate affect in ways that serve particular political and policy agendas. Very often, in times of crisis, 'affect is what states make of it' (Holland and Solomon 2014).

At these moments, very often, affect is what states make of it for two reasons. First, because crises often follow moments of (what Edkins has explored as) trauma; when language, culture, and Politics are temporarily suspended. And second, because crises concentrate agency in the hands of those with the requisite institutional power to have their words heard and accepted. And these words are central to establishing future solutions and the trajectory of the nation. The articulation of affect therefore tends to take place through the state, as the principal source of emergent dominant discourses (Hay 1999; Holland 2009). After the events of September 11, invalidation ('This has made everyone open their eyes'), ending ('We no longer appear to be chosen people'), and incomprehension ('I couldn't understand what was happening') characterised the affective experience of September 11 for many ordinary Americans. It was only later that policy-makers and practitioners retrospectively accounted for affect, and built on experience, in their formulation of resonant foreign policy discourse, which gave voice and reality to emotions such as 'fear' and 'anger'. Empirically, then, this chapter has begun to show how the Bush Administration accounted for three components of the prevalent affective American experience of 9/11 – 'senses' of foreignness, temporal rupture and incomprehension – which helped to affectively invest citizens in the emerging War on Terror discourse. This investment was vital to the resonance of the official account of 9/11 and the construction of the day as a moment and marker of crisis, which would underpin subsequent policy and legislative responses.

## Notes

1 The chapter broadly adheres to the practice of using the term 'September 11' to refer to the events of the day and '9/11' to denote a framed and constructed interpretation of those events.

2 The chapter draws on data collected in 2008 from the Witness and Response Collection of the Library of Congress, which records the thoughts of ordinary Americans in the days, weeks and months after 9/11. A network of amateur folklorists conducted the interviews, across the United States, in which members of the public reflect on how they think and feel about the events of September 11, 2001.

3 Exceptions, of course, exist. For example, feminist work in IR has long argued that the personal is political (Enloe 2000).

4 Accounts considering gendered narratives (e.g. Shepherd 2006) have explored narratives of 'saving women' which were seen to appeal to key audiences. They did more than this, however; such discourses were useful in silencing potential oppositional voices (Holland 2013a, 2013b).
5 Whereas the former, as we shall see, are socially conditioned.
6 Of course, as Solomon acknowledges, affect is not asocial; rather, affective dispositions are always already conditioned by previous encounters. As I go on to argue, affective dispositions are culturally (as well as biologically) produced.
7 As Connolly, amongst others, has noted, affect is biological and cultural (Connolly 2005). The layering of culture and biology in the establishment of neurological expectations is fascinating and important. This feedback loop features in the later empirical analysis of 9/11.

## Bibliography

Anderson, L. (2001) 'Witness and Response', Library of Congress, SR375, 13 September.

Bauch, A. (2001) 'Witness and Response', Library of Congress, SR380, 18 September.

Bleiker, R. and Hutchison, E. (2008) 'Fear no more: Emotions in world politics', *Review of International Studies*, 34(1): 115–135.

Bulley, D. (2008) 'Foreign terror? London bombings, resistance and the failing state', *British Journal of Politics and International Relations*, 10(3): 380–381.

Bush, G. W. (2001) 'Address to Joint Session of Congress and the American People', 20 September.

Bush, G. W. (2002a) 'President George W. Bush signs 9/11 Commission Bill', 27 November. Available online at: www.911memorial.org/sites/all/files/President%20Bush%20Signs%20911%20Commission%20Bill.pdf.

Bush, G. W. (2002b) Speech in Berlin, 23 May. Available online at: www.guardian.co.uk/world/2002/may/23/usa.georgebush.

Campbell, D. (1998) *Writing Security: United States Foreign Policy and the Politics of Identity*, revised edition. Minneapolis, MN: University of Minnesota Press.

Castello, V. (2001) 'Witness and Response', Library of Congress, SR321, 19 October.

Connolly, W. (2002) *Neuropolitics: Thinking, Culture, Speed*. Minneapolis, MN: University of Minnesota Press.

Connolly, W. (2005) 'The evangelical, capitalist resonance machine', *Political Theory*, 33(6): 869–886.

Crawford, N. (2000) 'The passion of world politics: Propositions on emotions and emotional relationships', *International Security*, 24(4): 116–156.

Croft, S. (2006) *Culture, Crisis and America's War on Terror*. Cambridge: Cambridge University Press.

Diken, B. and Laustsen, C. (2005) *The Culture of Exception: Sociology Facing the Camp*, International Library of Sociology. London: Routledge.

Diken, B. and Laustsen, C. (2008) '"We two will never twin": Fundamentalism and the politics of security', *Global Society*, 20(2): 199–221.

Edkins, J. (1999) *Poststructuralism & International Relations: Bringing the Political Back In*. Boulder, CO and London: Lynne Rienner.

Edkins, J. (2002) 'Forget trauma? Responses to September 11', *International Relations*, 16(2): 243–256.

Edkins, J. (2004) 'Ground Zero: Reflections on trauma, in/distinction and response', *Cultural Research*, 8(3): 247–270.

Enloe, C. (2000) *Bananas, Beaches and Bases: Making Feminist Sense of International Politics*, second edition. London and Berkeley, CA: University of California Press.
Farley (2001) 'Witness and Response', Library of Congress, SR242, 13 October.
Gaddis, J. L. (2004) *Surprise, Security, and the American Experience*. London: Harvard University Press.
Grayson, M. (2001) 'Witness and Response', Library of Congress, SR327, 1 November.
Hay, C. (1996a) 'From crisis to catastrophe? The ecological pathologies of the liberal-democratic state', *Innovations*, 9(4): 421–434.
Hay, C. (1996b) 'Narrating crisis: The discursive construction of the "Winter of Discontent"', *Sociology*, 30(2): 253–277.
Hay, C. (1999) 'Crisis and the structural transformation of the state: Interrogating the process of change', *British Journal of Politics & International Relations*, 1(3): 317–344.
Holland, J. (2009) 'From September 11 2001 to 9/11: From void to crisis', *International Political Sociology*, 3(3): 275–292.
Holland, J. (2010) 'Howard's War on Terror: A conceivable, communicable and coercive foreign policy discourse', *Australian Journal of Political Science*, 45(4): 643–661.
Holland, J. (2012) 'Blair's War on Terror: Selling intervention to Middle England', *British Journal of Politics and International Relations*, 14(1): 74–95.
Holland, J. (2013a) *Selling the War on Terror: Foreign Policy Discourses after 9/11*. London and New York: Routledge.
Holland, J. (2013b) 'Foreign policy and political possibility', *British Journal of Politics and International Relations*, 19(1): 48–67.
Holland, J. and Jarvis, L. (2014) '"Night fell on a different world": Experiencing, constructing and remembering 9/11', *Critical Studies on Terrorism*, 7(2): 187–204.
Holland, J. and Solomon, T. (2014) 'Affect is what states make of it', *Critical Studies on Security*, 2(3): 262–277.
Hutchison, E. (2010) 'Trauma and the politics of emotions: Constituting identity, security, and community after the Bali bombing', *International Relations*, 24(1): 65–86.
Jackson, R. (2005) *Writing the War on Terrorism: Language, Politics, and Counter-terrorism*. Manchester and New York: Manchester University Press.
Jarvis, L. (2009) *Times of Terror: Discourse, Temporality, and the War on Terror*. Basingstoke: Palgrave Macmillan.
Katzenstein, P. (ed.) (1996) *The Culture of National Security*. New York: Columbia University Press.
Lundborg, T. (2012) *Politics of the Event: Time, Movement, Becoming*. London: Routledge.
Massumi, B. (2007) 'Potential politics and the primacy of preemption', *Theory and Event*, 10(2). doi: 10.1353/tae.2007.0066.
McCrisken, T. (2003) *American Exceptionalism and the Legacy of Vietnam*. London: Barnes & Noble.
Moe, J. (2001) 'Witness and Response', Library of Congress, SR380, 18 September.
Nabers, D. (2009) 'Filling the void of meaning: Identity construction in US foreign policy after 9/11', *Foreign Policy Analysis*, 5(2): 191–204.
Peker, E. (2006) 'Following 9/11: George W. Bush's discursive re-articulation of American social identity', Master's thesis, Department of Management and Economics, Linköpings Universitet.
Ross, A. (2006) 'Coming in from the Cold: Constructivism and emotions', *European Journal of International Relations*, 12(2): 197–222.

Sato, K. (2001) 'Witness and Response', Library of Congress, SR247, 16 October.

Senor, J. (2001) 'Witness and Response', Library of Congress, SR015, 11 October.

Shepherd, L. (2006) 'Veiled references: Constructions of gender in the Bush administration discourse on the attacks on Afghanistan post-9/11', *International Feminist Journal of Politics*, 8(1): 19–41.

Shouse, E. (2005) 'Feeling, emotion, affect', *Media and Culture Journal*, 8(5). Available online at: http://journal.media-culture.org.au/0512/03-shouse.php.

Silberstein, S. (2002) *War of Words: Language, Politics, and 9/11*. London: Routledge.

Solomon, T. (2012) '"I wasn't angry, because I couldn't believe it was happening": Affect and discourse in responses to 9/11', *Review of International Studies*, 38(4): 907–928.

Waters, N. (2001) 'Witness and Response', Library of Congress, SR025, 27 October.

Weber, C. (2002) 'Flying planes can be dangerous', *Millennium: Journal of International Studies*, 31(1): 129–147.

Weber, C. (2008) 'Popular visual language as global communication: The remediation of United Airlines Flight 93', *Review of International Studies*, 34(1): 137–153.

Weldes, J., Laffey, M., Gusterson, H. and Duvall, R. (1999) 'Introduction: Constructing insecurity', in *Cultures of Insecurity*, Weldes, Laffey, Gusterson and Duvall (eds). Minneapolis, MN: University of Minnesota Press.

Williams, P. (2007) 'From non-intervention to non-indifference: The origins and development of the African Union's security culture', *African Affairs*, 106(42): 253–279.

# 14 Photographing war

## Don McCullin, Vietnam and the politics of emotion

*Thomas Gregory*

> Few are equipped to remain unmoved by the spectacle of what war does to people. These are sights that should, and do, bring pain, and shame, and guilt.
>
> (Don McCullin, *Unreasonable Behaviour*)

This chapter began its life in the special exhibition hall at the Imperial War Museum North on a cold winter's morning in January 2011. My partner and I had taken the short bus ride from our apartment in Hulme to see a collection of photographs by Don McCullin, whose haunting images of war have earned him the World Press Photo Award, the Cornell Capa Award and the Royal Photographic Society's Special 150th Anniversary Medal. The exhibition, which was rather appropriately titled 'Shaped by War', brought together almost all of the iconic images that have shaped his career, taking visitors on a journey from his humble beginnings in London's East End to his more recent work in Syria and Iraq. But the ride is anything but easy. From his early black-and-white shots of 'The Guv'nors' standing in the ruins of an abandoned building in Finsbury Park, London (which earned him his first contract with *The Observer* in 1959), to a more vivid colour portrait he took in El Salvador of three corpses being dragged from the back of a pick-up truck in 1981, the path that McCullin followed throughout his career is one that is strewn with mutilated corpses, injured bodies and grieving relatives.

As we sauntered around the dimly lit room, we were bombarded with images of death and destruction. Around every corner we were confronted with another conflict, another body, another image of grief. In the space of two hours, we had seen Congolese troops abusing prisoners in 1964; injured troops from both sides taken amidst the fighting in Vietnam between 1968 and 1969; and Phalangists posing around the body of a dead Palestinian girl in Beirut, 1962. Interspersed amongst these images of war were other icons of suffering that were no less disturbing: the emaciated figure of a small albino child from an orphanage in Biafra, still clinging to an empty tin of corned beef; a small child feeding on the shrivelled breast of his malnourished mother; homeless men scratching for a living in London's East End during the economic turbulence of the late 1960s. The only respite was a series of personal trinkets that McCullin had picked up along the way: a collection of passports with details of his travels, various press cards that had been issued to him at one time or another, and the mangled remains of a Nikon F camera, which had saved his life when it was hit by a bullet in 1968.

Reflecting on his experiences some years later, McCullin admitted that the violence he had seen continued to haunt him:

> Now that I have stopped going to wars I still struggle with the meaning of all those experiences. Wars have dreadful differences, but also a dreadful sameness. You sleep with the dead, you cradle the dead, you live with the living who become the dead.
>
> (McCullin 2002: 4)

It is perhaps not surprising that, in his retirement, McCullin only photographs the Somerset countryside. Although his dark and brooding tones remain, his landscapes lack any sign of human life. There are no victims or perpetrators to be seen, no pain and suffering, no death and destruction, just the snow-covered trees, waterlogged fields and overcast skies that seem to dominate the countryside in that part of rural England. Even now, he is still haunted by the scenes of violence, misery and despair that he has witnessed over the years. As he explains, 'the ghosts in my filing cabinets sometimes seem to shock me – the ghosts of all those dead in all those wars, especially that little Biafran boy' (McCullin 2002: 285).

As we left the Imperial War Museum North and traipsed back to the bus stop in the cold Manchester rain, we couldn't help but mull over what we had just seen. It is hard to describe how I was feeling on the journey home, but it certainly seemed like a huge burden had been placed on my shoulders as the mangled bodies of the victims raced through my mind. But the sense of despair that I was feeling, and the anger and sadness that seemed to accompany it, also got me thinking: Why do certain images of war seem to provoke such feelings whilst others do not seem to affect us in the same manner? Is it something about an exhibition like this, where you are bombarded with so many images of suffering, that triggered my despair? It also made me think about the images of death and destruction that we see – and don't see – today. Why is it that we remain so indifferent to the loss of some lives, but not others? Why do certain photographs seem to shake us to the very core, whilst others fail to resonate? How is it that we can simply turn the page on other people's suffering and ignore images of their plight? The purpose of this chapter, therefore, is to think about the emotionality of McCullin's photographs, focusing particular attention on his most famous images from the Vietnam War.

## Photographing war

In his book *Camera Lucida: Reflections on Photography* (1981), Roland Barthes reflects on the emotional impact that certain photographs seem to have and the failure of others to provoke similar kinds of feelings. To illustrate what he means, Barthes describes a scenario with which we will all be familiar: flicking through an illustrated magazine when, for whatever reason, one photograph just seems to make you stop (1981: 23). For Barthes, the photograph in question was from the rebellion in Nicaragua in 1979, which showed two nuns crossing a road as three soldiers strolled through the rubble. The photograph, he argues, was nothing extraordinary: there were no dead bodies on display or anything that might be considered particularly gruesome or ghastly. For the most part, the scene that was depicted captured little more than the everyday banalities of the war and was no different from the thousands of other photographs that were taken of the conflict and reproduced in the pages of newspapers around the world. What stood out for Barthes was the 'co-presence of two discontinuous elements, heterogeneous in that they did not belong to the same world': the nuns and the soldiers (ibid.: 23). Although other photographs of dead and injured bodies stirred a general interest, they failed to create the 'internal agitation' that this particular photograph caused.

To explain why this might be, Barthes differentiates between the *stadium* and the *punctum* of a photograph. The former refers to a general interest in or commitment to a particular topic without any sort of acuity, whereas the latter can be understood as a break with this more superficial concern or, as Barthes himself explains, an 'element which rises from the scene, shoots out of it like an arrow, and pierces me' (ibid.: 26). In other words, the *punctum* is something about the photograph that seems to prick our interest, to arouse some sort of emotional response that goes beyond the more casual concern. In the photograph of the rebellion in Nicaragua, it is the co-presence of the military and the holy sisters that provides this prick, but we can also find plenty of examples in McCullin's work that might explain why his photographs capture our attention. His photographs of the civil war in Cyprus, for example, always managed to capture quite discontinuous elements within the same scene. In one image of a street fight in the southern city of Limassol, a man is seen wandering the streets in a suit and tie, as if he had just popped out the office for lunch – except that he is also wearing a balaclava and carrying a gun. In another photograph, this time of the war in Beirut, a group of Christian militia-men are shown standing around the body of a dead girl as one of them plays a lute. Likewise, in one of his most famous photographs of The Troubles in Northern Ireland, we see a snatch squad armed with billy clubs charging down a street just as a scared housewife opens her front door. The appearance of these seemingly incongruous elements within McCullin's photographs might help explain why it is that his work seems to leave such a mark on those that see them.

His photographs of the war in Vietnam are no exception to this rule, and often contain things that seem to leap out from the image and seize our attention. One of his most famous celebrated photographs from the Vietnam War captures an injured marine as he is carried through the ruins of a house by two of his colleagues. At first glance, it is difficult to explain why it is that this image seems so striking, as it seems to portray a relatively mundane battlefield scene that has been seen in countless other photographs of war. If you look a little more closely, it is clear that McCullin has managed to capture something quite special. As numerous commentators have observed, the photograph of the marine is strangely reminiscent of the crucifixion and religious paintings of Jesus as he was taken down from the cross (Evans 2003: 13). In another photograph from the war, we see an army chaplain – with a crucifix dangling from his helmet – carrying a petrified old woman through the wreckage of her village. Following Barthes, therefore, we might try to explain the emotional responses that these photographs engender on the basis of discontinuities that they depict: soldiers interrupting the mundane routines of domestic life; combatants playing musical instruments around the body of a dead girl; messianic scenes in the midst of war.

The problem with this understanding of the photograph is that it assumes that our emotional responses are triggered – or not triggered – by aesthetic qualities that exist within the photograph itself. It also presumes that all those who see the photograph will be pricked in the same way. Others have also sought to explain the emotionality of McCullin's work by drawing attention to visual qualities intrinsic to the individual photographs. In an essay that accompanied a retrospective of his work, Susan Sontag argued that 'in this great tradition of photojournalism, sometimes labelled "concerned photography" or "the photography of conscience", no one has surpassed – in breadth, in directedness, in intimacy, in unforgettability – the exemplary, gut-wrenching work produced by Don McCullin' (Sontag 2001: 16). For many, it is not just the *punctum* that explains why McCullin's photographs are so affective, but the sheer brutality of the scenes that he depicts. In contrast to the more sanitised images of war that appeared in magazines and print at the time, McCullin does not try to mask the blood, the guts and the gore that seem to saturate the battlefield (Sylvester 2011: 2).

## Photographing Vietnam

> If I ask myself if I have done any good or changed anything, I actually don't believe I've changed anything at all.
>
> (Don McCullin, *Shaped by War*)

When McCullin first arrived in Vietnam in 1968, he was intending to cover the Battle of Khe Sanh in the north-western province of Quang Tri, where a US Combat Base had been surrounded by the North Vietnamese Army and subjected to a barrage of artillery attacks (McCullin 2002: 93–104, 2010: 77). But he soon discovered that David Douglas Duncan had already departed for Khe Sanh, so he jumped aboard a convoy of trucks heading towards the Imperial Citadel in Hue (McCullin 2010: 77). Arriving in Hue, McCullin had nothing but the fatigues he was wearing – no helmet, no flak jacket and no water bottle – but his destination turned out to be one of the bloodiest battles of the entire war, claiming the lives of approximately 5,000 North Vietnamese and at least 668 Allied Forces, including 216 Americans. At least 3,800 civilians are believed to have died as a result of the battle and another 116,000 made homeless (Turse 2013: 102–104, see also Tirman 2011). His photographs of the violence that was unleashed in Hue – along with the work of other photographers, such as Larry Burrows, Horst Faas, Philip Jones Griffiths, Catherine Leroy, Eddie Adams and Nick Ut – are often praised for providing new forms of intimacy with the pain and suffering caused by war, and blamed for transforming public attitudes towards the conflict in Vietnam (Hallin 1986; Brothers 1997; Knightley 2004). As President Nixon complained some years later, 'whatever the intention behind such relentless and literal reporting of the war, the result was a serious demoralisation of the home front, raising the question of whether America would ever again be able to fight an enemy abroad with unity and strength of purpose at home' (quoted in Hallin 1986: 3).

By the time he had returned to his darkroom in Da Nang, McCullin had with him 'thirty rolls of the most powerful film I've ever taken in my life' (2010: 80). Perhaps the most famous of these was the photograph of a shell-shocked marine, who is seen hunched in the ruins of the citadel, seemingly overcome with fear and anxiety. This attention to the emotions generated by war is something that comes in much of his work and McCullin talks very openly in his autobiography about his own emotional experiences of war. Despite all of the horrors that he has witnessed and all the pain and suffering he has seen, McCullin argues that he has never been able to switch off his own feelings, and at times these feelings would reach an 'unbearable pitch' (McCullin 2002: 4). One incident that continues to haunt McCullin happened when he found himself caught in a forward position with a group of marines in Vietnam. A supply truck – which looked 'more like a moke or dune-buggy than a lorry' – overshot their position in the dark and the driver was killed by a sniper. All night his body lay slumped at the wheel whilst the engine continued to run. McCullin recalls how he could clearly see the body thanks to the bright green, yellow and orange tracer flares illuminating the night sky but was unable to reach him (ibid.: 104).

At other times, he describes the sense of guilt he always felt when he encroached upon the emotions of others, including the time he was caught photographing the remains of three dead men by the family of the deceased. As McCullin explains, 'it wasn't just trespass in the legal sense [because … ] I had trespassed on death and emotion too' (ibid.: 46). The reason why he was prepared to trespass on the emotional experiences of others was his belief that part of his role was to capture and convey the emotionality of war and the human consequences of the violence he was witnessing. During the early stages of his career, for example, he operated under the assumption that the main purpose of his photographs was 'to share other people's emotional experiences, live with them silently, transmit them' (ibid.: 48). Following his first assignment to Berlin, he describes how he had been seduced by the political and emotional significance of the photograph: 'I thought to myself that, for once in my life, I had a purpose. I had to use it. I thought I could turn people's minds and even change situations' (McCullin 2010: 39).

Since his retirement, however, McCullin has become much more ambivalent about the impact of his photographs, telling one reporter in a recent interview that 'the last fifty years of my life has been wasted photographing war' (Cade 2014). Reflecting on how his attitudes towards war photography have evolved over the course of his career, McCullin seems strangely unsatisfied with the arrogance and naïveté he had displayed in his youth. To illustrate what he means, he points to the famous photograph that Eddie Adams took of the South Vietnamese General Nguyen Ngoc Loan executing a prisoner on a street in Saigon, which is often cited as a key turning point in American attitudes towards the conflict in Vietnam (McCullin 2010: 39). Although the photograph eventually became a prominent symbol in the anti-war movement, McCullin reminds us that 'after Eddie Adams took the famous photograph of the police chief in Saigon shooting a man in the head, the war raged on for another seven years' (ibid.). It is also worth pointing out that when the image was first published, it was presented as a 'brutal but understandable [act of] revenge against a man who had murdered many Americans' (Taylor 1998: 22). Adams himself viewed the general as 'hero' and later apologised to him for the damage his photograph had done to his reputation (Adams 1998).

## Seeing war/feeling war

As well as trying to capture the emotional trauma of war, McCullin also paid close attention to the dead and injured bodies that littered the battlefield. By the end of his tour of duty in Vietnam, McCullin claimed to be something of 'an expert on what a bullet can do to a frail human body as it zips through flesh and fragments on bone' (1994: 52). The idea that photographs of dead and injured bodies will automatically cause the viewer to recoil in horror – or provoke outpourings of anger, sadness and grief – has been the subject of much debate within academic literature as well. In her book *On Photography* (1977), Susan Sontag questions the capacity of the photograph to generate the intensity of feeling that we might expect. Although photographs seem to furnish us with incontrovertible proof of the pain and suffering experienced by distant others, Sontag warns that people's reactions to these images is contingent upon the wider political consciousness within which they appear (Sontag 1977: 19). To illustrate what she means, Sontag notes that during the latter stages of the Vietnam War – when opposition to the conflict was at its peak – images of the conflict were sufficient to provoke significant levels of public outrage. However, during the Korean War and the early stages of the Vietnam War, she argues that there was little 'ideological space' for images of American atrocities. Even when they did appear, these photographs were usually dismissed as fakes, fabrications or forgeries (ibid.: 19, 2003: 10). In other words, our emotional, moral and political reaction to these images was not determined by the scenes of violence that they depicted but the wider narrative that had been constructed around these events.

As well as questioning this 'presumption of validity' that these photographs are supposed to present, Sontag also voiced concerns about the proliferation of these images, suggesting that the public sphere had become so saturated with pictures of war that people were becoming de-sensitised to the suffering of others (1977: 19–21, see also 2003: 21). According to Sontag, our capacity to be affected by these images was dependent to a large extent on our exposure to them, so the sheer number of these photographs now in circulation was having an anaesthetising effect, deadening our emotional responses rather than arousing them (1977: 20–21). As she explains, 'the quality of feeling, including moral outrage, that people can muster in response to photographs of the oppressed, the exploited, the starving, the massacred also depends on the degree of their familiarity with these images' (ibid.: 21). Similar themes have also been picked up by a number of other commentators. At the height of the Kosovo War, for example, Michael Ignatieff warned that 'war photography, thanks to television, has now become a nightly banality' (quoted in Sontag 2003: 16–17). Likewise, Roland Bleiker and Amy Kay have warned that images of suffering tend to reify existing stereotypes about the lives of those depicted, reinforcing the distance between us and them, the viewer and the viewed (2007: 142–144).

To try to mitigate the effects of this, Sontag suggested that we ought to try to ration our exposure to these photographs by establishing an 'ecology of images', thereby preserving their emotional tug (1977: 180). Towards the end of her life, Sontag was a little more circumspect about her proposals for restricting our access to these images, arguing that 'no committee of guardians is going to ration our exposure to the almost-unbearable-to-look-at' (2001: 17). But her central concerns about the de-sensitising effects of these images, their failure to generate the emotions that we might desire, and the failure of photographs to 'speak for themselves' remained constant (2003: 9). Although photographs of dead and 'mutilated bodies certainly can be used … to vivify the condemnation of war' it is perfectly possible and quite common for other people to see the same images and find 'no evidence, none at all, for renouncing war' (ibid.: 10–11). In addition, she warned that even when they do trigger an emotional response in the viewer, whether by moving them to tears or inciting them to anger, the intensity of these feelings will be negligible and their duration only fleeting (ibid.: 90). After the initial shock dissipates, people will quickly forget about the violence they have just seen and return to normality.

Our capacity to be moved by images of war has also been challenged by a number of other commentators, who warn that these photographs can be rather depoliticising in their effects. In his work on the iconography of famine, for example, David Campbell has warned that we are bombarded with very stylised images of starving women and children, but the larger social, economic and political technologies that cause or precipitate these issues remain invisible (2012: 80, see also 2007: 369; Bleiker and Kay 2007: 149–150). Drawing on the work of Allen Feldman, Campbell argues that we are suffering from a form of 'cultural anaesthesia' that increases the social capacity not only to inflict pain on the other, but to render this pain inadmissible to public discourse (Campbell 2003: 67–73; see also Feldman 1994: 406; Rosler 2006: 174–176). Others have suggested that photographs of such violence are depoliticising not because we remain unaffected by what they show, but because they affect us too much, engulfing us in the suffering of distant others at the expense of more meaningful forms of political action (Berger 1991: 42–43).

McCullin's work is certainly not immune from these criticisms. It is worth noting, for example, for all the bodies that have been mangled by war, we rarely catch a glimpse of the sniper who pulled the trigger, the soldier who threw the grenade, or the guard who delivered the fatal blow. There are, of course, always exceptions to the rule. In one photograph we see three soldiers humiliating a Vietnamese civilian, who is kneeling in front of them with a blindfold around his face and his hands tied behind his back. In another photograph, two marines are seen rummaging through the possessions of a dead soldier, searching for souvenirs (although I can find no evidence that the latter was published at the time). Similarly, Robin Anderson has argued that his work on the Biafran famine stripped the victims from their social context and failed to implicate or accuse those who are responsible for their plight (cited in Campbell 2003: 70). And finally, John Berger has suggested that McCullin's attention to 'sudden moments of agony' is sufficient to provoke feelings of indignation or despair, these feelings seem 'hopelessly inadequate' to the events that are depicted (1991: 43). Whilst his photographs of war are capable of provoking an emotional outburst, they cannot sustain our commitment once the initial shock dissipates (ibid.: 42–43).

## Frames of war

> War sustains its practices through acting on the senses, crafting them to apprehend the world selectively, deadening affect in response to certain images and sounds, and enlivening affective responses to others.
>
> (Judith Butler, *Frames of War*)

Although McCullin's photographs have been widely praised for trying to capture and communicate the emotional impact of war, the arguments presented in the previous section clearly complicate the suggestion that photographs of dead and injured bodies will be sufficient to incite an emotional response. Some have warned that images of war can be profoundly depoliticising because they tend to camouflage the wider problems that have enabled this violence, and erase the perpetrators from view. Others have suggested that the proliferation of these images has deadened our senses to the suffering of others by normalising the violence that is depicted, reproducing stereotypes of the oppressed and the victimised, and reinforcing the distance – both physical and emotional – that separates us. In contrast, some have warned of a real danger that people will be so overwhelmed with their emotions that they end up drowning in feelings of pity, sorrow or despair, rather than seeking to transform this into more concrete forms of political action. Clearly, these are all issues that might, in one way or another, affect the affectivity of the photograph, but they do not quite get to grips with the questions that I outlined at the beginning. Why is it that certain photographs seem to prick us emotionally, whilst others fail to affect us at all? Why is it that the pain and suffering experienced by certain groups of people will generate mass outpourings of anger or sorrow, whilst images of other losses fail to replicate this success? What does it mean to become emotionally and ethically responsive to the suffering of those who are photographed?

In the final part of this chapter, I want to try and tackle these questions from a slightly different perspective, by drawing on Judith Butler's recent work on the politics of grief and the ethics of photography. What interests Butler is not so much the content of the photograph itself, or the aesthetic concerns that might account for why it is that some images are more engaging that others, but the wider field of representability that helps to condition our emotional responses to the suffering that is depicted and the lives that have been lost. In the previous section, we touched upon some of Sontag's concerns about the limitations of photographs for arousing the emotions of those who view them. As well as pointing to the anaesthetising effect of these images, Sontag cast doubt on the claim that photographs of war will be sufficient to mobilise the population against it. Although some will undoubtedly recoil in horror at the violence that is depicted, others will view these images in an entirely different manner (2003: 10).

One of the more controversial aspects of Sontag's argument was the idea that photographs cannot 'speak for themselves' (1977: 108–109, 2003: 9). Although these images can provide a visual record of something that has happened, they cannot provide an interpretation of that event but must 'wait to be explained or falsified by their captions' (ibid.: 9). Moreover, the structural ambiguity of any photograph means that it is vulnerable to multiple interpretations. An image of a civilian casualty, for example, cannot tell us much about what happened by itself, because it provides only a glimpse of what has happened. As a result, the image could easily be used as evidence to condemn the indiscriminate use of force by those responsible, or as evidence that enemy combatants are placing civilians at risk by using them as human shields (see Gregory 2012: 329). Alter the caption, Sontag argued, and the meaning of the photograph can be easily changed; the evidence it is supposed to provide can be re-figured, re-interpreted and re-used to show precisely the opposite (2003: 9).

Although she is largely sympathetic to Sontag's analysis, Butler takes issue with the idea that photographs are unable to provide an interpretation of the events they depict. Countering Sontag's view that photographs can be understood as punctual, atomistic and discrete entities, Butler argues that photographs are always already interpretations of the events portrayed (2007: 952). Even before we have a chance to see the photographs, decisions are being made about what should be seen and what should not, and these decisions are shaped – in part – by a set of interpretive structures that decide whose lives matter and whose do not. As Butler explains, 'prior to the events and actions that are represented within the frame, there is an active, if unmarked, delimitation of the field itself, and so a set of contents and perspectives that are not shown, never shown, impermissible to show' (ibid.: 953). In this respect, these norms work to govern the field of perceptible vision, not only controlling what can and cannot be seen, but helping to orchestrate how these images will be seen and understood. Crucially, these frames also act to regulate and control the affective responses that may or may not be triggered by a particular image, stifling our emotional responses to certain forms of suffering whilst arousing feelings of anger, outrage or anguish towards others (Butler 2009: 39).

One way that these frames can regulate affect, therefore, is by limiting what kinds of images come into view, either through more explicit forms of censorship or more insidious forms of control. In her own work, Butler has focused on attempts by the state to orchestrate the visual field by embedding journalists within military units, thereby limiting what they are likely to see and what kinds of images they can take (2005: 822; see also Kennedy 2008: 285–286; Campbell 2011). Although these examples seem particularly salient given the present conditions, we can also point to examples from McCullin's own career where his work has been censored before he has even had a chance to unpack his kit. The most obvious incident here is the travel ban that was placed on McCullin and many other leading journalists during the Falklands War in 1982, despite telling him that arrangements for his travel had already been confirmed (2010: 172–173). In a letter to *The Times*, McCullin complained that 'their excuse was that there was not enough accommodation on board any of the ships, even though they managed to accommodate three million Mars bars' (ibid.: 174). Even during his tour of Vietnam, McCullin often found that the photographs he took never materialised in print (McCullin 2002: 70; Campbell 2011: 8; see also Hallin 1986: 129–130; Brothers 1997: 203).

By restricting the visual field in this manner, our emotional response to the suffering of others is stifled not by the prevalence of these images, but by the absence of an image. Our emotions have not been pricked because there was nothing there to prick us; no photographs of the pain and suffering experienced by those on the frontlines, no images of the death and destruction that was caused, and no mutilated corpses to shock and disturb us. But it is important to understand how these frames might circumscribe our emotional reactions even when we do see graphic photographs of the pain and suffering caused by war. As well as drawing attention to the prohibition on certain kinds of images, Butler is equally concerned with the ways in which these interpretive frames work to produce and maintain an exclusionary conception of the human, helping to establish an emotional hierarchy that will animate our emotional responses to certain forms of suffering whilst deadening our responses to others (2004: 35). In her own work, Butler has shown how the de-realisation of enemy combatants in Afghanistan and Iraq means that they do not have access to a publicly grievable death, ensuring their passing cannot be mourned in quite the same way as our own soldiers (ibid.: 74–78). As Butler explains, 'if certain lives do not qualify as lives or are, from the start, not conceivable as lives within certain epistemological frames, then these lives are never lived nor lost in the full sense (2009: 1). Others have expanded her analysis to show how civilian casualties are also ungrievable within the prevailing frames of war (Gregory 2012).

It is this observation that might be helpful to understand why it is that McCullin's work never quite had either the emotional or the political impact that he had expected. Throughout his career, McCullin always maintained that his job was as an 'independent [but] not unemotional' witness, even when he was embedded with American troops in Hue (McCullin 2002: 96). Part of his role, he claimed, was to try to communicate the harm caused by war, no matter who the victims were. On his second trip to Vietnam, for example, he came across a group of South Vietnamese soldiers rejoicing over the death of an enemy fighter and pretending to urinate over his dead body. Next to the corpse he discovered a small red diary that he brought home and published in *The Sunday Times* in an attempt to re-humanise 'the enemy' (ibid.: 185). Likewise, the only photograph that McCullin ever 'faked' was of a dead North Vietnamese soldier he found in Hue, with his personal possessions scattered around him. In an effort to 'say something about the human costs of this war', McCullin re-arranged his personal items – a tin of family portraits, a letter home and a picture of his girlfriend – into a collage around the victim's body (ibid.: 102).

Despite the best intentions of the photographer, there is no guarantee of course that those viewing this image will see the victim as a fellow human being or that they will feel anything about his passing. As I have indicated above, our emotional responses are not spontaneous operations of the mind or unmediated bodily reactions but are conditioned by a 'nonthematised background' of cultural assumptions about what counts as a human and who does not (Butler 2007: 953). It is worth remembering that, at the time, the bodies of those killed and injured in Vietnam were not always guaranteed the same recognition as American casualties of war because they had been marked by a series of racial assumptions about what qualifies as human and what does not. Against this backdrop of normative assumptions, the emotional responses of those viewing images like this would be tempered by the fact that this was 'just another dead gook' (McCullin 2002: 96–97; see also Hallin 1986: 158; Turse 2013: 49–51). As Butler explains, 'if violence is done against those who are unreal, then, from the perspective of violence, it fails to injure or negate those lives since those lives are already negated' (2004: 33). One only needs to think about the relatively muted response to the photographs of the My Lai Massacre to realise that graphic portraits of the victims are not always sufficient to trigger the emotional responses that we might expect (Oliver 2006; see also Lewinski 1978: 213–214; Schlegel 1995). As Kenderick Oliver explains, 'the empathetic connection that many Americans made during the national debate about My Lai ... was not with the victims shown in the massacre photographs, but with the perpetrators from whose perspectives such images had been shot' (2013: 80).

## Conclusion

The aim of this chapter is to think about the emotions that may or may not be triggered by images of war. Focusing on McCullin's graphic imagery of the war in Vietnam, I have explored some of the arguments that have been put forward to explain why photographs often fail to deliver the emotional blow that we might expect. Some have focused their attention on the explicit content of the photographs themselves, and aesthetic concerns about the way in which this content is presented, arguing that photographs often reproduce pre-existing and profoundly de-politicising stereotypes of distant others. Others have suggested that the sheer proliferation of images had de-sensitised us to their plight and deadened our emotional responses to the pain and suffering caused by war. Although I am sympathetic to both sets of arguments, I have suggested that we need to focus on the regimes of affect that condition how we might feel about the death and destruction that we see – the background conditions that produce feelings of anger, sadness and compassion when we see certain dead and injured bodies, but leave us strangely unaffected when we are confronted by other bodies in similar states of distress. Understanding how it is that photographs fail to elicit the emotions we expect cannot be explained, therefore, simply by looking at the explicit contents of the individual photograph or by pointing to the sheer numbers of similar images. Instead, we must turn our attention to the regimes of affect that animate our responses to some images of war but leave us strangely indifferent to many others.

## Bibliography

Adams, E. (1998) 'Eulogy: General Nguyen Ngoc Loan'. Available online at: http://content.time.com/time/magazine/article/0,9171,988783,00.html (accessed 18 May 2014).

Barthes, R. (1981) *Camera Lucida: Reflections on Photography*, Howard (transl.). New York: Hill & Wang.

Berger, J. (1991) *About Looking*. London: Vintage.

Bleiker, R. and Kay, A. (2007) 'Representing HIV/AIDS in Africa', *International Studies Quarterly*, 51(1): 139–163.

Brothers, C. (1997) *War and Photography: A Cultural History*. London: Routledge.

Butler, J. (2004) *Precarious Life: The Powers of Mourning and Violence*. London: Verso.

Butler, J. (2005) 'War, photography, outrage', *PMLA*, 120(3): 822–827.

Butler, J. (2007) 'Torture and the ethics of photography', *Environment and Planning D*, 25(6): 951–966.

Butler, J. (2009). *Frames of War: When is Life Grievable?* London: Verso.

Cade, D. L. (2014) 'Interview with Don McCullin'. Available online at: http://petapixel.com/2014/01/29/incredible-must-see-interview-iconic-conflict-photographer-don-mccullin/ (accessed 18 May 2014).

Campbell, D. (2003) 'Cultural Governance and Pictorial Resistance', *Review of International Studies*, 29(S1): 57–73.
Campbell, D. (2007) 'Geopolitics and Visuality: Sighting the Darfur Conflict', *Political Geography*, 26(1): 357–382.
Campbell, D. (2011) 'How has photojournalism framed the war in Afghanistan?' Available online at: www.david-campbell.org/wp-content/documents/Framing_the_war_in_Afghanistan.pdf (accessed 18 May 2014).
Campbell, D. (2012) 'The iconography of famine', in *Picturing Atrocity: Reading Photographs in Crisis*, Batchen, Gidley Miller and Prosser (eds). London: Reaktion, 79–92.
Evans, H. (2003) 'Introduction', in *Don McCullin*, McCullin (ed.). London: Jonathan Cape, 12–15.
Feldman, A. (1994) 'On cultural anaesthesia: From Desert Storm to Rodney King', *American Ethnologist*, 21(2): 404–418.
Gregory, T. (2012) 'Potential lives, impossible deaths: Afghanistan, civilian casualties and the politics of intelligibility', *International Feminist Journal of Politics*, 14(3): 327–347.
Hallin, D. C. (1986) *The 'Uncensored War': The Media and Vietnam*. Oxford: Oxford University Press.
Kennedy, L. (2008) 'Securing vision: Photograph and US foreign policy', *Media, Culture and Society*, 30(3): 279–294.
Knightley, P. (2004) *The First Casualty: The War Correspondent as Hero and Myth-Maker from the Crimea to Iraq*. Baltimore, MD: John Hopkins University Press.
Lewinski, J. (1978) *The Camera at War: War Photography from 1848 to the Present Day*. London: W.H. Allen.
McCullin, D. (1994) *Sleeping with Ghosts*. London: Jonathan Cape.
McCullin, D. (2002) *Unreasonable Behaviour: An Autobiography*. London: Vintage.
McCullin, D. (2010) *Shaped by War*. London: Jonathan Cape.
Oliver, K. (2006) *The My Lai Massacre in American History and Memory*. Manchester: Manchester University Press.
Oliver, K. (2013) '"I would too, wouldn't you?" Regarding the deaths of others during the Vietnam War', in *Liberal Democracies at War*, Footitt and Knapp (eds). London: Bloomsbury, 67–88.
Rosler, M. (2006) *Decoys and Disruptions: Selected Writings 1975–2001*. Cambridge, MA: MIT Press.
Schlegel, A. (1995) 'My Lai: We lie, they die', *Third Text*, 31(9): 47–66.
Sontag, S. (1977) *On Photography*. New York: Picador.
Sontag, S. (2001) 'Witnessing', in *Don McCullin*, McCullin (ed.). London: Jonathan Cape, 16–17.
Sontag, S. (2003) *Regarding the Pain of Others*. London: Penguin.
Sylvester, C. (ed.) (2011) *Experiencing War*. London: Routledge.
Taylor, J. (1998) *Body Horror: Photojournalism, Catastrophe and War*. Manchester: Manchester University Press.
Tirman, J. (2011) *The Deaths of Others: The Fate of Civilians in America's Wars*. Oxford: Oxford University Press.
Turse, N. (2013) *Kill Anything That Moves: The Real American War in Vietnam*. New York: Metropolitan Books.

# 15 Exposed images of war

*Emmanuel-Pierre Guittet and Andreja Zevnik*

> There are so many images moving around and again in the world that we believe we possess them because we saw them …
>
> (Panh 2013: 12)

The common understanding of war is strongly influenced by cogent but codified visual narratives: be it heroism and triumphalism when the American flag was raised on Iwo Jima (Rosenthal 1945)[1]; be it the distress of a shell-shocked GI lost in the middle of the Vietnam war (McCullin 1968); be it the genuine pain of a weeping soldier seated in a helicopter and grieving for a fallen comrade in Iraq (Turnley 1991); or be it civilian suffering caught in a close-up portrait of a woman burned by napalm (Avedon 1971). Landscapes of ruins and desolate battlefields (Fenton 1855; Hoffman 1945), derelict and deserted barracks of the Cold War (Roemers 2010) and close-up portrayals of the wounded all testify to the destructive force of war, and to photography's power to preserve such events for future generations. Scenes of imminent or instant death are common in war, but so are moments of tranquillity, particular wartime intimacy (Hetherington 2008) and joy (Velder 1973), or madness (Greene 1995) and humiliation (Abu Ghraib 2003; Bouju 2003), which, fixed on paper and disseminated, reach the public eye. From pictures taken by professional photographers, via creative (Greene 1995; Blenkinsop 2001; Asburn 2002; Roemers 2010) and artistic use of war imagery (Loesch 1991; Lhuisset 2010), to pictures taken by ordinary civilians and service personnel, the context, content, format and intentions behind the images produced, edited, framed and distributed are multiple and sometimes contradictory.

'Images of war' is a complex photographic genre impregnated with emotion, which, unsurprisingly, carries enormous power in determining *reality*. In the context of politics and its engagement with the public, war imagery carries that extra weight. Not only are such images a tool of manipulation, they also challenge the idea of visual representation as Linfield (2010) suggests, namely, that images reflect and transmit some of the real-time and on-the-ground experience of war to those who are distant. Critique of representation (Benjamin 1997, 2007) and Feldman's theory of cultural anesthesia (Feldman 1994) are two common critiques of war imagery. While the former evaluates images through a prism of authenticity by raising questions about the staging of photo-shoots and the photographer's intention when taking these shots, cultural anesthesia focuses more on the effect images have on their audience, in particular on their emotional investment and voyeuristic engagement. The two critiques of imagery thus address two rather distinct areas: the conditions in which the photo was taken, and the intended effect it might have. More recent literature (Sliwinski 2009; Linfield 2010; Kozol 2012) has attached the emotive aspect of photography to arguments of pacifism and withdrawal from action. Here images' narratives seduce the public with their artistic expression, with emotional overload when suffering and pain are exposed, or with their humanitarian intent, and thus enable – anesthetise – the public's incentive to act. However, such a critique rests on the assumption that images are manipulated, have lost a sense of authenticity or reality, and thus have pushed the audience to seek out ways to re-connect and meaningfully re-engage with them. As they can no longer inform, audiences engage with images only at the level of the emotions (or affects) they evoke. In other words, that which is depicted in the photo can only be engaged with in an individual, emotional tête-à-tête. Whilst such an emotion-focused way around the aforementioned critiques perhaps bears some weight, photos are more than just devices for triggering emotional responses. They are traces of light, of something that was *there* and that was caught by a camera lens. Reducing such materiality to a frame, or the bare context in which the photo is taken (and to the photographer's intentions), or worse, to a context in which the photo is received, misses important power(s) of photography, one of which is a power of imagination. Instead of looking at the 'reality' of the photo, imagination considers that which a photo can be, or is a trace of. A photo, if conceived through a prism of imagination, can give life to spaces that would otherwise remain unexplored or hidden, or that are of a different *scopic regime*[2] and thus excluded per se from the existing regime of visibility. Such photos are *out-of-joint* with the context in which they were shot, or inherently displace common narratives about war. Tim Hetherington's series of photos portraying US marines in Afghanistan exemplifies such *out-of-joint* intervention as he draws out the banal everyday experiences of soldiers. They are seen playing golf, having fun, drinking; photos aestheticise and eroticise their bodies as well as depict moments of humility, emotional struggle and intimacy. Hetherington penetrates the war zone with glimpses of everyday life and thus displaces common narratives about war. What is to be learnt from such interventions is that photos cannot be reduced to emotional material. They are neither representations nor depictions of real-time events. They are very distinct narratives driven by the person behind the camera-trigger, but as Didi-Huberman reminds us (2005a), that makes them no less valid. With the developments in technology and ever-expanding scale of image reproducibility, the value of images is bound to come under scrutiny, but focusing on the emotion/anesthetic side of the critique and forgetting about their value is not a productive way of engagement.

Departing from the emotion-focused debates on the representation of war/wartime photojournalism and questions about photos' authenticity, this chapter looks at how images shape both what we know and how we learn about contemporary war, its landscapes, actors, actions and causes. In other words, we claim that photography can provide knowledge of wartime events, but only as long as its audience is interested in questions of what took place, and does not aim to seek personal connections with that which photography portrays. Or, as Didi-Huberman (2008: 80–88) writes in *Images in Spite of All*, photographs are openings of knowledge (not absolute knowledge), as for the gaps in knowledge we, as the audience, need to imagine. This chapter therefore contributes to the debate on the fragility of war representation at a time when we are saturated with images of violence. It is divided into three parts. Part 1 (Seeing) focuses on technological developments in war photography and on the emergence of radically new approaches to photography. The aim is to demonstrate that critique of war photography is interlinked with technological advancement in the photographic genre, and that a critique is viable only on the assumption that war photography was once authentic, and that authenticity of (war) photography is a question worthy of engagement. Part 2 (Looking) focuses on the image-riddled 'emotional blackmail' reality of war. By engaging with the critique of (war) photography, the section aims to show how emotion/affect and graphic disillusion are tautological and in fact redundant in the study of war photography, as the critique is concerned with what photography is not (namely an authentic representation of reality). Questions of authenticity, originality and truth are the wrong questions, as Didi-Huberman (2005a) reminds us. Part 3 (Registering) is designed as a reply to the disenchantment uncovered by the crisis of representation. What we suggest here is that images are indexes of warfare's mutation, admissible evidence of daily life in a war zone, war trophies and traces of actions taken in affect or records of camera-witnesses, of particular actions, from a particular point of view and at a very particular moment. Photography works as an imaginary *quilting point* or a common reference, which creates our collective imaginary of heroism, cruelty and suffering. It does not hold truth or absolute knowledge, it can never pass a test of authenticity, but that does not detract from it as evidence of something taking place; it is an index on which we can draw, it is a testimony to the event and to the photographer's intention.

## Seeing – in the eye of the storm[3]

Photography has recorded conflict from the early days of its invention. When photography discovered war in the mid-nineteenth century, and aimed to shoot, report and represent it, it established itself in opposition to thousands of years of heroic and glamorised war paintings, combining anecdotal accuracy with a charged romantic landscape. That is of course not to say that war photography was critical per se, but due to its ability to 'capture light' in a manner similar to the human eye, it was quickly perceived as an imprint of reality. One only needs to be reminded of a shocked individual when experiencing their photographic portrait for the first time. Suddenly, a reflection they had only seen in a mirror, and that constituted their image of who they were (their face and body), was materialised on a piece of paper. As what they had seen on the paper was no different from the reflection in the mirror, it led them believe that photography was an imprint of reality. With the first photographic portrayals of the epicentre of war, the tumultuous and frenetic clang of arms with dead and dismembered bodies remained supremely absent. War photography was all about preparation and a form of cruel uncertainty and expectation. But Roger Fenton and Alexander Gardner soon whitewashed centuries of heroic story-telling. Fenton brought the silence of desolation from the Crimean war (1853–56); Gardner and his assistant James Gibson were the first to bring back home the terrible reality and earnestness of war, with their exhibition of pictures of cadavers and dead horses from the bloodiest 1862 battle of the American civil war, Antietam. In some respects, Fenton and Gardner were the first to offer the public a different visual narrative from the more common narrative of classic glorious military history, using photography and its certificate of realism, *war as if you were there*, and contributing to the development of photography as a technique of testimony.

From its earliest days, the status of photography as a new medium drew from its alleged ability both to authentically record the truth and to present a radically new way of seeing the world. The emergence of a market for this new medium, which very importantly coincided with the rise of newspapers and a fostered appetite for up-to-date views of the outside world, gave an important impetus to the photographic industry. Photography became collectable, and photographic views of war provided the means for an unprecedented presence of war imagery in the contemporary public and private consciousness (Brothers 1997; Gervereau 2003). The global expansion of European and American Empires spurred the growth of photographic techniques, and despite unmanageable equipment and a certain inadequacy of photography to register the speed of action, it became a highly praised tool for gathering information about exotic places and native populations; it was an instrument for collecting, staging and displaying exotica and domesticating cultural otherness (Seremetakis 1993: 13); an instrument of surveillance and control (Tagg 1988); and a support to the European imperialist's sense of cultural and military superiority: 'Day in and day out, optical lenses were pointed at the combat zones alongside the mouths of rifles and cannon' (Junger 1993: 24). Thus the power of photography to change perspectives, tailor events and portray them in a different light was soon realised. It created and depicted 'home' and 'abroad', as it created heroes, villains and enemies (Lewinsky 1978). It captured war and its struggles, made them permanent and exposed them for interpretation, and illuminated 'the unbridgeable chasm that separates ordinary life from extraordinary experience of political trauma' (Linfield 2010: xv). As Peter Maslowski (1993: 4) writes: 'memories dim and ultimately die, but photographs remain clear and crisp. Pictures are time machines.' They turn into testimonies of events, death and conflict; they aid military and exploratory endeavours; they shape cartography and topography; and become an indispensable political and strategic tool.

Developments in mobile technology, light and small high-quality cameras, have taken images that extra step and further interlinked them with the strategic intentions of policy-makers. As Kennedy (2009) rightly suggests, the digitalisation of war imagery introduced uncertainty, which reinforced the disintegration of categories and genres. Not only has the war zone opened to the public gaze, cameras placed on guided missiles, drones or satellites have physically removed one part of human agency from the action of war. Some of the most talked-about images of the Gulf War were not photographs, but still frames from Department of Defense videos and snippets of video from CNN newscasts (Griffin 2010: 27). Cameras focused on the landscape, technology, and live reports from the battlefield where human subjects, at least visually, disappeared. What was important was that which could be seen: the tanks, the planes and the war machine. Soldiers were on the ground, but rarely portrayed. The Gulf War moved the representation of war from portrayals of on-the-ground action – the aftermath of a battle, soldiers' everyday life – to a highly computerised, distant yet live reporting of war, to seeing action as it is taking place, to 'experiencing' the moment the bomb strikes. With such a shift in the scopic representation of war in the direction of science, technological advances took place; the camera became a tool of dissection – a scalpel of vivisection as Baudrillard (2005: 184) puts it – of relational and social dimensions outside language and symbolic context. As everything was put on display, imagination was evacuated. It is as if photographic realism re-entered the scene; questions of objectivity and photographers' intentions were no longer relevant as the human element was no more. It is technology that is taking pictures, which is supposed to be *truer*. The war of projectiles and missiles was turned into a war of pictures and sounds (Baudrillard 1995; Virilio 1984). To illuminate war, to allow everything to be seen and known, at every moment and in every place, and to rule out any possibility of an accident, surprise or casualty, seems to have become a *new* direction in war photography (Gregory 2011; see also Virilio 1984). With no bodies, no blood, no other side, the war was sanitised and a simulation. As such, the representation of warfare in photography provided us with a disturbing example of the fading link between experience and knowledge, between that which is 'directly lived' and that which is representation.

But the rise of technology has also given life to a new frontline figure, the soldier-photographer, who contests the realism of drone or missile screenshots with their emotionally charged experience. Soldiers have turned one segment of war photography into wartime postcards sent home to loved ones, or into personal war memorabilia that was to remain hidden from the public gaze (Kozol 2012). A number of soldiers, as Kozol notes, took photos of comradeship, of their personal space, of their weapons or of their opponent (dead or alive), as a reminder of what they went through. These 'memorabilia photos' are driven by affection, and stand for a particular emotional artefact for a soldier or his/her family. But in the age of Twitter, Facebook, Instagram and other social networking sites, personal photos of war and soldiers' photographic practices overlap with tourism discourse and demonstrations of exhibitionism, voyeurism or simple expressions of 'I was there' and 'look what I have done'. At least as exhibitionist and voyeuristic as the soldiers', is the public's desire to seek out these photos and to see into the eye of the storm (and perhaps even to experience it). Trapped in the discourse of tourism, as Kozol (2012: 31) explains, these images are sent home to loved ones with an expectation of admiration or envy. With the same logic as tourists sending postcards to loved ones or posting images on social media sites, these soldiers invited viewers to participate in a regime of a particular military scopic domination; the framing of these photos presumed that viewers would appreciate the images and understand their intended meaning.

But photos meant for private use – sent back home or published on personal websites – were re-appropriated by the media with an aim to expose exceptional, problematic practices to the public eye, blurring the distinction between the private and public spheres. These 'private' photos could have been taken in affect, to show what was witnessed or experienced (very rarely to capture that which was seen), or taken out of context. It becomes very easy to judge soldiers' actions in affect from a distance; yet personal photographic practices have changed perceptions of soldiers' conduct. A growing number of instances in which soldiers face legal consequences for their actions come as a result of their own photographic practice. In particular, in instances of abuse (such as the Abu Ghraib scandal, where soldiers took photos posing next to naked and humiliated Iraqi prisoners, or of US soldiers urinating on the bodies of their dead opponents), photos from the frontline turn into evidence. They are no longer seen as carefully staged works of art and portrayals of personal experience. In such instances photos, because of their context, dismiss their otherwise ever-present critique of bias. They return to photographic realism and become knowledge-bearers. The emotional, affective context in which the photos were taken turns out to be irrelevant.

This section shows how the developments of war photography are closely interlinked with changes in technology, and how that shapes the ways in which we see, understand and relate to war. On one hand, images of war are treated as representations of reality, although looking throughout history it becomes clear that they have been everything but imprints of reality. On the other hand, images of war are impregnated with emotions and affect, as more recent photographic practices from the frontline have shown, but what is common to the two accounts (both realist and emotively driven photography) is the public's desire to seek knowledge, truth and authenticity in these images. That, as we have shown, is a fruitless exercise. The next section looks further into the reasons why this is the case by discussing two critiques of photography.

## Looking – Cultural anesthesia and graphic disillusion

The illusion that cameras produce objective knowledge about the actuality of war has been rapidly disproven. War photography as a form of documentation, representation and story telling was somehow pushed aside. Instead, all eyes turned to the other darker, manipulative side of photography that draws on personal portrayals, mug-shots, images of suffering and pain or momentary affective actions. The randomness with which these images and portrayals of war are taken is what is particularly intriguing. As Höijer points out: 'the camera explores faces twisted in pain, or lingers on wounds and bloody bandages, it zooms in on broken and mutilated limbs, or pools of blood, and the injured are not [only] soldiers but ordinary people' (Höijer 2004: 516). If the beginnings of photojournalism were marked by photographic realism supported by scientific knowledge and the assumption of objectivity, which arose from a one-on-one relationship between observer and observed (Feldman 1994: 406), the advancements in technology, fast production of images, ease with which they are taken, and their accessibility have lost the illusion of closeness and the pre-assumption of an objective or value-free photographer. If early war imagery rested on the assumption of objectivity and authenticity (although, as shown earlier, this assumption is nothing more than an illusion), the massive reproduction of images and the ability to manipulate not only the shot but also the product (to artificially construct the photo by adding or deleting elements) has seen the end of illusive authenticity and alleged closeness. An often-asked question became: 'If a photo can no longer be trusted, then what is its role?' The most common response to this problem is to focus on the content, on that which the photo depicts.

Is it a play of light caught in a lens of a camera, an illusion, or an actual existing object? Roland Barthes claims that all photography proclaims 'there-have-been', which alludes to some material presence and a registration of light (Barthes 1981: 77). Yet the image is also displaced, as it is not really *there* while at the same time it has been *there*. This renders the photograph 'a mad image, chafed by reality' (Barthes 1981: 115). On one side of the camera lens there is a material object, while on the other side, the lens transforms this object into a registered reflection of light, in a copy or an original trace of light, transforming its object into materiality of a different kind (Tagg 1988: 3). While both views acknowledge the materiality of the photo, the frame in which they emerge is somehow different. Barthes, for example, would argue for the presence of 'something' in the photo, its 'representation' or 'depiction', a photographic frame, whereas Tagg (1988), Campbell (2007), Sliwinski (2009) and others emphasise the context in which the photo emerged, or where it was put on view. Thus the photo is shaped by who looks, and how and why they do it. Instead of a photo emerging from a unique proximity to the real (embodying a trace), for Sliwinski (2009: 308): 'photographic meaning is thought to depend upon the circulation and context in which the image is viewed'. The context of the image is what makes and builds its effect/affect.

Stanley Greene's capture of a trace of a body in the snow in the midst of the conflict in Chechnya, or Rosenthal's raising of the American flag on top of Iwo Jima mountain, are two such different portrayals. Greene's is siding with the notion of 'chafed by reality' (Greene 2003), whereas Rosenthal's power is in the context. The two, however, point towards two different responses to war photography. Greene plays on imagination and on 'documentary versus art', a binary in which images of war are often caught (to which we return in the final section); Rosenthal counts on emotion, to which we turn now.

The sheer amount of images that aim to evoke emotions, emotional responses, feelings of sympathy, responsibility or empathy, as the emotion-focused argument goes, defeats their purpose. The viewer/audience, instead of becoming politically engaged in a situation, becomes numb. Society, as Allen Feldman (1994) argues, becomes anesthetised. When war photography produces familiarity without understanding, intimacy without sympathy, information without knowledge, at that moment, as Sontag (2003) argues, an image can no longer play a progressive role. How, then, should we position ourselves in relation to the growing reproduction, saturation and perception of perceived emotion-driven images? The problem that Sontag and many others identify is the seductive power of images, and indeed images are seductive to the point at which one becomes blind to their political potential. Even if the audience consciously aims to remain emotionally detached, an inclination to give in to the aesthetic power of an image remains. That is no surprise, as photography is always driven by some purpose or with intent, but Sontag and Feldman see a problem in audiences' emotional attachment to what is depicted in the photo. Barthes also brilliantly points to this problem when he observes that every time he reads about photography, he thinks of an image he likes or that is particularly close to him; and what drives him to that image is not the photo – its composition or the technicality of it – but rather its referent object, that which the photo portrays. 'Myself, I only saw the referent, the desired object, the beloved body', as Barthes (1981: 7) writes.

The audience of war photography is not interested in the photo per se, but always, understandably, in its referent, with its actions and states of distress, to which the person looking can relate. Such a desire or curiosity to seek out the familiar or disturbing is unsurprising (Sontag 1977: 167). Morbid curiosity driving the excess of imagery and emotive responses is what Sontag (1977) and Feldman (1994) see as the crux of cultural anesthesia. However, it is not the excess of images, their emotive appeal, or manipulation (all critiques that link photography to developments in technology) that drives such an anesthetic state, but the perverted voyeuristic tendency which distinguishes between the investment-worthy body of the spectator as opposed to the lost, disfigured and wasted body of those looked at. It is the complacency with, or a sensory colonisation of, a scopic regime that leads to cultural amnesia, and that subsequently poses questions about the purpose of the photo or what a 'photo should do' (Feldman 1994: 415). Ultimately, in such a scopic regime, a photo can no longer just *be*, it is commodified, displaced, and serves a purpose (Feldman 1994: 407).

'How can we see without looking?' to follow Barthes (1981: 111), is a question in need of an answer if war photography is to turn away from cultural anesthesia. In looking at photography of strangers suffering, as Sliwinski (2009) and Sontag (2003) argue, we need to recognise the responsibility in looking, the responsibility of recognising that suffering has taken place, but also – and this is crucial, and often forgotten even by writers engaging in photography critique – that this suffering is not for us. It is crucial that in search of authenticity, the viewer does not inhibit what is not intended for them, embrace if not voyeuristically indulge in images of suffering and distress. In other words, images can point, reveal that which took place; they can transmit knowledge, to the extent that the audience knows something took place; but for what is to follow, the image has no answer. One has to stop looking for connection and the subject's own recognition of the image.

Thus a critique of representation in war photography is in place, but is ultimately redundant as authenticity was never something photography claimed to be. Equally, the emotionally driven response that drives the critique is out of sync. Photography, war photography in particular, can be judged only on grounds of the context (the situation in which the photo was taken) or the authorship (who took the photo). These are the two realms, if one is to talk about the critique of representation, where one can judge and examine emotional or affective aspects of war photography, and both can be dealt with only in relation to the technological advancements discussed earlier. If the focus is on the content of the photo, the offered engagement can amount to nothing else but pure voyeurism (if approached through an artistic lens) or to narcissism (if we are to seek sympathy/empathy or seek out our responsibility). If critique of representation is to be taken seriously, the ethical force of the photograph, that is, 'to mirror and to call to a halt the final narcissism of our habits of visual consumption' (Butler 2005: 826), has to be re-examined. An overly emotion-driven engagement with photography has to be re-tracked, and instead attention should be given to the technical and representational value of photography. That is photography not as a testimony of reality, but as a caption per se, a trace of something that the camera caught, or an invitation to engage our imagination. The insistence on emotion feeds the desire for imagery and its excesses, and it searches the content of photography for something that might not be there in the first place.

Instead of dwelling on emotion, research on war photography, as we suggest, should return to the referent of the photo, that which the camera caught in its lens. Floods of images did not entirely sap out the capacity to react; but such an exaggerated focus on emotion has depoliticised images and numbed spectators' ability to engage politically. A return to the image as such does not deny the misery or the graveness, the suffering in war, and it does not reduce war photography to a set of aesthetic concerns. In fact, only if one puts aside the emotive element of war photography can one engage with photos politically (as a growing number of war photographs are used as evidence to counter wartime abuses). Such new visibility, as Thompson (2005) named it, renders a photo as a frame, a trace or a document over its capacity to provoke. It turns photography and a photo into an act of registering.

## Registering – Art, documentary, evidence, trace

Photography reveals unpleasant facts, unimaginably harrowing scenes, but also enjoyable and ordinary realities. It is a simple registration of light, but behind the click of the shutter there is much more. In the words of self-taught French photographer and filmmaker Raymond Depardon:

> [L]ight, time, distance, choice, nothing is neutral. It is subjective, emotional, it is political, it is incomplete … I am trying to speak with my photography and that has nothing to do with information. I am not a reliable human being, I have got my fears, my curiosity, my desires, I am not impartial.
>
> (Depardon 2004: 16)

Photographers, whether professional or not, deal with intrinsically contingent materials (random events are what snapshots are made of) and impose themselves from a distance and from their choice of perspective on the portrayed object/subject; they are imposed in the act of clicking the shutter, and, finally in the choice of whether to archive, publicise the image or to ignore and delete it. A photographer is at once passive and active; medium and actor; recorder and creator. Every picture is the product of a disjointed encounter of several protagonists: a photographer understood in their own cognitive, intellectual and emotional environment; the photographed knowing or ignoring camera's focus on them; the camera as an imperfect technological medium operating and framing the photographer's own field of vision; and the more-or-less remote spectator, be it in terms of time and/or space. The point is not that war is 'unrepresentable', but rather that war itself is partly a contest between different paradigms of representation that are not easily coordinated with one another (Mieszkowski 2012: 35). Or, as David Campbell rightly suggests, 'images cannot be isolated as discrete objects but have to be understood as imbricated in networks of materials, technologies, institutions, markets, social spaces, affects, cultural histories and political contexts' (Campbell 2007: 361).

A photograph is thus never a neutral document or a pure source (Burke 2006); it can only be a fragile document that must be mistrusted as being subject to material, subjective and historical forces (alterations, errors, falsifications and off camera).[4] Despite the mistrust, understanding that a picture cannot give a full account of a situation, or that a photograph has failed to depict an event or situation fully, is still to accept that the event actually occurred. A photograph, as David Levi Strauss (2012: 74) observed: 'doesn't need to prove anything on its own; it corroborates and confirms what we already know'; it participates in the existing scopic regime and makes it that bit more believable. As spectators, we do not blindly accept images; the believability of an image is always squared with a story (historical or political) one is familiar with. Familiar photos are easier to accept and become unquestionable, everyday travel companions. A story with artistic, highly ideological or context-bound imagery is different. Some photos of demonstrations or combat carry a political message that governs/frames their composition. Those images are not less valid, they simply belong to a different regime of visibility. To understand their different vantage point, the micro-sociological aspects of conflict – where an image is a referent point rather than a bearer of absolute knowledge that is to uncover the hidden power relations or causes of war as Stallabrass 2013 argues – need to be looked at.

A play of light framed, captured and made visible by the camera is evidence of something that has been *there* and is now projected on the photo (Meskin and Cohen 2010). The type of evidence, and evidence for what the caption stands for, depends on cultural and discursive systems through which images are given historical, scientific and aesthetic worth. Thus images inhabit a space between art and documentary (Rouillé 2005), between imagination and registering, between that which calls for creativeness and that which copies. Images possess meaning only if, as Carl Einstein writes: 'one considers them as sources of energy and intersections of decisive experiences; … works of art only acquire their true meaning by dint of the insurrectionary force they contain' (Einstein 1934, quoted in Didi-Huberman 2007). Thus photography is caught in a struggle between art and documentation (Rouillé 2005); it is a slave to social and political categories, interpreted and understood in too close proximity to the political, to the truth and to the reportage; whereas artistic photography is much too easily dismissed as a form of abstraction, installation, performance or visual experimentation. But, despite its (over)reliance on imagination and experimentation, artistic photographic practice, especially in the context of war, cannot be a-historical or a-political. In a particular artistic way it speaks of the event and of the existing regime of visibility. As it is not obsessed with purity, artistic imagery cannot be dismissed in the study of conflict and war (Didi-Huberman 2007) as, even when staged, it allows for a re-engagement with the complex and tortuous problem of the questionable magnitude and geometry of warfare, inviting us to refuse the reduction of conflict to simplistic categories and to explore the blurring boundaries of violence, its actors and its legacy in terms of time, space and affect. It might be a peculiar relationship – between artistic photographer, suffering subject and the very act of defeating the mythology of photography as a neat authentic exposition of reality – that can unknot some of the issues of the representation of war. Indeed, finely tuned pictures of war usually prompt fresh questions on the nature of violence. Stanley Greene's black-and-white snapshots of war trigger unconscious associations of cruelty and emptiness (Greene 1995), whereas Roemers' pictures of derelict habitats of the Cold War summon up an entire bygone world, resurrecting ghosts of our imagination (Roemers 2010) and pushing forward an embarrassing question: have we entirely broken away from the diktats of the Cold War?

Imaginatively conceived and not simply perceived, artistic images are shifting away from traditional, objectifying practices towards more subjective explorations of identity and difference. Lhuisset's *Theatre of War* (2011–12) collection consists of carefully composed pictures of a group of Iranian Kurdish guerrillas. He deliberately deployed the style of the nineteenth-century iconography of Second French Empire war paintings to remind the viewer of the inevitability of their own demise. As such, Lhuisset's work is a wedge in the media reporting style, a deliberated artistic imposture playing on the illusionist *sfumato*,[5] the blurring of the lines between real and virtual, here and there, past and present. These images inform without telling, they say without speaking, they disclose without revealing, they add to the complexity of war. They pierce the camouflage of violence as much as they contribute to the shared smoke screen and distorted views about the scale of war. But, as war throws images into disorder (as much as one cannot tell between before and after), they in any case find reconstructing war impossible.

If the invention of photography profoundly altered the public's experience of war, it is nonetheless difficult to explain how war photographs differ from other photos, and how photographs of war differ from other representations of combat. To some extent, the problem lies in distinguishing between the violence that the photos represent and the violence that the photographic medium itself places upon its audience or its subject matter. As such, the image is neither a deficient simulacrum nor a transparent document, but an index and, in spite of everything, a trace (Didi-Huberman 2005b, 2008; Ginzburg 2002) of the political economy of war, its articulation of the historical understanding of war in general, of the mutations in the reality of war (Shaw 2005) and of our imaginary of war. Images are registrations of light and thus *admissible evidences* of daily life in a war zone, war trophies, *traces* of actions in affect, records of camera-witnesses, of particular actions, from a particular point of view at a particular moment, and *quilting points* in our collective imaginary of heroism, cruelty and suffering.

## Conclusion

Images suffer from what Walter Benjamin named the perceived 'disappearance of aura'; that is, a disappearance of the subject-specific experience of closeness with that which is portrayed in the photo. Technological development is again to blame for the ever-expanding gap between the subject and its object of engagement, leading to the perceived annihilation of aura. But as Benjamin and Didi-Huberman (2005a) remind us, the aura is not actually disappearing, instead it is turned into a process of constant becoming, constant change, which makes each subject's engagement with a particular object unique and equally authentic. In turn, such a becoming of aura also makes any attempt at reaching a real authentic experience impossible; every experience is always already both authentic and a copy. The same applies to photography: every photo is always already a copy, and as it is an imprint of light on paper, it is also in itself unique. As such, affectionate, emotional or in any other way, particular and individual engagements with the photo cannot make for a more authentic experience; in fact, a content-driven search to experience affect and emotion is per se always non-authentic. A way to engage with photography productively is, as this chapter suggests, to take war photographs as quilting points of common societal narratives of heroism, cruelty or suffering; as traces that can give insight to knowledge, as pieces of evidence, records and archives. Caught between documentary and art, they are indexes of something taking place.

## Notes

1 Iconographic references are in square brackets; they refer to the photographer and a year in which the photo or a series of photos were taken.
2 Martin Jay, in his piece 'Scopic regimes of modernity', defines scopic regime as a particular visual culture that frames ways in which we see and look at the world, but also how we look and how we make sense of that which we see. According to Jay (1988: 4), scopic regime is a contested terrain where visual theories and practices meet.
3 The title is a reference to Didi-Huberman's series of books *The Eye of History* [*L'oeil de l'histoire*] and Volume 1: *Where Images take Position* [*Quand les images prennent position*]. He opens the series with a powerful statement: 'To take knowledge is to take position'. In this statement Didi-Huberman implies that we often take knowledge, but what remains missing is to take the position and argue for a particular type of knowledge. An image (from the eye of the storm – war) can be a starting point for different narratives driven by different knowledge; what these narratives are depends on the viewer and their social and historical background. With this statement, Didi-Huberman aims to show the fluidity and perhaps also the randomness in which histories, knowledge and, at the back of that, different visual representations take place; but instead of simply taking knowledge from them, one should begin to argue for particular narratives, or one should recognise that the arguments have already taken place and are ongoing.
4 Off camera: As outside the view of the camera; from French *hors champ*, also outside the scope or field of vision; in the field of photography outside or beyond the scene caught by the photographic lens.
5 *Sfumato* is one of four canonical painting models of the Renaissance; the word is of Italian origin – *sfumare* – which means to evaporate like smoke or to be toned down. Da Vinci's *Mona Lisa* is one of the most famous examples of this style of painting, for the painting has no clear or sharp lines, the borders or lines disappearing in the manner of smoke.

## Bibliography

Baudrillard, J. (1995) *The Gulf War Did Not Take Place*. Bloomington, IN: Power Institute.

Baudrillard, J. (2005) *The Conspiracy of Art*. New York: Semiotext(e).

Barthes, R. (1981) *Camera Lucida: Reflections on Photography*. New York: Hill & Wang.

Benjamin, W. (1997) *Charles Baudelaire: A Lyric poet in the Era of High Capitalism.* London: Verso.

Benjamin, W. (2007) *Walter Benjamin's Archive: Images, Texts, Signs.* London: Verso.

Brothers, C. (1997) *War and Photography: A Cultural History.* Abingdon: Psychology Press.

Burke, P. (2006) *Eyewitnessing: The Uses of Images as Historical Evidence.* London: Reaktion Books.

Butler, J. (2005) 'Photography, war, outrage', *PMLA*, 120(3): 822–827.

Campbell, D. (2007) 'Geopolitics and visuality: Sighting the Darfur conflict', *Political Geography*, 26: 357–382.

Depardon, R. (2004) *Images politiques* [*Political images*]. Paris: La Fabrique.

Didi-Huberman, G. (2005a) 'The supposition of the aura: The now, the then, and modernity', in *Walter Benjamin and History*, Benjamin (ed.). London: Continuum, 3–18.

Didi-Huberman, G. (2005b) *Confronting images: Questioning the Ends of a Certain History Of Art.* University Park, PA: Penn State University Press.

Didi-Huberman, G. (2007) 'Picture = rupture: Visual experience, form and symptom according to Carl Einstein', *Papers of Surrealism*, 7: 1–25.

Didi-Huberman, G. (2008) *Images in Spite of All: Four Photographs from Auschwitz.* Chicago, IL: University of Chicago Press.

Didi-Huberman, G. (2011) *Quand les images prennent position (L'œil de l'histoire, 1).* Paris: ed. de Minuit.

Feldman, A. (1994) 'On cultural anesthesia: From desert storm to Rodney King', *American Ethnologist*, 21(2): 404–418.

Gervereau, L. (ed.) (2003) *Voir/ne pas voir la guerre. Histoire des représentations photographiques de la guerre* [*To see/Not to see the War. History of photographic representations of War*]. Nanterre: BDIC/Somogy.

Ginzburg, C. (2002) *Wooden Eyes. Nine Reflections on Distance.* London: Verso.

Greene, S., Glucksmann, A. and Caujolle, C. (2003) *Open Wound: Chechnya 1994 to 2003.* London: Trolley Books.

Gregory, D. (2011) 'From a view to a kill: Drones and late modern war', *Theory, Culture & Society*, 28(7/8): 188–215.

Griffin, M. (2010) 'Media images of war', *Media, War & Conflict*, 3(1): 7–41.

Höijer, B. (2004) 'The discourse of global compassion: The audience and media reporting of human suffering', *Media, Culture, & Society*, 26(4): 513–531.

Jay, M. (1988) 'Scopic regimes of modernity', in *Vision and Visuality*, Foster (ed.). Seattle, WA: Bay Press, 3–23.

Junger, E. (1993) 'War and photography', *New German Critique*, 59: 24–26.

Kennedy, D. (2009) 'Soldier photography: Visualising the war in Iraq', *Review of International Studies*, 35(4): 817–833.

Kozol, W. (2012) 'Battlefield souvenirs and the affective politics of recoil', *Photography and Culture*, 5(1): 21–36.

Levi Strauss, D. (2012) *Between the Eyes. Essays on Photography and Politics.* New York: Aperture.

Lewinski, J. (1978) *The Camera at War: A History of War Photography from 1848 to the Present Day.* London: WH Allen.

Linfield, S. (2010) *The Cruel Radiance. Photography and Political Violence.* Chicago, IL: University of Chicago Press.

Maslowski, P. (1993) *Armed with Cameras: The American Military Photographers of World War II*. New York: Free Press.

Meskin, A. and Cohen, J. (2010) 'Photographs as evidence', in *Photography and Philosophy: Essays on the Pencil of Nature*, Walden (ed.). Malden, MA: Blackwell.

Mieszkowski, J. (2012) *Watching War*. Stanford, CA: Stanford University Press.

Panh, R. (2013) *L'image Manquante* [*The Missing Picture*]. Paris: Gallimard.

Rouillé, A. (2005) *La Photographie, entre document et art contemporain* [*Photograph, between document and contemporary art*]. Paris: Gallimard.

Seremetakis, N. C. (1993) 'The memory of the senses: Historical perception, commensal exchange and modernity', *Visual Anthropology Review*, 9(2): 1–18.

Shaw, M. (2005) *The New Western Way of War*. London: Polity Press.

Sliwinski, S. (2009) 'On photographic violence', *Photography and Culture*, 2(3): 303–315.

Sontag, S. (1977) *On Photography*. New York: Picador.

Sontag, S. (2003) *Regarding the Pain of Others*. New York: Picador.

Stallabrass, J. (ed.) (2013) *Memory of Fire: Images of War and the War of Images*. Brighton: Photoworks.

Tagg, J. (1988) *The Burden of Representation. Essays on Photographies and Histories*. Amherst, MA: University of Massachusetts Press.

Thompson, J. (2005) 'The new visibility', *Theory, Culture & Society*, 22(6): 31–51.

Virilio, P. (1984) *War and Cinema: The Logics of Perception*. London: Verso.

# 16 Grief and the transformation of emotions after war

*Emma Hutchison and Roland Bleiker*

War leaves a powerful emotional mark.[1] Indeed, violence endured during war – whether experienced directly or witnessed from a far and safe distance – shatters a community's sense of normalcy and safety to the extent that powerful emotions generated often linger long after the immediate threat and conflict have passed. A once united society may be left divided, or an already divided society may descend into even deeper hostility, resentment and anxiety.

The trauma associated with violence and war thus has a profound, sometimes dislocating and destructive, communal impact. Haunted by memories of pain and suffering, post-conflict communities paradoxically search to 'forget' the horror of war while simultaneously becoming emotionally fixated, and constituted, by it (Edkins 2002). A particular emotional politics – centred on loss, humiliation, anger and even guilt – binds a community closer together. But in doing so, this response to trauma also triggers forms of remembering that preclude the possibility of properly working through the legacies of war. Dealt with in this way, wartime traumas come to inscribe and perpetuate exclusive and often violent ways of configuring community. Rather than solving the problems at stake, ensuing political attitudes generate new antagonisms that increase rather than reduce the propensity for violence.

This prototypical response to the traumas of war is, however, not the only way for societies to move on after war. Some scholars and practitioners now speak of an alternative: the possibility of, and potentials immanent in, 'grieving' societal trauma (see Fierke 2004; Yoder 2005; Mollica 2006; Schick 2011). Key here is the opportunity to critically engage with and properly mourn the realities of war and, in so doing, 'work through' painful memories and understandings (La Capra 2001). By confronting the injuries of war head-on, communities can actively reflect upon rather than internalise and co-opt the ensuing trauma (Schick 2011: 11–17). More cathartic and less maladaptive, redemptive forms of community are thought to result.

This chapter picks up on the potentials immanent within the politics of grief and applies them to rethinking the nature and shaping of collective identity and community after war. We do so by drawing attention to the intensely emotional nature of post-war trauma, and by underlining the need to acknowledge and work through the various emotions – from fear, anxiety and anger to humiliation and guilt – that inevitably circulate after conflict. We see doing so as critical, for if communities are to move from conflict-prone patterns towards the possibility of grieving and healing, a thorough understanding of the powerful but often neglected role emotions play in adhering post-war communities is necessary.

While for many the need for a society to work through painful post-war emotions is commonsensical, we are yet to fully appreciate the roles emotions play in rebuilding war-affected communities. Until recently, emotions were largely assumed to be personal and irrational reactions, and thus of little relevance to conceptualising political issues. Those approaches that do look at emotions, particularly in understanding the emotional roots of ethnic violence, have thus far not examined extensively how emotions as well as broader forms of affect can be consciously and actively engaged after violence in order to try to rebuild communities in more conciliatory ways (see e.g. Kaufman 2001). As a result, emotions are seldom engaged as positive political forces, even while key political events – war, in particular – are so evidently emotional. Indeed, in the aftermath of war the logic of fear and anxiety have been normalised to the point that we can hardly recognise, let alone deal with, the emotions that lie at the origin of the events in question.

Our argument takes shape in two parts. The first part concerns the linkages between the traumas of war, emotions and community. Specifically, we argue that dealing with the legacy of war more effectively requires paying closer attention to how particular emotions are linked to notions of identity, belonging and community after war. Here we show that emotions that typically accompany war and its trauma, such as fear, anger, anxiety, humiliation, shame and even guilt, help to shape an image of the trauma that redefines the community at stake in an insular manner, thus preserving a perception of threat (see also Stein 2013). Second, we explore and propose a politics of grief as a way to work through the legacy of war in an alternative manner. Significant here is a type of active engagement with post-war emotions that is consonant with a more genuine attempt to both grieve the horrors of war and, in turn, critically reflect upon their origins. An ideal – and longer-term – result would be the cultivation of empathy and compassion, which could in turn help to rebuild and adhere communities in more inclusive, rehabilitative and non-violent ways. Yet foremost, and central to a politics of grief, is the need to question pre-conceived ideas about how individuals and societies can best deal with past violence and suffering. Embracing concrete practices that refuse the habitual, reflex-like push to memorialise (and gloss over) the traumas of war, and instead enable the potentially alternative expression, acknowledgment and acceptance of the profound and frequently reciprocal emotional impact of violence and suffering, is thus key.

A short chapter cannot provide a definitive account of how the emotional legacy of war that perpetuates violence can be replaced with a more transformative grieving and healing process. Doing so would entail tackling the unique emotional and psychological legacy that each particular conflict leaves. It would also necessitate consideration of other crucial factors in each post-conflict setting, such as questions of power, inequalities, justice and rights. Our purpose here is therefore far more modest: to identify the broad contours of how emotions matter in the aftermath of war and, more specifically, to understand how collective emotional dispositions influence the possibilities for working through the deep-seated wounds and injustices that both precede and follow from conflict.

## Constituting community after the traumas of war: from fear, anger and anxiety to loss, guilt and humiliation

War is a deeply emotional form of political action. Whether experienced as a combatant or as a civilian, the conflict it instigates causes both immediate and long-lasting forms of violence and trauma. It involves a profound and often prolonged period of social disruption. In some instances, the social and communal impact is so shocking that a normal understanding of how the world works is impossible. The comfort and stability of normal habits and social expectations are stripped away. The social context individuals ordinarily place themselves in feels 'betrayed' (Edkins 2002: 247); the fabric of community is shattered.

Wartime violence may thus not be processed in the same way as other political events. The often unpredictable and lengthy period of conflict prompts feelings of anxiety, fear and terror. Cathy Caruth (1995: 153) describes this kind of trauma as 'the confrontation with an event that, in its unexpectedness and horror, cannot be placed within the schemes of prior knowledge'. The horrors and trauma reaped by war thus not only uproot deeply entrenched political patterns and expectations; they also mark a community or wider society with physical and mental scars that continue to injure long after the conflict has ceased. It is in this way that the period following war is a critical period for constituting individual and collective subjectivities and, ultimately, a sense of community (Fierke 2004).

Emotions play a central role in these processes, for they help construct a sense of identity and solidarity that can emerge despite – or, rather, as a direct response to – the feelings of pain, loss and fragmentation that are generated by the memory of war. Traumatic events can pull people together, giving them a sense of common purpose. Dominant ways of representing, commemorating and remembering are significant here, in that they shape an image of the war that is accepted and hence readily able to be incorporated into existing communal narratives (Edkins 2003). Some commentators suggest that prevailing images of past violence are so powerful that they become a 'chosen trauma': the memories of violence and injustice become unconsciously co-opted and internalised within a large group's identity such that they are then to a large part defined by them (Volkan 1997: 48, see also 2001). The ensuing dynamics decisively shape the political patterns ahead. They play a crucial role in determining whether conflict or peace will prevail in the long run. This is why it is important to gain a better understanding of the emotional factors that are involved in setting up these patterns in the first place.

The disruptive and intensely emotional social conditions that follow conflict and wars constitute a unique political opportunity to construct new forms of identity and community – forms that are less likely to lead to violence and new conflict. In reality, though, such opportunities are far too often lost. In most cases, the experience of dislocation and injury wrought by such events is swiftly countered with political projects that seek to mobilise the unleashed emotional energy for projects aimed at regaining political authority and control (Humphrey 2000: 13). Certain forms of emotions – hatred, fear, anger, anxiety and even guilt and humiliation – often 'take over' and become central to the contours of post-war identity and community, while others, such as compassion and wonder, become marginalised (see Volkan 2002; Kirmayer 2010). The consequences are often fatal, leading to new sources of resentment and hate, which can in turn spiral into new forms of conflict.

While an attentiveness to the politics of fear is thus central here, so too is the recognition that numerous other emotions are also at play. Through representations, war dislocates an entire society manifesting a range of intense emotions. Anxiety often remains intact at an individual and collective level long after a conflict has ceased to exist openly (Rae 2013). A community may feel grievous, angered and even humiliated at their losses (Fontan 2006; Fattah and Fierke 2009). Resentment may collectively circulate.

A classic example here is the collective emotions that emerged in Germany after World War I, where widespread feelings of defeat and humiliation gradually led to a political climate ripe for resentment, manipulation and, ultimately, violence, war and genocide. More recent examples of complex links between emotion and war can be seen in how terrorist attacks affect subsequent societal dispositions and state policies. Although the situation is completely different from that in the inter-war period, consider the emotional effects of the attacks on New York and Washington in 2001, the Bali bombing of 2002, and the attack on London in July 2005. In each case, media and political discourses were suffused with emotions such as anger and fear (Edkins 2002; Martin 2004; Hutchison 2010). The discourse of anxiety and resentment that emerged created not only highly problematic cultural stereotypes, but also an emotional discourse of 'us' versus 'them', one that pitted people against whatever or whoever is perceived to threaten them. In the US, for instance, this emotional discourse facilitated a gradual shift from confronting terrorism through police and law-enforcement mechanisms, which was the prevailing approach until the Clinton era, towards a strategy based on countering terrorists and rogues through military means, including war (Tsui 2014). The enduring consequences of this shift will not be known for many years, but already at this stage we know that it has neither eliminated the threat of terrorism nor brought stable peace and security to the two countries that were the object of military intervention: Afghanistan and Iraq.

To highlight the political consequences of such emotional dynamics is not to condone terrorism, or to equate the German role during World War II with the more recent War on Terror. Rather, the point is that war, and violence in general, leaves a series of complex emotional legacies which, if left unaddressed, can easily be passed down and generate new conflicts. No matter what the political context is – authoritarian or democratic, stable or chaotic – numerous problematic scenarios emerge when emotions such as fear, anger and hatred form the basis for new forms of political identities and communities. The most worrying of these is that a political community constituted by feelings of anger and fear of the outside will inevitably be dragged into new forms of conflict. Communities become shaped solely around the need to cordon off and secure a safe inside – often through military means – from a threatening outside.

Some commentators, such as Robert Kaplan, speak of so-called intractable conflicts: situations where antagonisms have persisted for so long that they have created a vicious cycle of violence. From the Middle East to Afghanistan, from Sri Lanka to Somalia, from Iraq to East Timor, and from Rwanda to Kashmir, years and often decades of conflict have left societies deeply divided and traumatised. New forms of violence constantly emerge, generating yet more hatred. Kaplan (2005) illustrates the issues at stake through the ethnic conflict that devastated the Balkan region during the first part of the 1990s. Kaplan believes that the political volatility that followed the break-up of Yugoslavia was linked to old ethnic and religious hatreds between Croats, Serbs and Muslims. These deeply seated antagonisms, he stresses, go back hundreds of years to the clash between the Ancient Roman and Byzantine Empires, between a Christian European West and a Muslim Ottoman East (see also Volkan 1997; Galtung 2001: 72–74). While drawing attention to the dangers of deeply entrenched emotional wounds, Kaplan's analysis also has problems. Some scholars find the very notion of an intractable conflict problematic. They locate the roots of violence not in ancient hatreds, but in much more recent political manipulations (Naimark 2002). David Campbell, for instance, provides an interpretation of the conflict in the Balkans that differs fundamentally from Kaplan's. For Campbell (1998: xi) the problem did not lie in ancient ethnic hatreds. The conflict, he believes, was linked to the recent actions of political elites.

The key point, then, is not to label some conflicts as intractable, but to identify the emotional dynamics that seem to make it impossible for the respective societies to move on from a discourse of fear, hatred, anxiety or humiliation (Bleiker 2013). Without unravelling the impact of the various emotions associated with war and political trauma, the often long-standing issues that cause conflict in the first place remain concealed and therefore unaddressed. Healing the wounds of war may become a matter of retribution and revenge, rather than a project begetting a mutually considered peace and emotional catharsis.

## The politics of collective emotions

A central part of understanding the legacy of war thus starts with appreciating emotions, particularly the roles they can play in constituting destructive or retributive forms of identity and community. This is why we now take a brief conceptual detour before examining how fragile post-war communities may be able to work through trauma and emotions in a more reflective and potentially positive manner.

Prevalent scholarly approaches to war and security have only recently begun to pay attention to emotions. This is because, traditionally, emotions were considered subjective and irrational reactions of an individual being. They were seen to involve neither thought nor knowledge and thus had no perceived relevance for public and political deliberations.

During the past decade, numerous International Relations scholars have started to engage the role of emotions more seriously. They did so in part by drawing upon well established emotions research in fields such as psychology, anthropology, sociology, philosophy and feminist theory (for a previous survey of the field see Bleiker and Hutchison 2008). The respective debates are complex and there are numerous disagreements. Nevertheless, there are at least two prominent themes which we would like to discuss here briefly, in an attempt to map out the role emotions can play in cultivating a more adequate political mindset and adequate approach to rehabilitating and rebuilding community in the wake of war.

First is the recognition that emotions are more than mere personal reactions. They play an important social and political role, and are fundamental to the constitution of identity and community attachments. Rather than considering emotions as simply biologically grounded, as was once thought, emotions are formed and structured within particular social and cultural environments. They are constituted through socio-cultural interactions and traditions, such as language, habits and memories. In this way, the ways we feel emerge from, and are constitutive of, the social and institutional processes that bind society together. Emotions are thus not just internal individual experiences. They are derived from and intrinsically linked to a social context (Lutz 1988; Nussbaum 2001: 107–109, 175–181). Important here is the notion that feelings are an active component of identity and community (Scheff 1994; Berezin 2001; Ahmed 2004).

Seen from such a perspective, emotions play a key role in establishing the kinds of collective political attitudes that shape all aspects of war: the reasons why conflict emerges in the first place, how it is being waged, and how societies deal with its aftermath. Emotions are pervasive social forces that influence attitudes, behaviours and actions. Thus an appropriate understanding of war can emerge only once one takes seriously the role of collective emotions.

The second key point is that emotions are more than just irrational impulses. A substantial body of literature now rejects the traditional dichotomy of rational/irrational, and dismisses the connotations this duality ordinarily imposes on the cultural sociology of emotion (see e.g. Nussbaum 1995b; Mercer 1996; Crawford 2000). Like other aspects of culture, emotions can be seen as an element of all social interaction. Emotions accompany so-called 'rational' actions as much as 'irrational' ones, positive experiences as much as negative. Robert Solomon (2003) and Martha Nussbaum (2001: 1–22) go even further and stress that emotions are important forms of knowledge and evaluative thought. They argue that emotions can tell us certain things, providing insights that could be of use in our attempts to address social and political challenges. 'Emotions are not irrational pushes and pulls', Nussbaum (1995a: 374) argues, 'They are ways of viewing the world.' Emotions are always about something, or are directed at something for specific reasons. They can be seen as elements of appraisal. Anger implies that something thought to be bad or wrong has happened; fear can be attributed to the feeling that something untoward may happen; and similarly, joy and happiness imply something good.

Not everyone agrees with this so-called cognitive approach. Others see emotions not primarily as thoughts, judgements and beliefs, but as manifest through more subconscious bodily sensations and affects (e.g. Massumi 2002; Thrift 2004). We do not enter these debates here, but only draw attention to a more fundamental underlying point: that emotions are not just irrational reactions, but can play a key role in understanding and perhaps even shaping how war affects communities.

## Transforming post-war emotions: from fear to empathy

Taking these two simple points to heart – that emotions are more than individual and irrational impulses, and thus play a significant collective and political role – we have previously advanced a straightforward argument: that engaging the dilemmas of post-war reconstruction can be done more successfully by exploring how the whole spectrum of emotions – not only anger and fear, for instance, but also empathy, compassion and wonder – may facilitate more lasting and ingenuous forms of social healing and reconciliation (Hutchison and Bleiker 2008a). Moving from negative to positive emotions, and from fear to empathy in particular, is a simple but important proposition, one that would gain further significance through processes of institutionalisation (Crawford 2014). This is the case even though it is self-evident that post-war societies are more likely to regain a peaceful political climate if they replace fear and anger with empathy. But the obvious and compelling logic of this move is often concealed by the relative absence of engagements with emotion. If scholars and politicians have a better understanding of the role that emotions play in war and post-war contexts, then they would also be able to promote the type of grieving (and working through of emotions) that helps affected communities to come to terms with, and heal effectively following, the trauma. Emotions may thus in turn be employed more effectively in attempts to promote long-lasting reconciliation.

What, then, can emotions tell us about the possibilities of constructing an alternative, less divisive sense of identity and community in the wake of war? Before such a move is possible, one must face difficult questions concerning how individuals and groups divided by conflict can initially be brought together, and thus how personal and collective feelings of fear and outrage can be transformed into emotions that may help to confront the very differences that cause conflict. The point here is not to just forget trauma, or to pretend that anger and fear will simply fade away. Rather, the point is to aim for an emotional 'turning point' that allows war-torn societies to cultivate new ways of thinking about past suffering and to envisage harmonious or at least non-violent forms of political order (Gobodo-Madikizela 2002: 15; Schaap 2006: 7, 87, 90–4).

Two issues are central here. First is the question of what kinds of emotions may help to facilitate the collective reckoning with and healing of war. An obvious and much discussed response here is, of course, that emotions such as empathy and compassion may help to generate a social space conducive to the collective acknowledgment and attempted healing of trauma (Gobodo-Madikizela 2002; Halpern and Weinstein 2004; Schaap 2006: 3–4). Empathy generally involves the ability to identify with (to at least some degree) the experiences and situation of another. Scholarly writings often suggest that empathy is key to reconstructing social relationships and communal bonds after mass violence and trauma. The respective reasoning behind this is that individuals and groups divided by conflict must be able to see the situation from the complex perspective of another, one who traditionally has been considered an adversary. In so doing, the suffering and trauma of others may 'resonate emotionally', providing an understanding of how another feels and why they may feel the things they do (Halpern and Weinstein 2004: 579–82). Victims and perpetrators may, as Gobodo-Madikizela (2002: 23) contends, be able to see each other as above all 'human'. This recognition may then lead to processes of re-humanisation – of both victim and perpetrator – and in turn inspire the agency needed to successfully embrace reconciliation. Implicit within this approach is that a form of empathetic identification – with the suffering other – can help to break down the antagonisms that caused the initial conflict. Feelings of empathy – and perhaps similarly, sympathy and compassion (see Whitebrook 2002) – may therefore prompt the shared understanding that is needed to take responsibility for and, in turn, resolve the conflict for the betterment of all.

Second is the task of implementing such a set of positive emotions. How can politicians, diplomats and mediators create a space where grievances can be freely expressed, and corresponding emotions can be collectively and empathetically worked through? At stake here is not simply the suspension or cessation of violence, but also, and crucially, that adversaries are encouraged to come together in the hope that their relations can be realised anew. Once again, this is not to suggest that the emotions of direct victims can be instantly transformed. Rather, the aim would be to draw out and work through the collective, politicised forms of emotion that may unknowingly constitute animosity and divisive political relations. During times of violence, the need for such a space becomes pertinent. Indeed, it would provide the conditions through which present-day politics and associated configurations of community can be reconsidered in light of injustices and exclusions (Schaap 2006: 98–101). Being able to stop and critically reflect upon what has led events to be as they are is therefore fundamental. Recognising the profoundly emotional and damaging nature of violence and ensuing trauma may provide an impetus to do so. The ensuing process would involve leaders in politics and the media becoming more aware of the implications involved in the proliferation of fear and suspicion. Rather than constructing community and formulating policy around fear alone, the strategy we propose suggests that feelings of vulnerability can be considered in a politically enabling way. Indeed, the sense of contingency that ensues after trauma – the sense of insecurity – can be thought as creating a space for political change.

## In lieu of conclusion: grief as a strategy to work through the traumas of war

We have made a relatively simple dual point in this chapter: one having to do with the basic but important need to understand how emotions shape war and post-war communities; the other with the ensuing political task for war-torn communities to work through emotions of anxiety, fear, resentment and humiliation – sentiments that are likely to produce new conflict – towards an environment defined by a search for collective empathy and compassion.

For us, the need for a society to work through emotions accompanying war is commonsensical. Just as an individual's sense of normality, structure and safety is shattered by extreme violence, so too is a community's. And, just as an individual must come to terms with and, to an extent, make peace with the often profound loss and grief after such violence, so too must a community. Should they fail to do so, the trauma and ensuing emotions may become internalised in a way that inhibits an individual and community from reflecting upon and potentially learning from the past (Yoder 2005; Mollica 2006; Schick 2011). Instead of moving on, the traumatised individual and community internalise painful memories and emotions and become unconsciously defined by them (Volkan 1997: 36–49). 'Ritualised' mourning processes in this case often ensue, which serve to re-enact (and thus perpetuate) the trauma rather than help accomplish the more gradual process of accepting loss by working through it (Volkan 1997: 183).

A move from fear to empathy does, of course, involve different challenges and processes in each unique conflict scenario. There is no pre-conceived universal emotional template that can be applied to the trauma of war. Nor are fear and empathy the only emotions involved in the drama of war and its aftermath. We pointed out that war-torn societies perpetuate violence through a range of complex emotions and associated behaviours: not just fear, but also anger, frustration, anxieties, humiliation, guilt. Although the literature on emotions and war is growing, we do not yet have sufficient insights to fully appreciate the political role that these emotions play. The same is the case with the type of emotions that might help post-war reconstruction. Here, too, empathy is not the only emotion at play, nor can fear and humiliation simply be erased. The very notion of positive versus negative emotions is, indeed, highly problematic. Fear, for instance, can be an essential emotion when it comes to maintaining adequate personal and collective security (McDermott 2014). Empathy, too, does not automatically lead to a more just society (Bloom 2013).

This is why we would like to make one final point here, one that appreciates the complexity of emotions, and highlights the need to understand how the traumatic nature of violence and remembering violence could be used as the very instrument to achieve a shift away from destructive and conflict-perpetuating emotions towards those that facilitate reconciliation. Key here is to understand how trauma and grief (and the diverging sense of loss associated with them) are distinct phenomena that orient communities in different ways (Volkan 2000; Fierke 2004). Reflex-like responses to the trauma of war, as we have pointed out, may simply memorialise the trauma in ways that keep it 'fresh' and unresolved for an affected community (see also Edkins 2002; Fierke 2004). Grief, however, may involve an emotionally and politically transformative 'working through' of trauma (La Capra 2001; Schick 2011). Indeed, a turn to grief recognises the inherent need for individuals and communities to confront intensely painful emotions and memories in order to be free of, rather than trapped by, past pain. Trauma and grief may thus be two sides of the same coin: they both shape emotional and communal attachments, but in profoundly different ways. A more nuanced understanding of the differences between them – and particularly the transformative potentials immanent in taking seriously, and in turn grieving, painful post-conflict emotions – might thus help scholars and policy-makers deal more successfully with the difficult aftermath of war.

## Note

1 This chapter draws and expands on work we have previously conducted on related topics, most notably Hutchison and Bleiker 2008a, 2008b.

## Bibliography

Ahmed, S. (2004) *The Cultural Politics of Emotion*. Edinburgh: Edinburgh University Press.

Berezin, M. (2001) 'Emotions and political identity: Mobilizing affection for the polity', in *Passionate Politics: Emotions and Social Movements*, Goodwin, Jasper and Polletta (eds). Chicago, IL: University of Chicago Press, 83–98.

Bleiker, R. (2013) 'Can we move beyond conflict?', in *Global Politics: A New Introduction*, Edkins and Zehfuss (eds). London: Routledge, 454–482.

Bleiker, R. and Hutchison, E. (2008) 'Fear no more: Emotions and world politics', *Review of International Studies*, 34(1): 115–135.

Bloom, P. (2013) 'The baby in the well: A critic at large', *New Yorker*, 89(14): 118–122.

Campbell, D. (1998) *National Deconstruction: Violence, Identity, and Justice in Bosnia*. Minneapolis, MN: University of Minnesota Press.

Caruth, C. (1995) 'Recapturing the past: Introduction', in *Trauma: Explorations in Memory*, Caruth (ed.). Baltimore, MD: Johns Hopkins University Press.
Crawford, N. C. (2000) 'The passion of world politics: Propositions on emotions and emotional relationships', *International Security*, 24(4): 116–156.
Crawford, N. C. (2014) 'Institutionalizing passion in world politics: Fear and empathy', *International Theory*, 6(3): 535–557.
Edkins, J. (2002) 'Forget trauma? Responses to September 11', *International Relations*, 16(2): 243–256.
Edkins, J. (2003) *Trauma and the Memory of Politics.* Cambridge: Cambridge University Press.
Fattah, K. and Fierke, K. M. (2009) 'A clash of emotions? The politics of humiliation and political violence', *European Journal of International Relations*, 15(1): 67–93.
Fierke, K. M. (2004) 'Whereof we can speak, thereof we must not be silent: Trauma, political solipsism and war', *Review of International Studies*, 30(4): 471–491.
Fontan, V. (2006) 'Polarization between occupier and occupied in post-Saddam Iraq: Colonial humiliation and the formation of political violence', *Terrorism and Political Violence*, 18(2): 217–238.
Galtung, J. (2001) 'The construction of national identities for cosmic drama: Chosenness-myths-trauma (CMT) syndromes and cultural pathologies', in *Handcuffed to History: Narratives, Pathologies and Violence in South Asia*, Udayakumar, (ed.). Westport, CT: Praeger, 61–77.
Gobodo-Madikizela, P. (2002) 'Remorse, forgiveness, and rehumanization: Stories from South Africa', *Journal of Humanistic Psychology*, 42(1): 7–32.
Halpern, J. and Weinstein, H. M. (2004) 'Rehumanizing the Other: Empathy and reconciliation', *Human Rights Quarterly*, 26(3): 561–583.
Humphrey, M. (2000) 'From terror to trauma: Commissioning truth for national reconciliation', *Social Identities*, 6(1): 7–27.
Hutchison, E. (2010). 'Trauma and the politics of emotions: Constituting identity, security and community after the Bali bombing', *International Relations*, 24(1): 65–86.
Hutchison, E. and Bleiker, R. (2008a) 'Emotional reconciliation: Reconstituting identity and community after trauma', *European Journal of Social Theory*, 11(3): 385–403.
Hutchison, E. and Bleiker, R. (2008b) 'Emotions in the war on terror', in *Security and the War on Terror*, Bellamy, Bleiker, Davis and Devetak (eds). London: Routledge, 57–70.
Kaplan, R. D. (2005) *Balkan Ghosts: A Journey Through History.* London: Picador.
Kaufman, S. J. (2001) *Modern Hatreds: The Symbolic Politics of Ethnic War.* Ithaca, NY and London: Cornell University Press.
Kirmayer, L. (2010) 'Peace, conflict, and reconciliation: Contributions of cultural psychiatry', *Transcultural Psychiatry*, 47(1): 5–19.
La Capra, D. (2001) *Writing History, Writing Trauma.* Baltimore, MD: Johns Hopkins University Press.
Lutz, C. A. (1988) *Unnatural Emotions: Everyday Sentiments on a Micronesian Atoll and their Challenge to Western Theory.* Chicago, IL: University of Chicago Press.
Martin, J. R. (2004) 'Mourning: How we get aligned', *Discourse and Society*, 15(2/3): 321–344.
Massumi, B. (2002) *Parables for the Virtual: Movement, Affect, Sensation.* Durham, NC: Duke University Press.

McDermott, R. (2014) 'The body doesn't lie: a somatic approach to the study of emotions in world politics', Commentary submitted as part of the Forum section on 'Emotions and World Politics', *International Theory.*

Mercer, J. (1996) 'Approaching emotion in international politics', paper presented at the Annual Meeting of the International Studies Association, San Diego, CA, 25 April.

Mollica, R. F. (2006) *Healing Invisible Wounds: Paths to Hope and Recovery in a Violent World.* Nashville, TN: Vanderbilt University Press.

Naimark, N. M. (2002) *Fires of Hatred: Ethnic Cleansing in Twentieth-Century Europe.* Cambridge, MA: Harvard University Press.

Nussbaum, M. C. (1995a) 'Emotions and women's capabilities', in *Women, Culture, and Development*, Glover and Nussbaum (eds). New York: Oxford University Press, 360–395.

Nussbaum, M. C. (1995b) 'Rational emotions', in *Poetic Justice: The Literary Imagination and Public Life.* Boston, MA: Beacon, 53–78.

Nussbaum, M. C. (2001) *Upheavals of Thought: The Intelligence of Emotions.* Cambridge: Cambridge University Press.

Rae, H. (2013) 'Civilizational discourses and the anxieties of liberalism', paper presented at the Millennium Annual Conference, London School of Economics, London, 19–20 October.

Schaap, A. (2006) 'Agonism in divided societies', *Philosophy and Social Criticism*, 32(2): 255–277.

Scheff, T. J. (1994) 'Emotions and identity: A theory of ethnic nationalism', in *Social Theory and the Politics of Identity*, Calhoun (ed.). Oxford: Blackwell, 277–303.

Schick, K. (2011) 'Acting out and working through: Trauma and (in)security', *Review of International Studies*, 37(4): 1837–1855.

Solomon, R. C. (2003) *Not Passion's Slave, The Joy of Philosophy: Thinking Thin Versus the Passionate Life.* Oxford: Oxford University Press.

Stein, J. G. (2013) 'Threat perception in International Relations', in *The Oxford Handbook of Political Psychology*, Huddy, Sears and Levy (eds). Oxford: Oxford University Press, 364–394.

Thrift, N. (2004) 'Intensities of feeling: Towards a spatial politics of affect', *Geografiska Annaler*, 86(1): 57–78.

Tsui, C.-K. (2014) 'Tracing the discursive origins of the war on terror: President Clinton and the construction of new terrorism in the post-Cold War era', PhD thesis, University of Otago.

Volkan, V. (1997) *Bloodlines: From Ethnic Pride to Ethnic Terror.* New York: Westview Press.

Volkan, V. (2000) 'Traumatized societies and psychological care: Expanding the concept of preventive medicine', *Mind and Human Interaction*, 11(3): 177–194.

Volkan, V. (2001) 'Transgenerational transmissions and chosen traumas: An aspect of large-group identity', *Group Analysis*, 34(1): 79–97.

Volkan, V. (2002) 'September 11 and societal regression', *Group Analysis*, 35(4): 456–483.

Whitebrook, M. (2002) 'Compassion as a political virtue', *Political Studies*, 50(3): 529–544.

Yoder, C. (2005) *The Little Book of Trauma Healing: When Violence Strikes and Community Security is Threatened.* Intercourse, PA: Good Books.

# 17 Concluding reflection

*Linda Åhäll and Thomas Gregory*

*Linda*: When I was working on my doctoral dissertation on how women's agency in political violence is communicated and culturally understood, it soon became apparent that emotions mattered, in multiple and diverse ways. Feminist scholars had already pointed out how women's violence tends to be discussed in terms of violent women's gender: *women* are not supposed to be violent (c.f. Elshtain 1995; Alison 2004; Sjoberg and Gentry 2007, 2008; Gentry 2009) but, I realised, such gender norms are specifically upheld through emotional communication; gendered ways of telling stories of are often specifically communicated through a sense of confusion, surprise or shock. In my own research, this was most obvious in the case of Lynndie England, the female Military Police officer who found herself at the centre of the so-called Abu Ghraib prison scandal where American soldiers were depicted abusing Iraqi prisoners in 2003. England was 'an enigma' and 'a mystery' simply because her behaviour did not fit with cultural ideas about women and war. Many expressed a feeling of disgust:

> When the first batch of photographs appeared, it was the picture of Private Lynndie England – giving the thumbs-up sign as she pointed at a naked Iraqi prisoner- that provoked most outrage. And as hundreds more photographs were released yesterday, the reservist stole the *sickening* show a second time, being pictured holding another naked prisoner at the end of what appeared to be a dog's leash.
>
> (Marks 2004, emphasis added)

The same day, *The Sun* used the following two headlines: 'Witch: Evil soldier Lynndie in new torture photo' and 'SICKENING new torture picture featuring an evil woman U.S. soldier shocked the world yesterday' (Flynn 2004). At the time, I argued that emotions and emotionality function in two different ways in representations of female agency in political violence: as 'women being emotional' and as 'being emotional about [violent] women' (Åhäll 2012, see also 2015). Yet, within the remits of the doctoral research project, there simply was not enough time or space to reflect on the politics of emotions more deeply. I remained intrigued with how we might make sense of emotional communication and affective representations in our analyses of global politics; how the politics of emotions matter to the study of IR and security studies more broadly; and how to, methodologically, bring emotions research into our discipline. This book is therefore, at least in part, the result of my personal lingering queries.

*Tom*: My interest in the politics of emotion is also rooted in my doctoral work, which focused on the discourses of humanitarianism that framed our understanding of Operation Enduring Freedom in Afghanistan. The focal point of my research was the way in which an exclusionary conception of the human had been produced and maintained within the justifications for military conflict, denying certain populations – particularly Afghan women – a politically qualified voice within the dominant frames of war. At the time, I was unaware of the increasingly important role they were playing in my work. Looking back now, it is clear that concerns about grief, anxiety, compassion, anger and empathy all loomed large in my research, but amidst the stresses and strains of the PhD they quickly disappeared into the background. Even when I did start to take more notice, I was not sure how to think about them, how to write about them, how to make use of them. And, like many schooled in the discipline of IR, I was not even sure they were legitimate concerns (Crawford 2000; Parashar 2013; Sylvester 2013). But an airstrike in Afghanistan in May 2009 forced me to take seriously the relationship between emotions and war (Gregory 2012: 330–331).

As many as 140 people were killed in the attack, after pilots mistakenly targeted buildings where civilians had been sheltering from the violence (Bumiller and Schmitt 2008). The families of those killed were so distraught at their losses that they packed thirty bodies onto the back of a truck and drove it to the provincial capital so that officials could see what had happened (Boone *et al.* 2009). What struck me was not the detail of what went wrong – a military investigation into the matter suggested that deviations from established procedure were to blame (CentCom 2009) – but the reaction of military officials reporting on these deaths. Although they expressed regret at the loss of life, it was the Taliban who were blamed for the violence. Moreover, officials seemed uninterested in the grief, sorrow or anger of those affected by this attack, questioning claims that so many died in the airstrike. As Col. Gregory Julian argued:

> Well I could give you 140 names too. The problem is there is no evidence of that number of graves … Are those real people? Did they ever actually exist? I can give you a list of 53 girls' names with their ages … There are no birth certificates and there are no death certificates.
>
> (quoted in Shalizi 2009)

This indifference towards those affected not only seemed to be at odds with the stated purposes of military operations, but also seemed to suggest that the lives of ordinary Afghan people were, to borrow Judith Butler's phrase, 'ungrievable' (2004; see Gregory 2012: 331–335). If certain lives, she argues, 'do not qualify as lives or are, from the start not conceivable as lives within certain epistemological frames, then these lives are never lived nor lost in the full sense' (Butler 2009: 1). As a result of this research, along with frustrations at my own emotional response, I found myself asking increasingly complex questions about the role of emotions in international politics, and the regimes of affect that seem to determine whose suffering is worthy enough to provoke feelings of anger, empathy and grief and whose suffering will remain unnoticed, undetected and unacknowledged.

## Putting emotions first

This book is one of few books in IR that puts emotions first. It shows how emotions matter in studies of politics and war but, because the ways in which the authors in this volume put emotions first differs, the book also offers various methodological insights into how one might study emotions, politics and war. Several chapters focus on representations as a way into 'the political', as *visions* of global politics. For example, Holland (Chapter 13) and Parr (Chapter 12) investigate representations of feelings/emotional states in relation to a particular political event and, especially, the link between emotional representations and official state policies. Welland (Chapter 9) draws on soldiers' self-representations in autobiographies to form her argument about compassion and identity construction through Judith Butler's use of interpellation. Gregory (Chapter 14) as well as Guittet and Zevnik (Chapter 15) explore the emotionality of visual representations through war photography. Howell (Chapter 11) and Hutchison and Bleiker (Chapter 16) deal with trauma and emotional aftermaths of war (and in Howell's case, also as preparations for war.) Howell (Chapter 11) and Parr (Chapter 12) both address political consequences of the repression of emotions in the form of stoic masculinity. Moreover, some authors approach emotion as something that happens *in* biological bodies, others are more interested in emotional processes *between* bodies, human ones, but also abstract ones such as states. How the authors approach 'the emotional' thus ranges from particular feelings such as grief or anger, to pre-conscious affective impressions. To some, emotion is an object of study, while to others – perhaps most obviously in the chapters by Parashar (6), Basham (10), Jauhola (7) and Zalewski (3) – emotions form an important part of, and are therefore written into, the research process. This diversity, to us, is one of the book's main strengths, as we are convinced that trying to define, once and for all, what emotions 'are' risks missing the point.

The chapters in this volume speak to each other in so many different ways; there are consequently several ways in which to sum up how these contributions show how emotions matter in contemporary research on politics and war. Elsewhere, we have mapped emotions research along how 'emotions' was used (as emotions, affect or feelings, see Åhäll and Gregory 2013), but alternative ways to sum up this book could be based on the chapters' argument, their topic, or levels of analysis (individual, group, state). In a recent Forum on 'Emotions and World Politics' published in *International Theory*, the focus is on 'the processes that render individual emotions collective and thus political' (Bleiker and Hutchison 2014: 491). In a survey essay, Hutchison and Bleiker suggest that the path forward for emotions research in IR could be 'the middle ground' between two opposing poles of 'macro approaches focused on identifying generalizable propositions about the nature and function of political emotions, and micro approaches that examine the political significance of specific collective emotions in specific situations' (Hutchison and Bleiker 2014: 507).

While we find the macro/micro distinctions in emotions research useful as a framework to understand links between emotional and affective phenomena and to map emotions research along different levels of analysis, the starting point and therefore also the outlook of this book is different. As the anecdotes at the start of this concluding chapter show, our own interest in the politics of emotions is a result of us asking feminist research questions, and from this background we are convinced that there is more to say, both about what is considered 'the political' and about 'emotions'. To answer a question posed in the Forum, we are not convinced it is possible, or desirable, to try to establish 'a general theory of emotions in international relations' (Hutchison and Bleiker 2014: 492), simply because the borders, barriers and boundaries of the academic field of IR itself are not fixed, but constantly re-negotiated.

In this concluding reflection, therefore, we are not so much interested in finding a common ground. On the contrary, we argue that an alternative way forward is to embrace methodological diversity, but above all *creativity*, while at the same time remaining focused on the particularity of the political puzzle chosen for analysis. We are much more interested in *how emotions function*, indeed what emotions *do*, in multiple and varied ways related to our area of research: as part of the research process, as part of shaping our understanding of 'the political', and as part of knowledge claims in IR and studies of war. Consequently, we map this concluding reflection around methods and methodology, not only because it is considered a 'pressing issue' (Bleiker and Hutchison 2008; Hutchison and Bleiker 2014) and that which is seen to be lacking in emotions research in IR, but also because, at least to us, it is the most confusing, challenging and messiest part of this topic itself. How can we study something often considered an individual experience as part of global politics? How can we study the both the tangible and intangible feelings, sensations, and bodily reactions to conflict without reifying the materiality of the human body or disregarding it entirely?

## Emotions and bodies

In Chapter 4, Karin Fierke problematises the well rehearsed dichotomies of emotion/reason and group/individual in the context of human dignity and argues that there is a global emotionology of norms that shape the appropriate expressions of emotion. She uses emotion as 'the glue that bind communities together' and argues that the meaning of human dignity travels between the global and the more local. Fierke talks about bodies when she compares human dignity of individuals to state sovereignty and autonomy to body politics. Both of these, Fierke argues, are existential values. Ty Solomon (Chapter 5) specifically calls upon IR not to disregard bodies and embodiment, and locates the body at the nexus of 'collective discourse and emotions'. In fact, to most of the authors in this book, 'putting emotions first' effectively mean a focus on 'bodies' and body politics. The preferred approach into emotions research, in other words, seems to be 'bodies', but to answer the questions above, we also need to think about what we mean by 'politics' more broadly. We need to think about how methodological choices made are linked to different knowledge claims.

As Fierke points out, emotions (and bodies) are shaped as much by context and socialisation as neurology. Within emotions research, there are subsequently two broader directions for finding, however partial, answers to questions on emotions and bodies: the cultural politics of emotions and neuroscience. As others have already mentioned, early emotions research in political science/IR drew on political psychology to explain human/political behaviour, for example in relation to foreign policy analysis. Today, neuroscientific discoveries provide 'concrete evidence for the idea that decisions and judgments are fundamentally imbued with emotion' (Hutchison and Bleiker 2014: 496), and neuroscience is therefore often seen as the appropriate (read 'scientific') 'way in' to emotions research in political science/IR. For example, the recent Forum is organised around two longer essays by 'two pioneers in this field', Jonathan Mercer and Neta C. Crawford, and subsequent shorter commentaries. What is important to us is that both essays draw on neuroscience. While some of the following commentaries offer a word of caution with regard to heading towards a subfield of 'neuro-IR', calls on us not to fall into 'the trap of thinking we humans are nothing but brains' (Jeffrey 2014: 584, 588) and to forget further excursions in neuroscience and psychology in lieu of 'creative reengagement with the insights and debates of global social and political theory and analysis' (Reus-Smit 2014: 573), our point is that the Forum's emphasis on pros and cons of neuroscience to study emotions and world politics risks reinforcing a particular, and dominant, approach to research on 'emotions and world politics'. We are not suggesting that there is anything wrong with experimental political science, and drawing on neuroscience and psychology as a way to explain emotions, politics and war, but we would like to emphasise that it is only one of several ways to claim/gain/create academic knowledge about emotions, politics and war.

## Knowledge claims in emotions research

Within IR and its subfield security studies, 'methods' is an increasingly hot topic. Some might even be compelled to talk about a 'methods turn', with recent publications of methods books (Shepherd 2012; Salter and Mutlu 2013; Aradau *et al.* 2015) and the popularity of a 'Methods Café' at the annual International Studies Association (ISA) conference, for example. At the same time, there has been a 'sensuous turn' in social sciences more broadly, and prior to that, an 'affective turn', in cultural studies at least (cf. Clough 2007; Gregg and Seigworth 2010; McSorley 2013).

The 2014 Millennium conference held at the London School of Economics was themed 'Quo Vadis IR: Method, Methodology and Innovation', and in his keynote address Patrick Thaddeus Jackson disentangled links between different types of knowledge claims in our discipline. He showed how there is more to 'science' than what is often considered 'the scientific approach', and that there is more to say about 'academic knowing' than 'objectively valid facts'.[1] Jackson contrasted 'the scientific method' – the 'impersonal view from nowhere' – with value-expressive knowledge claims to make the point that there are other ways of knowing than 'facts'. In the keynote, Jackson mentioned technic, aesthetic and ethical knowledge in addition to – and as different from – scientific knowledge. For studies in IR, the four different types of knowledge correspond to four different, legitimate ways of evaluating academic claims: scientific, technical, aesthetic and ethical.[2] Jackson argues that 'there are ways of thinking and practicing politics that inhabit each of these domains' (Jackson 2014: 16). Since politics is what we study from a variety of angles, he argues, 'it makes little sense to confine ourselves to one ex ante definition of that object if we want to give ourselves the best chance of expanding our knowing about it' (Jackson 2014: 17). Or, as Bleiker noted more than a decade earlier: 'The globe has become too complex a place not to employ the full register of human insight and intelligence to understand and address the political challenges of our day' (Bleiker 2003: 417). Because of this, though, to Jackson science is a diverse collection of ways of knowing, but each of which has its own type of internal validity. IR needs room for knowledge in all of these sites but, importantly, we must avoid 'category confusion' when making claims to knowledge, such 'as when a theological claim that belongs in the domain of Ethics is mistakenly treated as an impersonal, wordly claim of the sort appropriate to Science' (Jackson 2014: 23).

Encouraging creativity as a methodological starting point, we have not attempted to control or police how the authors in this book engage with either emotions or politics. The authors have their own ways into emotions, politics and war, they are interested in different levels of analysis and, method-wise, some draw on anthropology and ethnography, others on discourse analysis, visual analysis, experiments or narrative analysis. What we think is important for us as researchers of emotions, politics and war, however, is to get the intention right. We need to be clear about what kind of contribution to knowledge we are making. Are we aiming to make a scientific or aesthetic claim to knowledge in our research on emotions, politics and war? Are we basing our claim in subjective experiences, or is our claim ethical, of what should be, of what is just or righteous? Context is most important.

The chapters in this book make different claims to academic knowledge. Drawing on recent developments in psychology, McDermott's Chapter 8 on experiments is a great illustration of how to approach emotions research if one intends making a scientific claim to knowledge. To McDermott, the point with using experiments as a method in emotions research is to 'show generalisable regularities in human behaviour, insights into aspects of common humanity we all share'. To do this, aesthetic or ethical knowledge claims are of no use. Instead, the idea of experiments is to link 'micro-foundational mechanisms' to behaviour at the macro-level. This technique, McDermott argues, makes it possible to break down complex phenomena into component parts in order to discover the psychological factors that undergird the political outcomes we seek to understand.

In contrast to a scientific knowledge claim that presents 'objectively valid facts', an aesthetic claim to knowledge concerns that which is 'felt', and the argument is that this knowledge can also be 'true', even though it is not scientifically validated. In this book, this is perhaps best illustrated in Massumi's Chapter 2, on how affective threats legitimise particular security policies, domestically as well as abroad:

> A clear and present danger is observable and, in principle, objectively verifiable, whereas a threat only has to be felt to be. It has a visceral reality that is self-confirming. If you feel threatened, you are – end of story. On 9/11 we felt it.
>
> (Massumi, Chapter 2 in this volume)

Similarly, Zalewski's reflexive and anecdotal writing style (Chapter 3) equally well illustrates aesthetic knowledge claims as she puts into words her own 'uncomfortable moment' described as 'a sticky and dense entanglement of love, popular culture, security, embarrassment, theory, abhorrence and tension', and shows us that we might be missing something in our theorising of violence if we fail to reflect upon how these seemingly unconnected things are connected. In addition, the way in which some of the authors are writing emotions into the research process are other examples of aesthetic claims to knowledge; for example, Parashar's use of feminist storytelling (Chapter 6) as a way to understand not only the emotions, in this case anger, of her research objects, but also in herself as a researcher. Parashar calls upon us to acknowledge that emotional encounters are not just influencing research, but actually are part of research data itself. Similarly, to both Basham and Jauhola, fieldwork is an emotional experience. Both research 'boredom' and use 'waiting around' as a specific method, but whereas Basham's research is about the emotionality of soldiering as a practice, Jauhola combines embodiment and emotions through the method/idea of the mindful researcher, with the purpose of 'to go along' and 'to give in' to emotions.

Last, it is perhaps the contributions by Howell (Chapter 11) and Hutchison and Bleiker (Chapter 16) that best exemplify ethical claims to knowledge about emotions, politics and war, as both chapters focus on what should be, of what is just or righteous. Howell's chapter on the affective economies of military families' 'fitness' ends with a warning: this ultimately is preparation for unending wars. Hutchison and Bleiker's chapter is about how war-torn communities must/should 'work through shared emotions of anxiety, fear, resentment and humiliation – sentiments that are likely to produce new conflict – towards an environment defined by a search for collective empathy and compassion'.

In our introduction to this book, we asked, what do emotions do? And how should we, in IR, study emotions and the emotional? As we hope the book shows, these questions cannot generate simple answers. Instead, we hope that the book demonstrates the multiple and overlapping ways in which emotions and the emotional matter for studies of politics and war. Furthermore, thinking about methods and methodologies to study emotions showcases the wide variety of possible ways forward. In this way, emotion is not simply the object of study, but can also form part of the actual methods used to gain/create knowledge. We would like to end this concluding reflection by picking up on two themes that we believe the content of the chapters of this book draw us towards, precisely because both have expanded the horizons for what can be considered 'politics': aesthetics and feminism.

## Future research on emotions, politics and war

In addition to the more established path of building on neuroscience and psychology to study emotions in IR, future research on emotions, politics and war might suitably be situated within the intellectual traditions of 'aesthetics' and 'feminism'. To start with, even though we in this book are 'putting emotions first', it is the engagement with global aspects of politics/the political that presumably sets us apart from other academic disciplines engaged in emotions research. Thus we think it is important that emotions research in IR does not lose sight of 'the political'. Our prime scholarly interest should remain global politics (however one defines it), not emotions per se, but, crucially, we believe that emotions can offer alternative insights into politics/the political, previously ignored. As Roland Bleiker noted almost fifteen years ago, the aesthetic turn reorients our very understanding of the political: 'it engenders a shift towards an approach that generates a more diverse but also more direct encounter with the political' (Bleiker 2001: 511). We need to remember, though, that how we approach 'politics' and 'the political' impacts on how (method) we study emotions. In this volume, some authors use the more common understanding of politics as linked to states, governments and particular policy decisions, whether to do with counterinsurgency operations or mental health services to soldiers, while others engage with 'the political' much more broadly, perhaps more akin to the concept of 'power' and not as directly linked to 'the state', for example in relation to ideas about gender/sex or identity. Nevertheless, here we would like to suggest that thinking about politics as 'political puzzles' can usefully guide the research design, as Bleiker explains in an article discussing what IR can or should learn from art:

> If a puzzle is the main research challenge, then it can be addressed with all means available, independently of their provenance or label. A source may stem from this or that discipline, it may be academically sanctioned or not, expressed in prose or poetic form, it may be language based on visual or musical or take any other shape or form: it is legitimate as long as it helps to illuminate the puzzle in question.
>
> (Bleiker 2003: 420)

In the same way, we suggest that the thinking and theorising of emotions in IR should be guided by the political puzzle chosen for analysis. If one thinks that emotions or the emotional can help shed light on the particular puzzle in question, then it is not only legitimate methodologically, but it would be a serious omission to leave out, precisely because a focus on emotions and emotionality would add yet another piece to the puzzle in question. How to do this, though, will differ, and this is where it is important to remember intent and context, and think about what kind of claim to knowledge one wishes to make. For example, if we are using emotions to explain human behaviour in general terms, then we need a different research design and different tools to 'solve' the political puzzle in question than if we were to understand particular subjective emotional experiences.

Bleiker notes that aesthetic *sources* offer alternative insights precisely because they are linked to imaginative and creative ways of reading the international (Bleiker 2009: 2). Aesthetic sources, Bleiker argues, cultivate a more open-ended level of 'sensibility about the political' (Bleiker 2009: 2). To us, however, aesthetic interventions in the study of IR, politics and war go beyond a focus on aesthetic sources. In the introduction to a special issue in *Global Society* on 'Aesthetics and International Relations', Cerwyn Moore and Laura Shepherd suggest that 'approaching the study of IR with an *aesthetic sensibility* encourages scholars to pay analytical attention to affect rather than reason, judgement rather than fact, sensation rather than intellectualism' (2010: 299, emphasis added). Emotions research is, of course, precisely about the sensibility of the political, but within emotions research there is also scope to include different types of knowledge claims. The range in approaches to study the emotional therefore also generates different types of knowledge.

Furthermore, feminism offers another intellectual space for future research on emotions, politics and war, due to the interest in bodies and embodiment. As Parashar importantly points out in Chapter 6, 'the move to analyse emotions isn't really that 'new' or distanced for feminists who reject the emotional/rational divide anyway'. More specifically, feminist scholarship's interest in how the personal is political (and international) 'inadvertently negotiates interest in bodily experiences and emotional responses, very often by default'. Where neuroscience might reduce bodies to brains, feminism focuses on gendered – and gendering of – bodies. In addition, as the engagement with emotions and world politics still largely remains focused on 'classical' sites and obvious 'political' contexts, 'the personal is political' immediately puts focus on individuals, bodies and experiences in the everyday, aspects previously not considered part of IR. In this way, both affect theory and feminist research have the advantage that they focus on the everyday, which we believe is a too-often forgotten dimension of international/global politics.

Sara Ahmed suggests that '[t]o be affected by something is to evaluate that thing. Evaluations are expressed in how bodies turn towards things. To give value to things is to shape what is near us' (Ahmed 2010: 31). Thus, to pay attention to affect also forms part of critical thinking. Let's say we feel something without knowing why, we are affected but confused about how we feel. Perhaps such confusion might then challenge us to re-think, re-value attitudes and beliefs about that by which we were affected by in the first place. Thinking about politics and the political in this way might help us to catch something that touches our conscience, an idea that things could be different: a dream, a vision. Perhaps this way, and here we paraphrase Zalewski's concluding remark (Chapter 3), the over-inflated certainty which marks theory and policy production in contemporary International Politics/Relations is able to shift in a more humble direction, to look more closely, if uncomfortably, at more of the ways in which our everyday and worlds are compressed so tightly together into an illusory whole.

## Notes

1 We draw here on notes from the keynote address, but also Jackson's unpublished paper 'The bias of "science"' presented at ISA 2014.

2 In the earlier version of the paper presented at ISA 2014, the four distinctions made are labelled 'Science', 'Engineering', 'Ethics' and 'Art'.

## Bibliography

Åhäll, L. (2012) 'Confusion, fear, disgust: Emotional communication in representations of female agency in political violence', in *Gender, Agency and Political Violence*, Åhäll and Shepherd (eds). Basingstoke: Palgrave Macmillan, 169–183.

Åhäll, L. (2015) *Sexing War/Policing Gender: Motherhood, Myth and Women's Political Violence*. London: Routledge.

Åhäll, L. and Gregory, T. (2013) 'Security, emotions, affect', *Critical Studies on Security*, 1(1): 117–120.

Ahmed, S. (2010) 'Happy objects', in *The Affect Theory Reader*, Gregg and Seigworth (eds). Durham, NC: Duke University Press.

Alison, M. (2004) 'Women as agents of political violence: Gendering security', *Security Dialogue*, 35(4): 447–463.

Aradau, C., Huysmans, J., Neal, A. and Voelkner, N. (eds) (2015) *Critical Security Methods: New Frameworks for Analysis*. London: Routledge.

Bleiker, R. (2001) 'The aesthetic turn in International Political Theory', *Millennium: Journal of International Studies*, 30(3): 509–533.

Bleiker, R. (2003) 'Learning from art: A reply to Holden's "World literature and world politics"', *Global Society*, 17(4): 415–428.

Bleiker, R. (2009) *Aesthetics and World Politics: Rethinking Peace and Conflict Studies.* Basingstoke: Palgrave Macmillan.

Bleiker, R. and Hutchison, E. (2008) 'Fear no more: Emotions and world politics', *Review of International Studies*, 34: 115–135.

Bleiker, R. and Hutchison, E. (2014) 'Introduction: Emotions and world politics', *International Theory*, 6: 490–491.

Boone, J., MacAskil, E. and Tran, M. (2009) 'US airstrikes kill dozens of Afghan civilians', *The Guardian*, 6 May. Available online at: www.theguardian.com/world/2009/may/06/us-air-strikes-afghan-civilians (accessed 20 November 2014).

Bumiller, E. and Schmitt, E. (2008) 'Joint chiefs chairman criticizes Afghan air strikes', *The New York Times*, 18 May. Available online at: www.nytimes.com/2009/05/19/world/asia/19farah.html (accessed 20 November 2014).

Butler, J. (2004) *Precarious Life: The Powers of Mourning and Violence.* London: Verso Books.

Butler, J. (2009) *Frames of War: When Is Life Grievable?* London: Verso Books.

CentCom. (2009) 'U.S. Central Command investigation into civilian casualties in Farah Province, Afghanistan on 4 May 2009: US Centcom's Unclassified Executive Summary', Homeland Security Digital Library. Available online at: www.hsdl.org/?view&did=35748 (accessed 20 November 2014).

Clough, P. with Halley, J. (eds) (2007) *The Affective Turn: Theorizing the Social.* Durham, NC: Duke University Press.

Crawford, N. C. (2000) 'The passion of world politics: Propositions on emotion and emotional relationships', *International Security*, 24(4): 116–156.

Elshtain, J. B. (1995 [1987]) *Women and War.* New York: Basic Books.

Flynn, B. (2004) 'Witch: Evil soldier Lynndie in new torture photo', *The Sun*, 7 May.

Gentry, C. (2009) 'Twisted maternalism', *International Feminist Journal of Politics*, 11(2): 235–252.

Gregg, M. and Seigworth, G. J. (2010) *The Affect Theory Reader.* Durham, NC: Duke University Press.

Gregory, T. (2012) 'Potential lives, impossible deaths', *International Feminist Journal of Politics*, 14(3): 327–347.

Hutchison, E. and Bleiker, R. (2014) 'Theorizing emotions in world politics', *International Theory*, 6: 491–514.

Jackson, P. T. (2014) 'The bias of "science": On the intellectual appeal of neopositivism', paper presented at the International Studies Association 55th Annual Convention, 26–29 March, Toronto.

Jeffrey, R. (2014) 'The promise and problems of the neuroscientific approach to emotions', *International Theory*, 6: 584–589.

Marks, C. (2004) 'Images that shook the US and the wider world', *The Scotsman*, 7 May.

McSorley, K. (ed.) (2013) *War and the Body: Militarisation, Practice and Experience.* London and New York: Routledge.

Moore, C. and Shepherd, L. J. (2010) 'Aesthetics and International Relations: Towards a global politics', *Global Society*, 24(3): 299–309.

Parashar, S. (2013) 'What wars and "war bodies" know about International Relations', *Cambridge Review of International Affairs*, 26(4): 615–630.

Reus-Smit, C. (2014) 'Emotions and the social', *International Theory*, 6: 568–574.

Salter, M. B. and Mutlu, C. E. (eds) (2013) *Research Methods in Critical Security Studies: An Introduction.* London and New York: Routledge.
Shalizi, H. (2009) 'List of 140 Afghan dead includes 93 children', *Reuters,* 13 May. Available online at: http://uk.reuters.com/article/idUKTRE54C1S220090513?sp=true (accessed 20 November 2014).
Shepherd, L. J. (ed.) (2012) *Critical Approaches to Security: An Introduction to Theories and Methods.* London and New York: Routledge.
Sjoberg, L. and Gentry, C. E. (2007) *Mothers, Monsters, Whores: Women's Violence in Global Politics.* London: Zed Books.
Sjoberg, L. and Gentry, C. E. (2008) 'Reduced to bad sex: Narratives of violent women from the Bible to the war on terror', *International Relations,* 22(1): 5–23.
Sylvester, C. (2013) *War as Experience: Contributions from International Relations and Feminist Analysis.* Abingdon: Routledge.

# Index